Dissecting Cthulhu:

Essays on the Cthulhu Mythos

Edited by

S. T. Joshi

Miskatonic River Press

Contents

IV. The Landscape .149

V. Influences. 203

Introduction

When H. P. Lovecraft wrote "The Call of Cthulhu" in 1926, it is unlikely that he was aware of the degree to which his seemingly improvised mythology not only would become the dominant feature of his own subsequent work but would infuse the writings of dozens, perhaps hundreds, of writers who followed in his wake, starting with such of his own colleagues as August Derleth, Donald Wandrei, Robert E. Howard, Clark Ashton Smith, Robert Bloch, and Henry Kuttner. And yet, it is symptomatic that Lovecraft himself, even later in life, never bothered to give this fictional construct a name; it was left to August Derleth to devise (in Lovecraft's lifetime) the somewhat unwieldy sobriquet of "The Mythology of Hastur" and, after Lovecraft's death, the "Cthulhu Mythology," later amended to the Cthulhu Mythos.

It is nearly four decades since Richard L. Tierney, in a one-page essay called "The Derleth Mythos" (1972), rightly pointed out that many of the features of the Cthulhu Mythos that most readers assumed to have been invented or elaborated by Lovecraft were in fact concocted by August Derleth—and concocted in such a way as to present an antipodally different conception of the universe from the one envisioned by Lovecraft. This simple essay triggered a spate of other work in which more Derlethian incrustations on the Mythos were systematically stripped away; there were even attempts—valiant or quixotic as the case may be—to fashion some other name for the mythology, from the "Lovecraft Mythos" to the extremely inelegant "Yog-Sothoth Cycle of Myth." These attempts generally failed, although "Lovecraft Mythos" has some minimal foothold in critical discourse as a means of distinguishing the "pure" Lovecraftian conception from the elaborations (or, from one point of view, perversions) of later writers, extending all the way up to the present day.

The reason why the Cthulhu Mythos is so compelling to readers and critics alike is that it, along with Lovecraft as a whole, is a kind of fulcrum in the history of supernatural fiction. Even if we laugh at August Derleth's strange assertion that the mythology somehow began with Edgar Allan Poe ("Tekeli-li!") and was rudimentarily elaborated by Ambrose Bierce (Hali, Carcosa) and Robert W. Chambers, it is evident that Lovecraft himself drew upon these and other illustrious predecessors in the fashioning of at least some elements of his mythology—a mythology that, in turn, has infused the work of countless successors in the fields of horror and science fiction. And because Lovecraft has left such an immense paper trail—in the form of letters, essays, and other documents, and even, indirectly, in the form of memoirs of him by his friends and colleagues—critics have an immense array of documents to draw upon in identifying the exact origin and development of any given feature or concept of the Cthulhu Mythos.

But if the scholarship of the past four decades has accomplished anything, it is the confirmation that Lovecraft was far more than just a writer of clever tales of supernatural fiction; he was, instead, a keen and penetrating thinker who evolved an elaborate worldview, atheistic at its core and reliant on the findings of science to devise a system of ethics and aesthetics that could function viably in a modern world that had demonstrated the inefficacy of the concepts of God, the afterlife, and the very centrality of the human race and human history in the workings of a spatially and temporally boundless universe. It is this "cosmic" stance that gives Lovecraft's own writing the intellectual and aesthetic substance to continue being of relevance nearly a century after it was written, and that continues to inspire contemporary writers to evoke its most noteworthy features.

What are those features, as relate specifically to the Cthulhu Mythos? They can perhaps be classified under four broad headings:

1) *The books.* In Lovecraft's unusually intellectualized world, books are a means to the penetration of the secrets of the universe. And since, in the fiction, those secrets are appalling and soul-annihilating—in essence, the knowledge of our risible inconsequence in the vast vortices of space and time—the books themselves become "forbidden," because the truths they utter are all too capable of shattering the minds and hearts of the human beings who read them. As a result, we find a Lovecraftian library full of imaginary (and a few real) tomes such as the *Necronomicon, Unaussprechlichen Kulten,* and so forth. Lovecraft's suggestion in later tales that these books are themselves incapable of telling the truth about the cosmos except by means of symbol or metaphor is an interesting development of his mythology that relatively few subsequent writers have sought to emulate.

2) *The gods.* The perennial paradox of how the atheist Lovecraft could have fashioned such a constellation of "gods" in his stories has been neatly dissipated by Robert M. Price's sensible contention that these "gods" are not really gods at all but rather merely space aliens—worshipped as gods

by primitive humans who are incapable of grasping their immense powers and hoping against hope to harness these powers in the service of their own ends. Nevertheless, these "gods" have exercised a compelling fascination for subsequent writers and critics, and for a time it seemed that no purportedly Lovecraftian writer could resist inventing his or her own new god to add to the pantheon, even if the result were such absurdities as Shudde-M'ell or Cthugha. It appears that the creation of such gods has abated somewhat, as an understanding of Lovecraft's true motivations in creating these entities has penetrated even down to the level of fan writers.

3) *The landscape.* There is some debate as to whether the imaginary landscape so richly envisioned by Lovecraft—and populated with such locales as Arkham, Innsmouth, Dunwich, Kingsport, and a host of lesser cities—has any intimate connection with the cosmicism inherent in the Cthulhu (or the Lovecraft) Mythos. All one can say is that the majority of Lovecraft's own tales in which the mythology plays a major role are set in this realm, with the notable exception of "The Call of Cthulhu" itself. An argument could be made that the transmutation of the imagination from the earth to the cosmos is somewhat facilitated when the initial phases of that process are situated in such a richly conceived imaginary milieu; but it is also worth observing that Lovecraft himself had elaborated upon his mythical New England in a number of tales (notably "The Picture in the House" and "The Festival") that are only tangentially related to his subsequent mythological writing.

4) *Cosmicism.* This rubric is not exactly equivalent to the three previously discussed, which are more in the way of plot devices that lay the groundwork for the elaboration of the plots of the stories in which they figure. Cosmicism, on the other hand, is an abiding philosophical vision that underlies the bulk of Lovecraft's tales, mythological and non-mythological alike. It is this element that was so sorely lacking in the first several decades of post-Lovecraftian Mythos writing, when so many writers seemed content to invent a new god or book or locale and by that process fancied themselves "contributing" in some meaningful way to Lovecraft's original conceptions. We know differently now, and as a result the novels and tales that draw inspiration from Lovecraft's writings are in large part infused with a cosmic perspective that would have earned Lovecraft's approval—even when, as in Colin Wilson's *The Mind Parasites* (1967), the overall philosopical thrust is quite antipodal to Lovecraft.

This volume seeks to present the most noteworthy essays on the Cthulhu Mythos by some of the leading Lovecraft scholars and critics of the past forty years. Essays by Richard L. Tierney, Dirk W. Mosig, and myself seek to clear away the misconceptions of the Mythos fostered by August Derleth and others, while David E. Schultz's "Who Needs the 'Cthulhu Mythos'?" remains a vibrant screed calling, at a minimum, for a radical revision of our understanding of the role that the mythology played in Lovecraft's work. Simon MacCulloch suggests interesting connections between certain phases of the Mythos and Lovecraft's own philosophical conceptions, while Steven J. Mariconda's exhaustive article makes a strong case that the Mythos grew out of the collegiality between readers and writers fostered by *Weird Tales,* where a majority of Lovecraft's and his colleagues Mythos tales first appeared.

Discussions of the books, gods, and landscape of the Mythos are undertaken by Robert M. Price, Will Murray, Dan Clore, Robert D. Marten, and others. The existence of thousands of letters by Lovecraft has, as I have suggested above, made the work of correlating certain phases of the Mythos akin to the work of biblical scholars poring over sacred texts, but the end result is an illumination of the sources and development of a number of central Lovecraft elements. In a final section on influences, scholars study both the influence of past writers on Lovecraft and Lovecraft's influence on both his contemporaries and his successors.

The fact that so many of these articles first appeared in *Crypt of Cthulhu* and *Lovecraft Studies* in the 1980s and 1990s bespeaks the incredible fertility of Lovecraft scholarship in those decades. Robert M. Price, in particular, the editor of *Crypt of Cthulhu,* made the Mythos a central pillar of his scholarly endeavors, and if his conclusions were not always identical to my own, no one can gainsay that his work has been unfailingly cogent and provocative. But the most heartening development in recent years is the radically increased quality of neo-Lovecraftian weird writing—writing that is consciously and directly infused with a sound understanding of the fundamental tenets of Lovecraft's philosophy and the means by which he enunciated that philosophy in his fiction. The days of mechanical and unimaginative pastiches of Lovecraft are long over, and a new era of stimulating, aesthetically evolved novels and tales that use Lovecraft as a springboard—oftentimes ending in a place where Lovecraft himself might never have ventured—is underway. There can be no greater testament to the benefits of scholarship than this.

—S. T. JOSHI

Seattle, Washington
April 2011

I. Some Overviews

The Derleth Mythos

By Richard L. Tierney

T he "Cthulhu Mythos" is largely the invention of, not H. P. Lovecraft, but August Derleth.

Lovecraft, of course, did the groundwork. He invented most of the gods, demons and servitors—and, above all, he provided the spooky, Gothic atmosphere necessary to the genre. Yet it seems to me that it was Derleth. who established the concept of a "Mythos" to comprehend all the Lovecraftian concepts.

Lovecraft himself seems never to have entertained such a concept. His outlook on the supernatural and the cosmos seems to have been basically dynamic—it was constantly developing through out his life. Derleth's attitude on the other hand was largely static; he appreciated Lovecraft's concepts but cared less for developing them than for systematizing them. His efforts were interesting but less than successful from an aesthetic point of view. This is not to say that Derleth was unaesthetic but merely that, in my opinion, his basic outlook was non-Lovecraftian and his attempt to carry on the Lovecraft tradition left out something vital.

Derleth probably coined the term "Cthulhu Mythos." If he did not, he certainly developed the attitude that goes with that term. Consider the basic premises of the "Mythos": a cosmic cluster of "good guys" (Elder Gods) protecting the human race from the "bad guys" (Ancient Old Ones) who are striving to do us (humanity) in! Derleth maintains that this is all a parallel of the "Christian Mythios," with its bad against good, and with humanity the focal point of it all. Evil Ancient Ones are striv-ng to take our planet from us, but angelic Elder Gods always intervene in time to save us.

I grant Derleth the right to his view of the cosmos, but the sad thing is that he has made all too many believe that his view is that of Lovecraft also. This is simply not true. Lovecraft's picture of the universe and Derleth's are completely dissimilar.

Derleth seems determined to link the Cthulhu pantheon with

Christianity and the medieval tradition by making it a struggle between "good" and "evil" from an anthropocentric point of view. Too, the concept of "elemental forces" in the Mythos seems to be Derleth's own—borrowed from the ancient theory that all things known to us are compounded from the four elements: fire, water, earth and air. Derleth runs into many contradictions here. For instance, he makes Cthulhu and his minions water beings, whereas "The Call of Cthulhu" has them coming down from space and building their cities on land; only later are their cities submerged by geological upheavals, and this is a catastrophe which immobilizes the Cthulhu spawn. Hastur is portrayed as an "air elemental," while at the same time Derleth implies that he lives on the bottom of the lake of Hali. Yog-Sothoth and Nyarlathotep, probably the two most purely cosmic of all Lovecraftian entities, are squeezed into the "earth" category; while, finally, he invents the fire elemental, Cthugha, to round out his menagerie of elementals. (Lovecraft invented no beings that could be construed as "fire elementals.") Cthugha comes from the star Fomalhaut—presumably because Lovecraft once mentioned that star in one of his sonnets.

Elementals aside, the whole basic concept of Derleth's "good-versus-evil" Mythos seems as non-Lovecraftian as anything conceivable. Lovecraft actually regarded the cosmos as basically indifferent to anthropocentric outlooks such as good and evil. The "shocker" in his best tales is usually the line in which the narrator is forced to recognize that there are vast and powerful forces and entities basically indifferent to humanity because of their over whelming superiority to man.

Most writers continuing the "Cthulhu Mythos" in fiction or documenting it in scholarly articles are merely perpetuating the misconceptions begun by Derleth. I feel Lovecraft reached his highest imaginative peak in the two novels, "The Shadow out of Time" and *At the Mountains of Madness*. In both these tales Lovecraft turned the whole universe into a haunted house, so to speak, linking the findings of modern science to the flavor of Gothic horror. In so doing, he created a type of "creepy" story that twentieth-century man could continue to believe in even after the traditional trappings of cemeteries, crumbling castles, haunted mansions, etc. began to acquire the flavor of clichés. But Lovecraft's followers have never pursued this line of development. Without exception they all leave man and his values at the center, in the Derleth tradition, and most of them even continue to use the non-Lovecraftian devices of "Elder Gods," "elementals," etc., while writing endless variations on the basic Lovecraftian themes dealing with Dunwich and Innsmouth.

To sum up: The Cthulhu Mythos as it now stands is at least as much Derleth's invention as it is Lovecraft's. The line of Lovecraft's development remains open—no one has really taken up as yet where he left off—and it leads toward the cosmic. Yet if one wants to get to the heart of what Lovecraft felt about the cosmos, one must sidestep Derleth and his followers.

[Meade and Penny Frierson, ed., *HPL* (Birmingham, AL: The Editors, 1972), p. 53]

H. P. Lovecraft: Myth-Maker

By Dirk W. Mosig

"The oldest and strongest emotion of mankind is fear, and the oldest and strongest kind of fear is fear of the unknown," wrote H. P. Lovecraft in "Supernatural Horror in Literature" (*D* 365). But although it is obvious from even a cursory examination of his works that Lovecraft himself fully understood the meaning and implications of his assertion, it is amazing to note how little the same was appreciated by others who, as August Derleth and, more recently, Brian Lumley, decided to "expand" the Lovecraft ouevre by adding to it their own inferior and unimaginative pastiches, almost invariably marred by over-explanatory naïveté.

In his essay "Notes on Writing Weird Fiction," Lovecraft provided a series of guidelines and helpful advice which should have been seriously pondered by all prospective weird fictioneers, and in particular by those interested in adding to Lovecraft's own mythopoeic conceptions. This has not been the case—they seem to have been noticed by few, and followed by even less.

But most Lovecraft imitations fall short not merely on the account of poor writing. There is a deeper underlying problem, namely a serious misconception of the basic ideas and philosophical undercurrents permeating the Lovecraft oeuvre. And the principal culprit seems to have been Lovecraft's disciple and correspondent, August Derleth. Despite his role in the preservation and propagation of his mentor's writings, Derleth was apparently unable or unwilling to understand the essence of Lovecraft's dynamic pseudomythology. Promulgating his own elucidation of the same as obvious fact and dogma, Derleth succeeded in disseminating an extremely distorted interpretation of what he termed Lovecraft's "Cthulhu Mythos." His version was not only blindly followed by other writers, but uncritically accepted by most readers and critics; the results were disastrous.

To restore the proper perspective, it is necessary first to examine Lovecraft's philosophical stance. H. P. Lovecraft was a "mechanistic materialist," in the philosophical sense of the words, totally devoid of any dualistic belief in religion or the supernatural. Possessing a bright scientific mind, already manifest in his childhood interest in chemistry and astronomy, he clearly perceived man's abysmal insignificance and meaninglessness in the vast mechanistic and purposeless cosmos, governed by blind, impersonal ("mindless") streams of force. A believer in the inexorable action of causality, he stated as early as 1921, in a letter to Rheinhart Kleiner:

> Determinism—what you call Destiny—rules inexorably; though not exactly in the personal way you seem to fancy. We have no specific destiny against which we can fight—for the fighting would be as much a part of the destiny as the final end. The real fact is simply that every event in the cosmos is caused by the action of antecedent and circumjacent forces, so that whatever we do is unconsciously the inevitable product of Nature rather than of our own volition. If an act correspond with our wish, it is Nature that made the wish, and ensured its fulfillment. (*SL* 1.132)

Contrary to what is assumed by many, Lovecraft did not conceive the cosmos as basically inimical or beneficial to man. He stated in a letter to James F. Morton, dated 30 October 1929: "I am ... an *indifferentist* ... I do not make the mistake of thinking that the resultant of the natural forces surrounding and governing organic life will have any connexion with the wishes or tastes of any part of that organic life-process ... [The cosmos] doesn't give a damn one way or the other about the especial wants and ultimate welfare of mosquitoes, rats, lice, dogs, men, horses, pterodactyls, trees, fungi, dodos, or other forms of biological energy" (*SL* 3.39).

Lovecraft was pessimistic with respect to man's ability to cope with the realization of his own meaninglessness and insignificance in an indifferent universe. The first paragraph of "The Call of Cthulhu" reflects his doubts about man's capacity to preserve his precarious sanity in a confrontation with bleak and unpalatable reality: it is only "the inability of the human mind to correlate all its contents" (*DH* 125) which prevents our mental disintegration when we come across dissociated bits of knowledge about our frightful position in the black seas of infinity that surround us. Notice that here Lovecraft is *not* deploring knowledge, but rather, *man's inability to cope with it.*

Lovecraft's fiction, and in particular his pseudomythology (which I prefer to call the Yog-Sothoth Cycle of Myth, to differentiate it from the distorted version labeled "Cthulhu Mythos" by Derleth) was *not* a reaction *against* his austere and parsimonious materialistic philosophy, but instead formed the natural outgrowth of the same. Lovecraft wrote primarily to give himself "the satisfaction of visualising more clearly and detailedly and stably the vague, elusive, fragmentary impressions of wonder, beauty, and adventurous expectancy which [were] conveyed to [him] by certain sights . . ., ideas, occurrences, and images encountered in art and literature," as he stated in "Notes on Writing Weird Fiction," and chose weird stories "because they suit[ed his] inclinations best—one of [his] strongest and most persistent wishes [having been] to achieve momentarily the illusion of some strange suspension or violation of the galling limitations of time, space, and natural law which for ever imprison us and frustrate our curiosity about the infinite cosmic places beyond the radius of our sight and analysis" (*CE* 2.175–76). Inclined to write *weird fiction*, Lovecraft's rationalistic intellect could conceive no weirder or more bizarre happening than a dislocation of natural law—not ghosts, daemons, or the supernatural, but the suspension of the laws of Nature.

Predisposed to write imaginative fiction by temperament and environmental contingencies, Lovecraft became also aware of the fact that supernatural themes were rapidly losing their ability to evoke the emotion of fear needed to "create a convincing picture of shattered natural law or cosmic alienage or 'outsideness'" (*CE* 2.176), at least among the more educated and skeptical readers. Consequently he turned to the unplumbed abysses of space and the unknown and unknowable spheres of alien dimensions (as well as to the tortuous depths of the unconscious), for the source of horror in his tales. As George T. Wetzel and Fritz Leiber have pointed out, he developed the concept of the "mechanistic supernatural," and was, in a sense, a "literary Copernicus," producing a body of cosmo-centred fiction unlike most of the anthropocentred writings of his predecessors and, regrettably, of most of his successors. Being a materialist, Lovecraft created the materialistic tale of supernatural horror. Far from implying an unconscious rejection of his philosophy, it was highly consonant with the same—it was the only kind of fiction he could have written, in view of his intellectual genius, his *Weltanschauung*, and his aesthetic inclinations!

In a letter to Frank Belknap Long, dated 27 February 1931, Lovecraft stated:

> It is inevitable that a symbolic aesthetic outlet will be demanded . . . under all phases of cosmic interpretation, as long as a sense-chained race of inquirers on a microscopic earth-dot are faced with the black, unfathomable gulph of the Outside, with

forever-unexplorable orbs and its virtually certain sprinkling of utterly unknown life-forms. A great part of religion is merely a childish and diluted pseudo-gratification of this perpetual gnawing toward the ultimate illimitable void. Superadded to this simple curiosity is the galling sense of *intolerable restraint* which all sensitive people (except self-blinded earth-gazers like little Augie Derleth) feel as they survey their natural limitations in time and space as scaled against the freedoms and expansions and comprehensions and adventurous expectancies which the mind can formulate as abstract conceptions. (*SL* 3.295)

(Well did H.P.L. realise the limitations of his pupil!)

Lovecraft did not envision the various mythopoeic conceptions that were going to become integral parts of his oeuvre at the start of his writing career. Instead, the various elements involved in his pseudomythology gradually evolved and constantly changed during his lifetime. The Yog-Sothoth Cycle of Myth centers around a certain group of alien entities from "Outside"—from beyond the sphere of conscious human experience: the unplumbed abysses of space, other dimensions, other universes, and the nightmare depths of the unconscious. The main ones are Azathoth, Yog-Sothoth, Nyarlathotep, Cthulhu, and Shub-Niggurath, and these are known with the generic name of "Old Ones" (although it does not follow that they are related or belong to a similar "species"; with the possible exception of Cthulhu, each seems to be unique). These Old Ones were, are, and will be. They are not mere symbols of the power of evil, although they may appear to be inimical to man, in the same way that man would appear to be inimical to ants, should these get in his way, The Old Ones are above and beyond mankind—they transcend man, and care no more for him than he does for ants.

As the result of occasional and more or less fortuitous contacts between man and those forces from Outside which he could not control nor comprehend, cults, superstitions, legends, and books of forbidden lore (such as the *Necronomicon*) emerged. Several of Lovecraft's stories record the consequences of attempts to use such forbidden knowledge to meddle with the powers from Outside; man, essentially helpless and impotent in his encounters with the Unknown (although at first often unaware of the extent of his own helplessness), does not fare well. In the few instances in which he escapes annihilation or insanity, it is ironically due, not to his own efforts, but to some accident beyond his control (e.g., the second sinking of R'lyeh). And what could be more terrifying for man than the realization of his own impotent insignificance face to face with the Unknown and the Unknowable?

From the above sketch it should be readily obvious that there is *no* real parallel between the Christian Mythos and Lovecraft's pseudomythology, despite Derleth's assertions to the contrary. The "Elder Gods," as benign deities representing the forces of good, were entirely Derleth's invention. The expression "Elder Gods" does appear in Lovecraft's *The Dream-Quest of Unknown Kadath* and in "The Strange High House in the Mist," but only to denote the "weak gods of the earth."[1] It also occurs in *At the Mountains of Madness,* but only as a label for one of the extraterrestrial species which inhabited the earth aeons before man. Nowhere did Lovecraft use the expression to refer to any powerful benign deities which might intercede for man—in Lovecraft's indifferent universe, man cannot expect such outside help in his confrontations with the Unknown.

August Derleth, perhaps in part due to his Catholic background, was unable to share Lovecraft's bleak cosmic vision, and conceived instead an anthropocentred universe, wherein benevolent Elder Gods and malevolent Old Ones would engage in ludicrous battles for the sake and welfare of man, much in the same way as the Judaeo-Christian God and his angels confronted Lucifer and his demonic hordes. While Lovecraft's hapless protagonists were left alone and defenseless in their chilling confrontations with an incomprehensible Reality, Derleth supplied his heroes with ridiculous star-stone amulets which played the role of garlic and the crucifix in the hackneyed vampire tale, not to mention interventions by rescuing Elder Gods which arrived with a timing reminiscent of the U.S. Cavalry in cheap Western films. (Although star-shaped stones are mentioned in *At the Mountains of Madness,* their power as talismans was entirely Derleth's unimaginative contribution.)

Not satisfied with perpetuating his own myopic pastiches, Derleth attempted to force his interpretation on the Lovecraft oeuvre, prefacing major collections of Lovecraft's tales with expositions of his own views presented as dogmatic and self-evident truths. One of his favorites was the contention that the main entities in Lovecraft's Yog-Sothoth Cycle of Myth represented elementals, a notion clearly refuted by Richard L. Tierney in his critical essay, "The Derleth Mythos." Derleth viewed Cthulhu as a water elemental, not realizing that the presence of wings, the extraterrestrial origin of Cthulhu and his kin, and the fact that he was *imprisoned* or *trapped* in his watery grave, the sunken city of R'lyeh, all militated against the hypothesis that Cthulhu is an aquatic being! (And although Cthulhu is described as only a "cousin" of the Old Ones in the *Necronomicon* passage included in "The Dunwich Horror," and is perhaps one of the weakest

---

[1] [Actually, the term "Elder Gods" does not appear in these stories; rather, the expression is "Elder Ones."—Ed.]

and least important of the main entities involved in the Yog-Sothoth Cycle of Myth—save for his immediacy—Derleth became strangely enamored with him, bestowing upon Lovecraft's pseudomythology the singularly inappropriate sobriquet "Cthulhu Mythos," and writing countless pseudo-Cthulhuoid pastiches, collected in *The Mask of Cthulhu* and *The Trail of Cthulhu*.) In a similar way, the contention that Nyarlathotep is an earth-elemental is indefensible, for this entity is in no way restricted to subterranean activities, appearing under various guises in eight Lovecraft tales (including revisions), as well as in the celebrated sonnet-sequence, Fungi from Yuggoth. Hastur (a name appearing in Robert W. Chambers's "The Yellow Sign") was mentioned by Lovecraft in his fiction only twice, in "The Whisperer in Darkness," but without giving any indication of its being aerial, cosmic, a "half-brother to Cthulhu," or even an entity at all . . . much less an air elemental! All such meaningless categorizations were strictly Derleth's.

Lovecraft wisely allowed his fictional entities to remain mysterious and nebulous—the strongest emotion of mankind being fear of the unknown, the entities were to play the role of the Unknown and the Unknowable. Not so Derleth and his disciples. By their systematic attempts at categorization and over-explanation, they committed the cardinal sin of any writer of weird tales—the over-explained and dissected Unknown ceases to be mysterious and terrifying, becoming merely absurd and ridiculous. Nothing could illustrate this point better than the Derleth collections mentioned above, and Brian Lumley's more recent *The Burrowers Beneath* and *The Transition of Titus Crow*.

One of the main "proofs" or arguments advanced by August Derleth to push his interpretation of the Old Ones as powers of evil that were expelled in the same way that Satan was expelled from Eden was the following quotation (allegedly from a Lovecraft letter), which regrettably has received more attention and diffusion than any other single paragraph attributed to Lovecraft, both here and abroad: "All my stories, unconnected as they may be, are based on the fundamental tore or legend that this world was inhabited at one time by another race who, in practis. ing black magic, lost their foothold and were expelled, yet live on out. side, ever ready to take possession of this earth again." Which doesn't sound like Lovecraft at all—particularly that allusion to "black magic." Instead, it sounds like something one would have expected from Derleth himself! Naturally, this "quotation" did not go unchallenged, but when Richard L. Tierney requested that Derleth produce the Lovecraft letter containing such paragraph, the latter became angry and refused. After Derleth's death in 1971, and as the result of the heightened interest in H. P. Lovecraft and his works in recent years, several researchers examined Lovecraft's unpublished letters at Brown University's John Hay Library and elsewhere, including L. Sprague de Camp (author of the highly opinionated biography of Lovecraft released by Doubleday in 1975). De Camp arrived at the conclusion that the famous paragraph simply *did not exist* in any of Lovecraft's letters to Derleth, or in any of the Lovecraft letters at the John Hay Lovecraft collection! Instead, this is what Lovecraft wrote to Farnsworth Wright on 5 July 1927:

> All my tales are based on the fundamental premise that common human laws and interests and emotions have no validity or significance in the vast cosmos-at-large ... To achieve the essence of real externality, whether of time or space or dimension, one must forget that such things as organic life, good and evil, love and hate, and all such local attributes of a negligible and temporary race called mankind, have any existence at all. (*SL* 2.150)

Which sounds very much like Lovecraft, indeed! It is of course possible that the famous "black magic" paragraph was paraphrased by Derleth from memory of something he had read, but was now unable to locate (he never supplied any reference to the origin of the same, other than to say that it was a Lovecraft letter), but it is also possible that the most reprinted paragraph attributed to H.P.L. was a hoax, a fabrication by his ardent but misguided disciple, "self-blinded earth-gazer" August Derleth. The suspicion is strengthened by the realization that the controversial paragraph seems to fit with Derleth's anthropocentred conception of the so-called "Cthulhu Mythos" better than anything within the Lovecraft oeuvre. The reader must judge by himself.

Parenthetically, it should be pointed out that Lovecraft of course did write about the various struggles and conflicts that took place among the different races of extraterrestrial beings preceding man on this planet—these were detailed in two grandiose and separate accounts, *At the Mountains of Madness* and "The Shadow out of Time," with their vast scope of cosmic nemesis and history. Nevertheless, none of these conflicts resembled in the least the Derlethian battle between cosmic (or should that be *comic?*) Good and Evil, between the "Elder Gods" and the Old Ones.

Another point which deserves clarification is that the Yog-Sothoth Cycle of Myth (or YSCOM, and I propose that the inadequate label "Cthulhu Mythos" be permanently discarded) refers to various alien entities, cults, books, and places, but the tales themselves—whether by Lovecraft, Derleth, or anyone else—do not, and cannot "belong" to the myth-cycle! Practically all of Lovecraft's stories are loosely connected by common themes, locales, legendry, and philosophical undercurrents, but to state that some of these tales "belong to the Cthulhu Mythos" and others don't is largely meaningless and misleading. Instead, it would be correct to state that in some of the tales elements of the Yog-Sothoth Cycle of Myth are of pivotal importance, while in others they assume a marginal role, or are absent. With this criterion in mind, a careful examination of the Lovecraft oeuvre reveals a dozen stories and novelettes in which the pseudomythological elements form the core of the narrative. These are: "The Nameless City," "The Festival," "The Call of Cthulhu," *The Dream-Quest of Unknown Kadath,* "The Dunwich Horror," "The Whisperer in Darkness," "The Shadow over Innsmouth," *At the Mountains of Madness,* "The Dreams in the Witch House," "The Shadow out of Time," "The Haunter of the Dark," and the collaboration "Through the Gates of the Silver Key" (with E. Hoffmann Price). This list differs in some respects from the ones provided by Derleth and others. "The Colour out of Space," in my opinion Lovecraft's masterpiece, is not included because it does not contain any explicit YSCOM elements, while such elements are only of marginal importance in *The Case of Charles Dexter Ward* and "The Thing on the Doorstep." On the other hand, pseudomythological entities appear in prominent roles in the *Dream-Quest* (in which Lovecraft succeeded in connecting many of his previous tales), and in "Through the Gates of the Silver Key."

It should also be pointed out that Lovecraft did encourage some of his friends and correspondents to incorporate Yog-Sothoth Myth-elements into their own works, and in return mentioned some of the others' contributions in a few of his own tales, notably in "The Whisperer in Darkness." There was nothing wrong with such procedure, of course, and tales written by old and new aspiring writers including Lovecraftian pseudomythological elements can be interesting and entertaining, particularly if they stop short of servile imitation and do not misuse or distort Lovecraft's ideas beyond recognition. Regrettably, with some very few happy exceptions, such misuse, distortion, and slavish imitation have been the rule in the past, in part due to the misinterpretation of the Lovecraft oeuvre popularized by Derleth. How many would-be Lovecraft pastichists inadvertently wound up imitating Derleth's own inferior imitations! Hopefully the trend will be reversed in the future, now that the facts are out in the open.

Once all the distortions and misconceptions superimposed by Derleth on Lovecraft's work (and perpetuated by uncritical "fans" and disciples) are removed, what remains is a work of genius, a cosmic-minded oeuvre embodying a mechanistic materialist's brilliant conception of imaginary realms.and frightful reality "beyond the fields we know," a literary rhapsody of the cosmos and man's laughable position therein, which is likely to appeal to new generations of readers all over the world, for many years to come. The Lovecraft oeuvre can be regarded as a significant contribution to world literature—may it be remembered without the "adornments," "embellishments," and "improvements" contributed by his "self-blinded, earth-gazing" imitators!

[*Whispers* 3, No. 1 (December 1976): 48–55 (as "Myth-Maker"); rev. ed. in *H. P. Lovecraft: Four Decades of Criticism*, ed. S. T. Joshi (Athens: Ohio University Press, 1980), pp. 104–12]

Who Needs the "Cthulhu Mythos"?

By David E. Schultz

As to overdoing the "Hastur" idea—of course I realise the danger of this, & have dozens of notebook entries of a totally different character. The only reason these have been postponed in favour of the "Whisperer" & "Mts. of Madness" is that the plots of these latter veritably thrust themselves on my attention and demanded to be written first.
—H. P. Lovecraft to August Derleth, 23 May 1931 (ES 1.340)

Will Murray's modest proposal in *Lovecraft Studies* 12 (Spring 1986) offers another point of view in the debate over H. P. Lovecraft's so-called Cthulhu Mythos. As Murray says, the dispute as to which Lovecraft stories belong to the Mythos and which do not (the dubious "contributions" of other writers notwithstanding) has become rather heated, and it does not appear that the matter will soon be settled. We all agree, certainly, that Mythos fiction written after Lovecraft's death is not for significant consideration in the study of Lovecraft's writing. However, Lovecraft's comments about his pseudomythology, as he referred to it in his own writings and those of his contemporaries, are of great importance in understanding the development and proliferation of the mythological elements he used in his stories.

Murray suggests that we limit the "Mythos" to three of Lovecraft's most "cosmic" stories from a period just before he began to pollute his mythic concepts by borrowing from other writers and introducing his fictional elements into the stories he ghost-wrote for clients. Bold as this suggestion is, it ultimately compounds the problem and merely introduces yet another opinion regarding which Lovecraft stories do or do not belong to the "Mythos." The solution, I think, is far simpler and lies in cleanly severing the Gordian knot to eliminate the problem effectively and permanently. S. T. Joshi has said that my suggestion—to abandon the concept and term

22

WHO NEEDS THE "CTHULHU MYTHOS"?

"Cthulhu Mythos" (or Lovecraft Mythos, for that matter)—is "extreme" (59). Rather, I see ignoring August Derleth's ill-conceived term as taking the middle course between Scylla and Charybdis.

Before we discuss the problems of the "Cthulhu Mythos," we must understand why the term came into existence. Lovecraft himself never used such a term, and many would agree that he would have had no use for one. Lovecraft once tossed off the term "Arkham cycle" in a letter to Clark Ashton Smith (*SL* 2.246), but as far as we know, he never specified which stories belong to that location-based group of stories. Presumably "The Picture in the House" (1920), "Herbert West—Reanimator" (1921–22), and even "The Terrible Old Man" (1920) would belong to the "Arkham cycle"; ("The Terrible Old Man," though it does not mention Arkham, is set in the fictitious town of Kingsport, a town that figures into many stories set in the same geographical region as Arkham.) but these are never listed among Lovecraft's Cthulhu Mythos tales. Lovecraft made tongue-in-cheek reference to the mythic background of his stories with such names as "Yog-Sothothery" or "Cthulhuism," but at those times he was merely speaking humorously. He politely resisted an early attempt by August Derleth to attach the name "The Mythology of Hastur" to the potpourri of fact and folklore mentioned in "The Whisperer in Darkness" (1930). He wrote to Derleth:

> It's not a bad idea to call this Cthulhuism & Yog-Sothothery of mine "The Mythology of Hastur"—although it was really from Machen & Dunsany & others rather than through the Bierce-Chambers line, that I picked up my gradually developing hash of theogony—or daimonogeny. Come to think of it, I guess I sling this stuff more as Chambers does than as Machen & Dunsany do—though I had written a good deal of it before I ever suspected that Chambers even wrote a weird story! I feel flattered by your adoption of some of this background. Robert E. Howard is doing it too. In making your allusions don't forget Klarkash-Ton's accursed & amorphous **Tsathoggua,** whom I have adopted into our malignly leering family pantheon! I shall identify Smith's Hyperborea with my Olathoë in the land of Lomar. (16 May 1931; *ES* 1.336)

I quote this passage at length because it is one of several in which Lovecraft subtly explained the reason for the allusions he and other writers made to each other's stories, and because it shows Lovecraft's mock enthusiasm about the matter. It should be noted that it was at this time that Derleth was writing the first of his numerous "Mythos" stories, "The Lair of the Star-Spawn."

There is no denying that Lovecraft suggested that Derleth make continued reference to this expanding base of quasi-mythological background material. He was indignant when he learned that Farnsworth Wright of *Weird Tales* rejected Derleth's story "The Horror from the Depths" (i.e. "The Evil Ones")—at about the time Wright rejected *At the Mountains of Madness*—because of allusions to Lovecraft's mythological elements, even to the extent of lifting entire phrases from Lovecraft's stories. Lovecraft wrote:

> As for Wright's rejections, as so interestingly transcribed in your letter—it almost nullifies the sting of his latest rejection to see his irrational & inattentive capriciousness so amusingly revealed on a large scale! Of all Boeotian blundering & irrelevancy! And what pointless censure of the introduction of Cthulhu & Yog-Sothoth—as if their use constituted any "infringement" on my stuff! Hades! The more these synthetic daemons are mutually written up by different authors, the better they become as general background-material. I *like* to have others use my Azathoths & Nyarlathoteps—& in return I shall use Klarkash-Ton's Tsathoggua, your monk Clithanus, & Howard's Bran. Indeed, I shall tell Wright of my attitude when next I write him. You have not used the "Elder Ones" any more specifically than Smith uses them in "The Holiness of Azédarac" (where he speaks of "Iog-Sotôt" &c)—which Wright has taken. (3 August 1931; *ES* 1.353)

Derleth misconstrued what Lovecraft meant by his statement that he liked to have others "use" his material. Even though Lovecraft said his "Azathoths and Nyarlathoteps" had become "general background-material," his emphasis seemed to be toward encouraging people to write stories about those things, though that was not really the case.

Lovecraft extended similar encouragement to other young writers. He wrote to Willis Conover: "I'll be interested to hear of your own contribution to horrific bibliography. Perhaps I'll mention it some time in a tale, since members of the *Weird Tales* group frequently use one another's synthetic daemons and forbidden books as background accessories" (2 August 1936; *Lovecraft at Last* 40).

As Murray has shown, Lovecraft was certainly his own worst enemy when it came to the expansion of his mythological background. What had started as a casual gesture, much like the tipping of hats between gentlemen, was soon less gracefully done. Whereas Lovecraft and Smith would make tantalizing allusions to elements from each other's work without detracting from the integrity of their own work, many younger writers (Derleth was only twenty-two in 1931, Conover was but fifteen in 1937) aggressively sought to "contribute" to the myth pattern merely for the sake of making the contribution and, in their eyes, placing themselves in the same league as Lovecraft and Smith and other established professionals. They can hardly be blamed because it seemed to them that many other unknown writers (but actually Lovecraft himself ghost-writing stories for others) had successfully made such allusions themselves. As we can see, Lovecraft encouraged reference to his pseudomythology, but in the three quotations above the careful reader will note that Lovecraft says the pseudomythology provides *background* material to be used only sparingly.

Following Lovecraft's death on 15 March 1937, August Derleth, with breathtaking swiftness, began planning a memorial collection of Lovecraft's works. The full impact of his effort with Donald Wandrei to publish *The Outsider and Others* is scarcely comprehensible, but we know that in less than two weeks' time Derleth was already writing to Lovecraft's friends for material to publish. Not only did he devote much energy to *The Outsider,* but he also wrote a tribute and a poem in Lovecraft's memory and quickly completed what he would call a "Cthulhu Mythos" story that he had begun five years before. These events, stimulated by Lovecraft's death, accelerated the genesis of the "Cthulhu Mythos."

Derleth never used the term "Mythology of Hastur" after Lovecraft casually brushed it aside, but he did not understand why Lovecraft was less than enthusiastic about it. In fact, Derleth seems to have missed the entire point of Lovecraft's statement, otherwise he would not have devised another term in which he merely substituted the word *Cthulhu* for *Hastur.* Quite simply, Lovecraft recognized that a formal designation and structure would have been the worst thing for a mythic background that was fragmented and unstructured and only hinted at for effect. Only Clark Ashton Smith seems to have considered the possibility that Lovecraft's pseudomythology was intentionally unstructured for the purpose of creating a greater sense of realism, and that occasional ragtag references by other writers contributed to that sense. Smith suggested this possibility to Derleth when Derleth was compiling *The Outsider and Others,* but, as we will see in many other instances, Derleth ignored the advice of someone better attuned to Lovecraft's cosmic sense. Thus, it is no surprise that eleven of the final twelve stories in *The Outsider* are stories Derleth considered to be "of the Cthulhu Mythos," or that he ignored Smith's recommendation that "The Colour out of Space" not be included among them but instead somewhere among the other tales.

Smith wrote to Derleth:

> As to the varying references to the mythos in different tales: I wonder if they weren't designed to suggest the diverse developments and interpretations of old myths and deities that spring up over great periods of time and in variant races and civilizations? I have intentionally done something of the sort in my own myth-creation. I believe [such a] theory would account for the discrepant characters given to Azathoth, Nyarlathotep, etc., in different stories. Cthulhu contains the germ of the mythos; the Dunwich Horror introduces Yog-Sothoth; and I am inclined to think the first mention of Azathoth occurs in Fungi from Yuggoth and The Whisperer in Darkness. Evidently HPL developed and varied the mythos as he went on. I believe the theory I have outlined above will afford the best explanation of discrepancies: HPL wished to indicate the natural growth of a myth-pattern through dim ages, in which the same deity or demon might present changing aspects. (28 April 1937; *Selected Letters* 293)

Smith recognized that Lovecraft did not need to construct a rigidly structured pantheon for his stories to be effective. He realized that when Lovecraft used the words "pantheon" and "gods" in relation to certain of his stories, he was using them metaphorically as a way to convey the utter alienness of the creatures he conceived. Thus, Lovecraft did not "fail" to provide certain entities in his pantheon, necessitating that other writers make up for his various lapses. Lovecraft never intended for there to be such entities.

During Lovecraft's lifetime, his friends and colleagues often mentioned Lovecraft's "mythology," the "Lovecraft mythology" or even the "Cthulhu Mythology" in their correspondence, so although Lovecraft does not seem to have used any such terms, several were in use while he was alive. The earliest reference to the "Cthulhu Mythology" in print is found following Lovecraft's death in Derleth's article "H. P. Lovecraft, Outsider," which appeared in the June 1937 number of *River:*

> After a time there became apparent in his tales a curious coherence, a myth-pattern so convincing that after its early appearance, the readers of Lovecraft's stories began to explore libraries and museums for certain imaginary titles of Lovecraft's own creation, so powerful that many another writer, with Lovecraft's permission, availed himself of facets of the mythos for his own use. Bit by bit it grew, and finally its outlines

became distinct, and it was given a name: the Cthulhu Mythology: because it was in "The Call of Cthulhu" that the myth-
pattern first became apparent. It is possible to trace the original
inception of this mythology back through Robert W. Chambers'
little-known "The King in Yellow" to Poe's *Narrative of A. Gordon
Pym* and Bierce's "An Inhabitant of Carcosa"; but in these stories
only the barest hints of something outside had appeared, and
it was Lovecraft who constructed the myth-pattern in its final
form. In his stories he merged fantasy with terror, and even his
poetry took on certain symbols of the mythos, so that presently
he was writing: ". . . all my stories, unconnected as they may
be, are based on the fundamental lore or legend that this world
was inhabited at one time by another race who, in practising
black magic, lost their foothold and were expelled, yet live on
outside ever ready to take possession of this earth again . . .", a
formula remarkable for the fact that, though it sprang from the
mind of a professed religious unbeliever, it is basically similar to
the Christian mythos, particularly in regard to the expulsion of
Satan from Eden and the power of evil. (88)

This extract is interesting for several reasons. In the first place, Derleth
clearly shows how he misunderstood the nature of Lovecraft's pseudomythology, particularly in his identification of Poe, Chambers, and Bierce
as key figures in the formulation of the "Mythos." Lovecraft admitted that
he *picked up* his theogony from Machen and Dunsany. When he said he
"slings this stuff" as Chambers did, he surely was referring to the way
Chambers dropped names in stories.

Derleth's article, written c. April 1937, contains what is probably a
spurious quote attributed to Lovecraft and apparently fabricated (without
intention to deceive) by Harold S. Farnese. In a letter to Derleth dated 11
April 1937 (ms., State Historical Society of Wisconsin), Farnese attributed
to Lovecraft the famous "Black Magic" quotation. Derleth immediately
latched on to the quote and used it at every opportunity to describe what
he believed was the essence of Lovecraft's work, for he believed it to be in
Lovecraft's own words. Unless we find Lovecraft's letters to Farnese, we
will never know if Lovecraft ever wrote such an unseemly description of
his work. However, it seems that Farnese may have had a penchant for
quoting from memory, as when he told Donald Wandrei that Lovecraft was
a major contributor to *Weird Tales* along with a writer he called "Bellknap
Jones," surely thinking of Frank Belknap Long. Dirk W. Mosig, in his article
"H. P. Lovecraft: Myth-Maker," quotes from several of Farnese's letters to
Lovecraft, and those letters show that it may have been Farnese who saw

Lovecraft's work as being concerned with black magic. Lovecraft's replies to Farnese (*SL* 4.69–71) provide information that is more nearly in keeping with the actual content and objectives of his stories, and it is noteworthy that he does not mention "black magic" as a typical subject.[1] Thus, Farnese innocently contributed to the birth of the "Cthulhu Mythos" as espoused by August Derleth.

In the face of a rather timid objection from Clark Ashton Smith, Derleth maintained that the Lovecraft mythology was remarkable because it resembled the "Christian mythos." This is remarkable only because there is no evidence whatsoever that Lovecraft founded his mythology with its "pantheon" of gods as a parallel to the monotheistic Christian religion, and also because, as Smith said, there is no reference to "expulsion" of Cthulhu in "The Call of Cthulhu." Even more remarkable is the fact that it occurred to Derleth to interpret the mythology in this way and that this interpretation went unchallenged for many years.

The "Cthulhu Mythos" as Derleth perceived it is, at best, an artificial, rigid grouping of Lovecraft's stories based upon a misinterpretation by someone not attuned to Lovecraft's philosophical outlook. In the nearly seventy-five years that the term has been in existence, there has been no consensus as to what stories are part of the "Mythos," nor has there been a clear idea of why some of Lovecraft's stories should belong to it and others should not. To become ensnared in Derleth's and Farnese's terminology and interpretation (later augmented by Francis T. Laney's "gods of water, of fire, of air, and of earth" which Derleth called "elementals") is to allow Lovecraft's expansive cosmic vision to become narrow and clouded. Lovecraft's stories were founded on his own philosophical outlook, whereas Derleth's interpretation is founded on his. For instance, Lovecraft was an atheist and Derleth was a Roman Catholic, and both had distinctly opposed philosophical points of view.

Let us take, for example, a letter from August Derleth to Robert Barlow dated 15 June 1934. In that letter, written three years before Lovecraft's death (indeed, Lovecraft may have seen the letter, for he was visiting Barlow in Florida at the time), Derleth wrote of his own stories using Lovecraft's mythological entities, and of his conception of what Lovecraft's mythology was about:

> According to the mythology as I understand it, it is briefly this: the Ancient or Old Ones ruled the universe—from their

[1] [Mosig's discussion of Farnese occurred in a footnote to "H. P. Lovecraft: Myth-Maker," appended after the article was first published. That footnote is omitted in the appearance of Mosig's essay in this volume. On this matter see David E. Schultz, "The Origin of Lovecraft's 'Black Magic' Quote" (p. 214).—Ed.]

authority revolted the evil Cthulhu, Hastur the Unspeakable, etc., who in turn spawned the Tcho-Tcho people and other cultlike creatures. The Star-Warriors are the condottieri of the Ancient Ones. Though your drawing is okeh, I personally had pictured the Star-Warriors as very human-like, save for an exalted and striking head. Besides all this, they shone, as from some great inner light. However, H. P. is the final court of appeal in all these matters. Of all my pieces, only THE THING THAT WALKED ON THE WIND is worth-while adding to the mythology. (Ms., State Historical Society of Wisconsin)

Derleth's feeble understanding of Lovecraft's stories written to that time is difficult to conceive. The alienness of his creatures was sheer genius in that they bore no resemblance to human beings or anything of this earth; yet Derleth envisioned his own Star-Warriors as being "human-like." It was Derleth who called Hastur "the Unspeakable." Indeed, Lovecraft mentioned Hastur only twice in a single story, "The Whisperer in Darkness" (1930), but it was Derleth who became obsessed with Hastur, using the creature as the focus of Lovecraft's pseudomythology for a time. (Lovecraft's letters of reply to Derleth from the summer of 1931 make repeated reference to "Hastur figures," obviously Derleth's term.) Lovecraft never indicated what significance Hastur had, if any. Robert W. Chambers, from whom Lovecraft borrowed Hastur, is equally vague in his mention of Hastur (if anything, Hastur is a place in Chambers; note the phrase "When from Carcosa, the Hyades, Hastur, and Aldebaran . . ." in the story "The Repairer of Reputations" from *The King in Yellow*), and Ambrose Bierce, who conceived of Hastur in his "Haïta the Shepherd," referred to Hastur only as "the god of shepherds"—surely a pastoral sort of god. (But see Lovecraft's reference to "the accursed cult of Hastur" in his description of Chambers's "The Yellow Sign" in "Supernatural Horror in Literature" [1925–27] and the cult of evil men in "The Whisperer in Darkness.") As Lovecraft pointed out repeatedly, Cthulhu is not evil. Smith reminded Derleth of this, but Derleth ignored him. Cthulhu's intentions regarding human beings are not evil, for evil is a human conception. We attribute evil as a motive to Cthulhu's actions because of his sheer alienness and because of his utter disregard for humanity, but we could not call Cthulhu intrinsically evil. Lovecraft mentioned Derleth's "Tcho-Tchos" only in passing in "The Horror in the Museum" (1933) and "The Shadow out of Time" (1934–35), so whatever Derleth meant in his letter cannot be attributed to anything Lovecraft wrote but only to Derleth's conception of his own creations. Whether Derleth ever went to the "final court of appeal in all these matters" is not known, but it would seem he did not. In fact, following Lovecraft's death, Derleth himself assumed that role, even to the extent of informing would-be "Mythos" writers that the Mythos was protected by copyright and that only with infrequently given permission could someone be allowed to write a Mythos story.

Since Derleth exhibited a poor understanding of Lovecraft's work, we should not have to defend what Lovecraft wrote on Derleth's terms. Defending an idea conceived by August Derleth on Lovecraft's behalf would be counterproductive. Such action would be akin to arguing about the interpretation of passages from the Bible on the basis of their translation into modern English. If we wanted to know what the writers of antiquity meant in any particular book in the Bible, we would first of all have to be familiar with their own language and culture and the audience for whom the book was written. So too is the case with Lovecraft. We should focus our attention on his writings as he himself wrote them and explained them. This is not to say that others may not be helpful in our understanding of Lovecraft and his work. Interpretation by learned scholars can be of great value. However, we must always keep the original in view and not deviate far from it.

If we examine Derleth's "Mythos" stories (of which he wrote more than thirty), we see that he interpreted very broadly Lovecraft's invitation to make allusions to his background material. The reason is that Derleth read what he wanted into Lovecraft's invitation, as seen in the following passage:

> Lovecraft began to write these stories without any overall plan; it is doubtful that he had even conceived the Cthulhu Mythos as it finally evolved when he began writing such tales as "The Nameless City" and "The Call of Cthulhu." When at last he began consciously to construct the pantheon, he invited some of his fellow writers to add to it, with the result that Clark Ashton Smith added Tsathoggua and Atlach-Nacha, Frank Belknap Long the Hounds of Tindalos and Chaugnar Faugn, Henry Kuttner Nyogtha, and I myself added Cthugha, corresponding to the fire elemental Lovecraft failed to provide, as well as Lloigor, Zhar, the Tcho-Tcho people, Ithaqua, etc. Lovecraft added Hypnos, god of sleep; Dagon, ruler of the Deep Ones, ocean depth allies of Cthulhu; Yig, the prototype of Quetzalcoatl; the "Abominable Snow-Men of Mi-Go," etc.
> ("Introduction" xiv–xv)

This statement is so full of inaccuracies as to make one wonder how ignorant of Lovecraft and his work his self-proclaimed disciple could have been. As noted, the mythology was probably intentionally unstructured. Smith told Derleth that Hypnos was the god of sleep in Greek mythology, not a Lovecraftian invention, but Derleth ignored him. Dagon and the Mi-Go are likewise founded in real myths. It is false to say that Lovecraft "invited some of his fellow writers to add to" the Mythos as an end in itself. Derleth's statement implies that only a certain privileged few—he among them—were allowed to contribute.

As we know, Lovecraft primarily borrowed terms—and only terms—from other writers, and he invited nearly anyone who wished freely to make allusions to things mentioned in his stories. He continually urged writers to develop their own ideas in their own milieux, but he never urged them to write about what was essentially his unique vision. No great artist tries to make other artists use the products of his imagination in their works. What Lovecraft did was urge writers to make glancing references to his own or Smith's or Howard's myth-creations, merely to magnify the expansiveness of what they may have been writing about. Surely *urge* is too strong a word to use to describe this phenomenon. It might better be said that Lovecraft was amused by such references; he did not direct any campaign to extend his pseudomythology, as Derleth seems to have believed when he wrote in 1943 that "I am at last heeding his [Lovecraft's] admonition to develop the vein he opened" (*Weird Tales*, March 1944, p. 104). This statement is Derleth's rather arrogant interpretation of Lovecraft's letter to him of 3 August 1931.

Derleth remained incredibly ignorant of how various names were assimilated into Lovecraft's stories. Clark Ashton Smith did not "add" Tsathoggua to Lovecraft's myth-pattern. Lovecraft made allusions to Tsathoggua in his work; Smith did not actively add anything. Derleth knew this because it was explained to him by both Lovecraft and Smith. Lovecraft read Smith's "The Tale of Satampra Zeiros" in manuscript in December 1929 and was so impressed by the story, which he thought was going to be printed soon in *Weird Tales,* that he made a nodding reference to Tsathoggua in "The Mound" and "The Whisperer in Darkness." But Smith's story was rejected, so Lovecraft's reference to Tsathoggua actually appeared in print before Smith's. Even so, Lovecraft did not "adopt" Smith's creation, he merely mentioned it. In the same way, Frank Belknap Long did not "add" the hounds of Tindalos to Lovecraft's pseudomythology, nor did Lovecraft adopt them—he merely referred to them in "The Whisperer in Darkness."

Derleth himself made numerous intentional contributions to the Lovecraft canon, for his Lloigor, Cthugha, Ithaqua, Tcho-Tcho people, and others are all found in stories that do not reflect any mode of fictional expression natural to Derleth. They are found in what can only be called Lovecraft pastiches. Although Lovecraft did not encourage writers to contribute to his mythology, neither did he discourage writers like Derleth from making overt use of his ideas. Following Lovecraft's death, Derleth made continued use of Lovecraft's material, while other so-called Mythos writers ceased. After all, the exercise of making references to each other's stories was something of an inside joke, and with Lovecraft gone, there was little fun in continuing the game. Derleth himself perversely had little regard for his numerous "Mythos" stories. He continually said they were entertainments not worth the effort to read more than once. Nevertheless, Derleth regularly wrote new Mythos stories because they sold easily, especially when he shared a byline with the deceased Lovecraft.

As noted, the pseudomythological elements to which Lovecraft referred were only part of the fictional background of his stories. They were never the subject of his stories, but rather part of the background against which the main action occurred. That is to say, Lovecraft did not write *about* Cthulhu, Yog-Sothoth, the *Necronomicon,* or any of the other places or creatures or books found in his stories. The subject of his stories was typically the small place that man occupies in an uncaring cosmos, and his fictional creations were only part of the means by which he sought to demonstrate that.

For instance, "The Shadow out of Time" is not strictly *about* the Great Race (or any of the elements from Lovecraft stories alluded to within it), although their history forms a large and significant part of the story. The story is *about* Nathaniel Wingate Peaslee's breakdown in his conception of reality and his place in it; and therefore, of necessity, our place in the universe. Lovecraft is saying that we tend to look at the world and ourselves in a very narrow way. If we looked beyond ourselves—or, as in this story, if we are forced to look beyond—we may not be able to comprehend or bear the significance of what really exists. The horror in the story is that Peaslee is not in total control of his life; everything he knew prior to his realization that the Great Race once occupied a significant though unknown part of our past has been shattered. Worse still, we find we are actually more akin to the Great Race than we might suspect; especially because we both have reason to fear an unknown elder race hinted at in the story.

Likewise, *At the Mountains of Madness* (1931)—Lovecraft's version of a "dinosaur egg" story—is an analysis of the reaction of a group of men to the discovery of an ancient, alien race that predates humanity and that once occupied the earth. There has been no record of their existence, save strange allusions in a book not taken very seriously. The men discover the book was correct, and to their horror they discover that the ancient race was not entirely dead; they themselves are responsible for freeing the Old Ones from their icy prison. The focus of the story is Prof. Dyer's musings about the significance of their discovery. It would have a startling effect on our thoughts regarding our place in the history of this planet.

In other words, Lovecraft's stories are about people, not exotic monsters from strange places. His stories address how we might be affected by knowledge of such things, but they are not *about* those things. The unfortunate fact is that most of Lovecraft's imitators, under the tutelage of August Derleth, have tended to write only about the monsters.

By May 1937 August Derleth had seen only about half of the stories he later referred to as Lovecraft's "Mythos" stories. It was Derleth who, on the basis of only a very sketchy background, felt that Lovecraft needed to name and organize the mythology about which Lovecraft had written only occasionally. Whereas Lovecraft was essentially indifferent to his pseudo-mythology, Derleth was quite obsessed with it. With the proliferation of more and more Mythos stories by writers in amateur publications, the term "Cthulhu Mythos," an ill-conceived expression from the beginning, has acquired a pejorative connotation. Lovecraft scholars have tried to avoid this by using the term "Lovecraft Mythos," but too many people still associate the substitute term with what August Derleth originally meant by "Cthulhu Mythos." My suggestion to dispense with reference to a "Cthulhu Mythos" is not new by any means. Richard L. Tierney and Dirk W. Mosig have both suggested abandoning the term as being inappropriate in the discussion of Lovecraft's works, but their suggestions have been ignored largely because they have been misunderstood and because they appeared merely to have supplanted the offending term with another one to no particular advantage.

Tierney's article, "The Derleth Mythos," was one of the early attempts to address Derleth's lack of understanding of Lovecraft's work. By referring to a "Derleth Mythos," Tierney was somewhat sarcastically saying that the "Mythos" was nothing more than Derleth's incorrect and earthbound interpretation of Lovecraft's cosmic vision. In exposing the Mythos for what it was, Tierney sought to convince us to look back to Lovecraft's words to determine what he actually wrote about and to ignore Derleth's mistaken and authoritarian interpretations. It seems Tierney preferred we not use the term "Cthulhu Mythos" because it conjured up Derleth's mistaken interpretation of Lovecraft's work, as well as the growing body of second-rate fiction based on that interpretation as well. However, many misunderstood Tierney's intent, and even now we see professed distinctions being made between a "Derleth Mythos" and a "Cthulhu Mythos" when Tierney had indicated that they were one and the same (see Price).

Dirk W. Mosig, inspired in part by Tierney's essay, explored the shortcomings of the ongoing misinterpretation of Lovecraft's pseudo-mythology. Because Derleth described the "mythos" in terms of the stories that "belonged" to it, what Lovecraft wrote about and the vehicles in which he discussed it were referred to by the same term. In an attempt to eradicate the inaccurate and vague term "Cthulhu Mythos," Mosig encouraged Lovecraft scholars to adopt the term "Yog-Sothoth Cycle of Myth" to refer to the myth cycle itself, with its attendant creatures and books and places, much as we would use the expression "Greek mythology" to embrace the legends of the Greek gods and heroes. Any works that mention characters, places, or artifacts from Greek mythology, such as the *Iliad* or *Odyssey* of Homer, would not be referred to as the "Greek Mythos." It would be equally inappropriate to say that the "Cthulhu Mythos" consists of "The Call of Cthulhu," "The Dunwich Horror," and so on. Unfortunately, nearly everyone (this writer included) construed the term "Yog-Sothoth Cycle of Myth" to be a mere substitute for "Cthulhu Mythos," and so the term never was accepted because of its cumbrousness and because of the comfortable familiarity of Derleth's term.

If we simply abandon the term "Cthulhu Mythos," where might we turn for ways to describe the content of Lovecraft's stories? Let us examine a few key descriptions written by Lovecraft himself that can give us a foundation on which to base study of his writings. One is from his now-famous letter to Farnsworth Wright which accompanied the second submittal of "The Call of Cthulhu" for publication in *Weird Tales:*

> All my tales are based on the fundamental premise that common human laws and interests and emotions have no validity or significance in the cosmos-at-large. To me there is nothing but puerility in a tale in which the human form-and the local human passions and conditions and standards-are depicted as native to other worlds or other universes. To achieve the essence of real externality, whether of time or space or dimension, one must forget that such things as organic life, good and evil, love and hate, and all such local attributes of a negligible and temporary race called mankind, have any existence at all. Only the human scenes and characters must have human qualities. *These* must be handled with unsparing *realism,* (not catchpenny *romanticism*) but when we cross the line to the boundless and hideous unknown—the shadow-haunted *Outside*—we must remember to leave our humanity and terrestrialism at the threshold. (*SL* 2.150)

Another is from his "Biographical Notice" of 1928: "[My] serious literary efforts [are] now confined to tales of dream-life, strange shadow, and cosmic 'outsideness', notwithstanding sceptical rationalism of outlook and keen regard for the sciences" (*CE* 5.286).

These two quotations provide ample basis for the study of Lovecraft's work. Any discerning reader can see that these statements apply to nearly all of Lovecraft's works, and so can be considered genuine expressions of Lovecraft's intent in his fiction. It is telling that Lovecraft does not say that his literary efforts are confined to attempts to create a new mythology, since nearly every story written after 1928 is considered by Mythos enthusiasts to be a "Mythos" story. It may amaze some readers to learn that Derleth used both of the quotations above in essays about Lovecraft right beside the familiar "Black Magic" quote and Derleth's own typical Mythos descriptions, even though it is clear that those viewpoints are incompatible.

Derleth's unflagging forty-year campaign for a "Cthulhu Mythos" has had far-reaching consequences. In reference books Lovecraft invariably is dubbed the inventor of the Cthulhu Mythos—what Derleth called Lovecraft's "crowning achievement." Lovecraft deserves better recognition than that. Derleth may have thought he was doing Lovecraft the dubious favor of assigning a name to and structuring (and even completing) what he erroneously assumed to be the most significant aspect of Lovecraft's work, and then stepping aside to let Lovecraft bask in the glory of the recognition of his creation. This action has done more harm than good. Lovecraft's stories offer much more than exotic extraterrestrials and occult books. They challenge us to consider the world in which we live in light of what science has told us about it. To wrestle with ambiguous, or downright incorrect, terms and concepts foisted upon Lovecraft by a well-meaning but misguided admirer of his work is to waste our time and to allow ourselves to be distracted from the grander vistas opened to us in Lovecraft's stories. Let us lay the unwieldy "Mythos" aside and go directly to Lovecraft's works if we mean to grasp its essence.

Works Cited

Derleth, August. "H. P. Lovecraft, Outsider." *River* 1, No. 3 (June 1937): 88–89.

———. "Introduction" to *The Dunwich Horror and Others*. Sauk City, WI: Arkham House, 1963. ix–xx.

Joshi, S. T. "The Development of Lovecraftian Studies, 1971–1982 (Part III)." *Lovecraft Studies* No. 11 (Fall 1985): 54–65.

Murray, Will. "An Uncompromising Look at the Cthulhu Mythos." *Lovecraft Studies* No. 12 (Spring 1986): 26–31.

Price, Robert M. "H. P. Lovecraft and the Cthulhu Mythos." *Crypt of Cthulhu* No. 35 (Hallowmass 1985): 3–11.

Smith, Clark Ashton. *Selected Letters of Clark Ashton Smith.* Edited by David E. Schultz and Scott Connors. Sauk City, WI: Arkham House, 2003.

[*Lovecraft Studies* No. 13 (Fall 1986): 43–53]

Lovecraft Waits Dreaming

By Simon MacCulloch

"What is the Cthulhu Mythos?" is a question which has persisted to the point of obsession in discussion of the fiction of H. P. Lovecraft. Answers have ranged from Will Murray's provocative suggestion that "The true Mythos exists in only three Lovecraft stories—the three rightfully considered his greatest: 'The Call of Cthulhu,' 'The Colour out of Space,' and 'The Dunwich Horror'" (31), to Stefan Dziemianowicz's equally bold assertion that "The Cthulhu Mythos is that nebulous network of amateur and professional fiction in which stories achieve some sort of fellowship through the superficial traits they share" (38): not to mention those who "find HPL's 'mythos' a useful paradigm in gaining access to the deeper, non-human areas of the subconscious" (Lyons 75).

Why bother? Well, the short story "The Call of Cthulhu," written in the summer of 1926, occupies a central position both chronologically and thematically in Lovecraft's fiction, consolidating a concept towards which he has been working as early as "Dagon" (1917) and which he would be elaborating as late as "The Haunter of the Dark" (1935). The extent to which that concept has captured the imaginations of readers and writers (not to mention practising occultists—and we shan't again in this essay) remains the most convincing measure of his artistic achievement. And that achievement is viewed by many as the greatest to which twentieth-century horror literature can lay claim.

"The Great Old Ones . . . lived ages before there were any men, and . . . came to the young world out of the sky. Those Old Ones were gone now, inside the earth and under the sea; but their dead bodies had told their secrets in dreams to the first men, who formed a cult which had never died . . . There were arts which could revive Them when the stars had come round again to the right positions in the cycle of eternity. . . . They all lay in stone houses in Their great city of R'lyeh, preserved by the spells of mighty Cthulhu for a glorious resurrection when the stars and the earth might once more be ready for Them . . . and the secret priests would take great Cthulhu from His tomb to revive His subjects and resume His rule of earth. The time would be easy to know, for then mankind would have become as the Great Old Ones; free and wild and beyond good and evil . . . and all the earth would flame with a holocaust of ecstasy and freedom" (*DH* 140–41).

In this extract from "The Call of Cthulhu" we can identify two essential elements of the fictional matter on which whatever it is we call the Cthulhu Mythos is based. These are, firstly, the Great Old Ones themselves—sorry, Themselves—secondly, the means by which and context in which They are perceived by the human race. The former has yielded a tribe of extraterrestial entities—principally Azathoth, Yog-Sothoth, and Nyarlathotep—together with their diverse exotic avatars, minions, rivals, and habitats. The latter has generated a library of textbooks, Abdul Alhazred's *Necronomicon* chief among them, and fuelled activities ranging from the primitive worship of the Cthulhu cult to the scientific procedure of the Miskatonic University, typified in individuals such as the "dark and goatish" Wilbur Whateley and his adversary, the "erudite Henry Armitage (A. M. Miskatonic, Ph.D. Princeton, Litt. D. Johns Hopkins)." Obviously, the above extract takes the viewpoint of the former, so in terms of Lovecraft's concept of the Mythos, as opposed to its fictional constituents, it gives us only half the picture.

To appreciate the full picture, we ought to begin by asking what Lovecraft's use for these inventions was. Presumably, it was to assist his fiction in the performance of that which he regarded as the essential function of supernatural horror in literature—the creation in the reader of a sense of cosmic dread, awe mixed with horror. As a guide to the writing of a fictional recipe which might produce this effect. Lovecraft no doubt had regard to other writers whom he held in esteem. But more importantly, we can assume he relied as any writer does upon his own responses to imaginative stimuli.

Lovecraft wrote that "My most poignant emotional experiences . . . concern the lure of unplumbed space, the terror of the encroaching outer void, and the struggle of the ego to transcend the known and established order of time, space, matter, force, geometry and natural law in general." Equally: "Time, space and natural law hold for me suggestions of intolerable bondage, and I can form no picture of emotional satisfaction which does not involve their defeat—especially the defeat of time, so that one may merge oneself with the whole historic stream and be wholly emancipated from the transient and the ephemeral."

These statements indicate a powerful emotional desire to transcend the finite viewpoint of the mortal individual so as to be one with the cosmos, coupled with an equally powerful intellectual conviction that the cosmos is arranged so as to frustrate that desire. Lovecraft's understanding was that "common human laws and emotions have no validity or significance in the vast cosmos-at-large" (*SL* 2.150), and this philosophy of "cosmic indifferentism" was the fundamental premise of his stories. What happens in them is designed to convey that understanding and its implications for the way in which human beings exercise the faculty of their imagination, collectively and midividually, with regard to their place in the scheme of things.

In "The Call of Cthulhu," Lovecraft presents the activity of dreaming, perhaps the oldest and most universal exercise of the human imagination, as humanity's channel of communion with the vast indifferent forces of the cosmos-at-large, symbolised by the Great Old Ones. His point is that there is a long-established and widespread tendency—sometimes conscious, more often unconscious—of the human mind to seek some kind of self-transcendant merging with something greater than the self, and thereby ultimately with the cosmos. He also suggests that this impulse, a valid universalisation own "lure of unplumbed space," acquires exceptional momentum when it is pursued collectively. And in the form of the Cthulhu cult, he represents its foremost vehicle of expression in the society of his own day and no doubt of our own: religion and mysticism in all its forms.

If the Cthulhu cult's vision of a "holocaust of ecstasy and freedom" is identified with Lovecraft's own desire to "be wholly emancipated from the transient and the ephemeral," we can easily see in the opponents of the cult the counterbalancing intellectual conviction of their creator's that the cosmos simply will not entertain such presumption on the art of its biological ephemera. The scientifically-minded investigators who view the Great Old Ones in their true perspective as indifferent engines of mankind's destruction rather than anthropomorphic instruments of its salvation embody an impulse opposite to the religious/mystical urge towards self-transcendent merging: the scientific/rational inclination to delineate precisely mankind's true insignificant place in the cosmos and hold him strictly to it until new facts suggest otherwise.

So we can take "The Call of Cthulhu" and its followers in the Lovecraft oeuvre as its author's dramatisation, through the metaphor of a struggle between the "cultist" and the "investigator" responses to the existence of the Great Old Ones, of his own internal dichotomy between a desire for emotional satisfaction and an insistence upon intellectual clarity in the face of an indifferent cosmos—a dichotomy which he saw reflected in society at large by the usually polarised viewpoints of religion/mysticism and science/rationality.

The dramatic tension which Lovecraft creates and sustains through his careful balancing of the implications for human beings of pursuing to the extreme either of these two responses is a major factor in the success of these stories. On the one hand, those who seek to be "as the Great Old Ones" are shown to be deluded, barbaric, depraved—less than human in all respects save one: the superhuman transports of emotional delight in which their delusion enables them to indulge together. Those who, by contrast, have "looked upon all that the universe has to hold of horror" with unblinking clarity are by virtue of their extraordinary perception set intellectually far above the ignorant mass of humanity, and stand nobly at the forefront of the forces of civilisation: yet their knowledge tends to render them emotional cripples, estranged from their fellows, suicidally depressed and nervously debilitated to the point of insanity. While the "cultist" sacrifices integrity of mind to a collective delusion, trading his sense of discrete identity for participation in an ecstatic dream, the "investigator" preserves integrity of mind by independently renouncing all sense of belonging in the cosmos, holding fast to an understanding of his place in the scheme of things whose price is alienation from a reality more starkly unsympathetic than his fellows can comprehend. Either the intellect or the emotions must be denied; the individual is either devoured utterly by dream, or exiled eternally from it.

Lovecraft himself preferred the stance of the alienated rationalist to that of the committed believer. It is Armitage and his ilk, after all, who are right about the nature of the Great Old Ones and the consequences for mankind of their awakening; in the end, it is chance, not the preparation of the cultists, which releases Cthulhu, and there is no "ecstasy and freedom" for mankind in His resurrection, only casual destruction. Nevertheless, as S. T. Joshi has pointed out, Lovecraft "was a scientist at heart, and that gave him a love of clarity. But he was also a dreamer . . ." (43). And he felt the desire to "merge oneself with the whole historic stream" with sufficient acuity to declare "I Am Providence"—a statement of self-transcendent faith whose value to his imaginative life is emphasised not least by its appearance on his gravestone. It need not surprise us that he sought a third option whereby the seemingly irreconcilable aims of emotional joy and intellectual truth might be united, not that he found that option in the imaginative exercise which the readers and writers of literature regularly perform.

In reading aesthetically successful fiction we seem temporarily to transcend our time-and-space-bound perspective to partake of the dream of another, perhaps greater (certainly different), imagination than our own.

If the fiction is supernatural horror as Lovecraft practised it, that merging of minds will bring with it the illusion of being "wholly emancipated from the transient and the ephemeral" which he regarded as the apogee of emotional fulfilment. At the same time, Lovecraft like any serious writer sought in his fiction to express the unmitigated truth about man's place in the order of things, thus maintaining the intellectual integrity which purely escapist fantasy lacks; he did not believe in the Great Old Ones, but he was convinced of the validity of what they represented, the cosmic indifference to mankind which was the core of his philosophy. With "The Call of Cthulhu," Lovecraft achieved a truthful delusion in which perception and delight are fused with such skill that the reader feels, with Lovecraft's Outsider, that "in my new wildness and freedom I almost welcome the bitterness of alienage" (*DH* 52).

As we have noted, Lovecraft was aware that the efficacy of the imagination was increased when it was exercised in concert. It was perfectly logical, therefore, that having evolved a satisfactory equation for achieving through his art a synthesis of the non-rational and rational approaches to the problem of an indifferent cosmos, he encouraged the active involvement of other writers in the production of further material based on his formula. Such involvement could and did enhance the lifelikeness, and thus the affective power, of the dream, in the same way that mutually held beliefs reinforce each other in society at large. The price was that the intellectual integrity of the fiction was correspondingly reduced, as different writers had the Great Old Ones represent different things, or nothing at all. This trend continued after Lovecraft's death, to the point where most Cthulhu Mythos fiction was not a fusion of emotional fulfilment with intellectual clarity, but an escapist indulgence which writers and critics sympathetic to Lovecraft's original aim rightly came to view with the same distaste registered by the author's fictional investigators when confronted with the identical self-gratifying delusions of the Cthulhu cultists.

Happily, there are enough writers and critics of this disposition working today to reinsert the viewpoint of the alienated rationalist in the equation to balance that of the committed believer. It may be that despite such work the Cthulhu Mythos can now be said to be nothing more than such fictitious history as may be derived from the sum of writings which have sought to reinforce, helpfully or otherwise, the verisimilitude of "The Call of Cthulhu" by explicit use or elaboration of its peculiar fictional constituents. But the achievement of "The Call of Cthulhu" itself will remain undiminished as long as readers can sense, behind the fake horror of the Great Old Ones, the true horror of a cosmos indifferent to mankind. Lovecraft's dream has not died, but has been preserved through the imaginations of its followers; whenever our own stars are right, our minds aligned with the pattern of Lovecraft's view of the cosmos, we can resurrect it in all its dread glory, and find to our surprise that it is not the idle wish-fulfilling daydream which its more credulous disciples have made of it, but a ruthlessly efficient nightmare. The type of nightmare which enables us to assimilate as far as possible those aspects of experience which disturb us most deeply, the better to face reality again upon awakening.

Works Cited

Dziemianowicz, Stefan. Review of *Tales of the Cthulhu Mythos* (Arkham House, 1990). *Crypt of Cthulhu* No. 73 (St. John's Eve 1990): 35–38.
Joshi, S. T., ed. *H. P. Lovecraft: Four Decades of Criticism*. Athens: Ohio University Press, 1980.
Lyons, Mick. Letter. *Lovecraft Studies* Nos. 19/20 (Fall 1989): 74–75.
Murray, Will. "An Uncompromising Look at the Cthulhu Mythos." *Lovecraft Studies* No. 12 (Spring 1986): 26–31.

[*Skeleton Crew* (October 1990): 22–27]

The Cthulhu Mythos: Lovecraft vs. Derleth

By S. T. Joshi

The "Cthulhu Mythos" (the quotations seem essential nowadays): What is it? Is it anything at all? Now that we have emerged from the shadow of August Derleth (although there are those who would plunge us back into the dark again), we can perhaps look at this whole phenomenon with a little less naïveté and a little keener critical scrutiny. Whether such a scrutiny will have any effect upon those many eager beavers out there who are so keen on writing "Cthulhu Mythos" stories is another question.

There is, to be sure, something going on in many of the tales of Lovecraft's last decade of writing: they are frequently interrelated by a complex series of cross-references to a constantly evolving body of imagined myth, and many of them build upon features—superficial or profound as the case may be—in previous tales. But certain basic points can now be made, although even some of these are not without controversy: 1) Lovecraft himself did not coin the term "Cthulhu Mythos"; 2) Lovecraft felt that *all* his tales embody his basic philosophical principles; 3) the mythos, if it can be said to be anything, is not the tales themselves nor even the philosophy behind the tales, but a series of *plot devices* utilised to convey that philosophy. Let us study each of these points further.

1) The term "Cthulhu Mythos" was invented by August Derleth after Lovecraft's death; of this there is no question. The closest Lovecraft ever came to giving his invented pantheon and related phenomena a name was when he made a casual reference to "Cthulhuism & Yog-Sothothery" (*ES* 1.336), and it is not at all clear what these terms really signify.

2) When Lovecraft claimed in a letter to Frank Belknap Long in 1931 that "'Yog-Sothoth' is basically an immature conception, and unfitted for really serious literature" (*SL* 3.293) he may perhaps have been unduly modest, whatever he may have meant by "Yog-Sothoth" here. But as the

rest of this letter makes clear, Lovecraft was utilising his pseudomythology as one (among many) of the ways to convey his fundamental philosophical message, whose chief feature was cosmicism. This point is made clear in a letter written to Farnsworth Wright in July 1927 upon the resubmittal of "The Call of Cthulhu" to *Weird Tales* (it had been rejected upon initial submission):

> Now all my tales are based on the fundamental premise that. common human laws and interests and emotions have no validity or significance in the vast cosmos-at-large. To me there is nothing but puerility in a tale in which the human form— and the local human passions and conditions and standards— are depicted as native to other worlds or other universes. To achieve the essence of real externality, whether of time or space or dimension, one must forget that such things as organic life, good and evil, love and hate, and all such local attributes of a negligible and temporary race called mankind have any existence at all. (*SL* 2.150)

This statement may perhaps not be capable of bearing quite the philosophical weight that some (including myself) have placed upon it: in spite of the very general nature of the first sentence, the bulk of the passage (and of the letter as a whole) deals with a fairly specific point of *technique* in regard to the weird or science fiction tale—the portrayal of extraterrestrials. What Lovecraft was combating was the already well-established convention (found in Edgar Rice Burroughs, Ray Cummings, and others) of depicting extraterrestrials as not merely humanoid in appearance but also in language, habits, and emotional or psychological makeup. This is why Lovecraft created such an outré name as "Cthulhu" to designate a creature that had come from the depths of space.

And yet, the passage quoted above maintains that *all* Lovecraft's tales emphasise cosmicism in some form or another. Whether this is actually the case is another matter, but at least Lovecraft felt it to be so. If, then, we segregate certain of Lovecraft's tales as employing the framework of his "artificial pantheon and myth-background" (as he writes in "Some Notes on a Nonentity" [*CE* 5.209], it is purely for convenience, with a full knowledge that Lovecraft's work is not to be grouped arbitrarily, rigidly, or exclusively into discrete categories ("New England tales," "Dunsanian tales." and "Cthulhu Mythos tales," as Derieth decreed), since it is transparently clear that these (or any other) categories are not well-defined nor mutually exclusive.

3) It is careless and inaccurate to say that the Lovecraft Mythos *is* Love-

craft's philosophy: his philosophy is mechanistic materialism and all its ramifications, and if the Lovecraft Mythos is anything, it is a series of plot devices meant to facilitate the expression of this philosophy. These various plot devices need not concern us here except in their broadest features. They can perhaps be placed in three general groups: a) invented "gods" and the cults or worshipers that have grown up around them; b) an ever-increasing library of mythical books of occult lore; and c) a fictitious New England topography (Arkham, Dunwich, hinsmouth, etc.). It will readily be noted that the latter two were already present in nebulous form in much earlier tales; but the three features only came together in Lovecraft's later work. Indeed, the third feature does not appreciably foster Lovecraft's cosmic message, and it can be found in tales that are anything but cosmic (e.g., "The Picture in the House"); but it is a phenomenon that has exercised much fascination and can still be said to be an important component of the Lovecraft Mythos. It is an unfortunate fact of course, that these surface features have frequently taken precedence with readers, writers, and even critics, rather than the philosophy of which they are symbols or representations.

It is at this point scarcely profitable to examine some of the misinterpretations foisted upon the Lovecraft Mythos by August Derleth; the only value in so doing is to serve as a prelude to examining what the mythos actually meant to Lovecmft. The errors can be summed up under three heads: 1) that Lovecraft's "gods" are elementals; 2) that the "gods" can be differentiated between "Elder Gods," who represent the forces of good, and the "Old Ones," who are the forces of evil; and 3) that the mythos as a whole is philosophically akin to Christianity.

It does not require much thought to deem all these points absurd and ridiculous. The notion that the "gods" are elementals seems largely derived from the fact the Cthulhu is imprisoned under water and that he resembles an octopus, and is therefore supposedly a water elemental; but the facts that he clearly came from *outer space,* and that he is *imprisoned* in sunken R'lyeh, must make it obvious both that his resemblance to an octopus is fortuitous and the water is not his natural element. Derleth's attempt to make elementals of the other "gods" is still more preposterous: Nyarlathotep is arbitrarily deemed an earth elemental and Hastur (which is only mentioned in passing once in "The Whisperer in Darkness") is claimed to be an air elemental. Not only does this leave out what are, by all accounts, the two chief deities in Lovecraft's pantheon—Azathoth and YogSothoth—but Derleth is then forced to maintain that Lovecraft "failed" in some inexplicable fashion to provide a fire elemental, in spite of the fact that Lovecraft was (in Derleth's view) working steadily on the "Cthulhu

Mythos" for the last ten years of his life. (Derleth came to Lovecraft's rescue by supplying Cthugha, the purportedly missing fire elemental.)

Derleth, himself a practicing Catholic, was unable to endure Lovecraft's bleak atheistic vision, and so he invented out of whole cloth the "Elder Gods" (led by the Britanno-Roman god Nodens) as a counterweight to the "evil" Old Ones, who had been "expelled" from the earth but are eternally preparing to reemerge and destroy humanity. Derleth seems to have taken a clue from *The Dream-Quest of Unknown Kadath* (which, paradoxically, he then refused to number among "tales of the Cthulhu Mythos") whereby Nodens seems to take Randolph Carter's side (although actually doing nothing for Carter) against the machinations of Nyarlathotep. In any case, this invention of "Elder Gods" allowed him to maintain that the "Cthulhu Mythos" is substantially akin to Christianity, therefore making it acceptable to people of his conventional temperament. An important piece of "evidence" that Derleth repeatedly cited to bolster his claims was the following "quotation," presumably from a letter by Lovecraft:

> All my stories, unconnected as they may be, are based on the fundamental lore or legend that this world was inhabited at one time by another race who, in practicing black magic, lost their foothold and were expelled, yet live on outside ever ready to take possession of this earth again.

In spite of its superficial similarity with the "All my stories . . ." quotation previously cited (with which Derleth was familiar), this quotation does not sound at all like Lovecraft—at any rate, it is entirely in conflict with the thrust of his philosophy. When Derleth in later years was asked to produce the actual letter from which this quotation was purportedly taken, he could not do so, and for a very good reason: it does not in fact occur in any letter by Lovecraft. It comes from a letter to Derleth written by Harold S. Farnese, the composer who had corresponded briefly with Lovecraft and who, evidently, severely misconstrued the direction of Lovecraft's work and thought very much as Derleth did. But Derleth seized upon this "quotation" as a trump card for his erroneous views.

By now there is little need to rehash this entire matter: the work of such modern critics as Richard L. Tierney, Dirk W. Mosig, and others has been so conclusive that any attempt to overturn it can only seem reactionary. There is no cosmic "good vs. evil" struggle in Lovecraft's tales; there certainly are struggles between various extraterrestrial entities, but these have no moral overtones and are merely part of the history of the universe. There are no "Elder Gods" whose goal is to protect humanity from the "evil" Old

Ones; the Old Ones were not "expelled" by anyone and are not (aside from Cthulhu) "trapped" in the earth or elsewhere. Lovecraft's vision is far less cheerful: humanity is not at centre stage in the cosmos, and there is no one to help us against the entities who have from time to time descended upon the earth and wreaked havoc; indeed, the "gods" of the Mythos are not really gods at all, but merely extraterrestrials who occasionally manipulate their human followers for their own advantage.

This last point is worth examining specifically in relation to "The Call of Cthulhu" (1926), the first story that truly established the mythos as a (fairly) coherent entity. The outlandish story about the Great Old Ones told to Legrasse by Castro speaks of the intimate relation between the human cult of Cthulhu worshipers and the objects of their worship: "That cult would never die till the stars came right again, and the secret priests would take great Cthulhu from His tomb to revive His subjects and resume His rule of earth" (*DH* 141). The critical issue is this: Is Castro right or wrong? The tale when read as a whole seems emphatically to suggest that he is wrong; in other words, that the cult has nothing to do with the emergence of Cthulhu (it certainly did not do so in March 1925, since that was the product of an earthquake), and in fact is of no importance to Cthulhu and his ultimate plans, whatever they may be. This is where Lovecraft's remark about the avoidance of human emotions as applied to extraterrestrials comes into play: we scarcely know anything about the real motivations of Cthulhu, but his pathetic and ignorant human worshippers wish to flatter their sense of self-importance by believing that they are somehow integral to his ultimate resurrection, and that they will share in his domination of the earth (if, indeed, that is what he wishes to do).

And it is here that we finally approach the heart of Lovecraft Mythos. Lovecraft's remark in "Some Notes on a Nonentity" that it was Lord Dunsany "from who I got the idea of the artillcial pantheon and myth-background represented by 'Cthulhu', 'Yog-Sothoth', 'Yuggoth', etc." (*CE* 5.209–10) has either been misunderstood or ignored; but it is central to the understanding of what the pseudomythology meant to Lovecraft. Dunsany had crated his artificial pantheon in his first two books (and only there), *The Gods of Pegāna* (1905) and *Time and the Gods* (1906). The mere act of creating an imaginary religion calls for some comment: it clearly denotes some dissatisfaction with the religion (Christianity) with which the author was raised. Dunsany was, by all accounts, an atheist, although not quite so vociferous a one as Lovecraft; and his gods were, like Lovecraft's, *symbols* for some of his most deeply held philosophical beliefs. In Dunsany's case, these were such things as the need for human reunification with the natural world and distaste for many features of modern civilisation (business, advertising, and in general the absence of beauty and poetry in contemporary life). Lovecraft, having his own philosophical message to convey, used his imaginary pantheon for analogous purposes.

What Lovecraft was really doing, in other words, was creating (as David E. Schultz has felicitously expressed it [212]) an antimythology. What is the purpose behind most religions and mythologies? It is to "justify the ways of God to men" (Milton, *Paradise Lost* 1.26). Human beings have always considered themselves at the centre of the universe; they have peopled the universe with gods of varying natures and capacities as a means of explaining natural phenomena, of accounting for their own existence, and of shielding themselves from the grim prospect of oblivion after death. Every religion and mythology has established some vital connection between gods and human beings, and it is exactly this connection that Lovecraft is seeking to subvert with his pseudomythology. And yet, he knew enough anthropology and psychology to realise that most human beings—either primitive or civilised—are incapable of accepting an atheistic view of existence, and so he peopled his tales with cults which in their own perverted way attempted to reestablish that bond between the gods and themselves; but these cults are incapable of understanding that what they deem "gods" are merely extraterrestrial entities who have no intimate relation with human beings or with anything on this planet and who are doing no more than pursuing their own ends, whatever they may happen to be.

The rest of Lovecraft's career does not concern us at the moment; suffice it to say that he continued to elaborate—in a highly unsystematic way—upon the conceptions established in "The Call of Cthulhu," inventing additional "gods," books, and places, and eventually "demythologising" his mythos to make it very clear (as in *At the Mountains of Madness* [1931]) that the gods were really no more than extraterrestrials and that Alhazred's *Necronomicon* and other tomes are actually in error in attributing godlike stature to these entities.

It is claimed that Lovecraft "invited" other writers to contribute to his growing mythology. But what really happened is that other writers simply took it into their heads to write stories that played off of some of Lovecraft's conceptions (Frank Belknap Long was the first, followed by Clark Ashton Smith, Robert E. Howard, and others), and there was scarcely anything Lovecraft could do about it. The preposterous notion that Lovecraft was somehow "orchestrating" the growth of the mythos scarcely needs any attention these days.

The chief figurehead in all this was August Derleth; but it is interesting that, although he had written a variety of "mythos" tales in Lovecraft's lifetime, he conveniently waited until Lovecraft was dead to undertake his own co-opting of Lovecraft's ideas. As early as 1931, Derleth had become fascinated with Lovecraft's pseudomythology, seeking not only to add to it but investing it with the name "The Mythology of Hastur." Indeed, it was exactly at this time that Derleth wrote the initial drafts of several stories, both on his own and in collaboration with Mark Schorer, which—though most were published much later—put the seal on his radically different treatment of the mythos. One story in particular, "The Horror from the Depths" (written with Schorer in the summer of 1931; published in *Strange Stories* for October 1940 as "The Evil Ones"), is very illuminating. Farnsworth Wright rejected this tale not only because he though it too derivative of Long's *Horror from the Hills* but because

> you have lifted whole phrases from Lovecraft's works, as for instance; "the frightful *Necronomicon* of the mad Arab Abdul Alhazred," "the sunken kingdom of R'lyeh," "the accursed spawn of Cthulhu," "the frozen and shunned Plateau of Leng," etc. Also you have taken the legends of Cthulhu and the Ancient Ones directly out of Lovecraft. This is unfair to Lovecraft.[1]

When Derleth relayed Wright's complaints to Lovecraft, the latter gave them short shrift: "I *like* to have others use my Azathoths & Nyarlathoteps—& in return I shall use Klarkash-Ton's Tsathoggua, your monk Clithanus, & Howard's Bran." Derleth seemed to use this single sentence as justification for his subsequent "additions" to Lovecraft's mythos, but he seems to have failed to notice the very preceding sentence: "The more these synthetic daemons are mutually written up by different authors, the better they become as general background-material" (*ES* 1.353). The term "background-material" is critical here: whereas writers like Smith and Howard really did use various elements of Lovecraft's mythos merely as random allusions to create atmosphere, Derleth set about resolutely writing whole stories whole very core was a systematic (and, accordingly, tedious) exposition of the mythos as he conceived it.

Relatively few of the stories Derleth was writing at this time actually got into print before Lovecraft's death, since they were repeatedly rejected. "Lair of the Star-Spawn" made it into *Weird Tales* for August 1932; its mention of the Tcho-Tcho people was picked up by Lovecraft in "The Shadow out of Time." "The Thing That Walked on the Wind," also written in 1931, was published in *Strange Tales* for January 1933. This tale actually does refer to the various components of the Lovecraft mythos in a random and allusive way, and is a relatively competent piece of work. One comment

---

[1] Farnsworth Wright to August Derleth, 13 July 1931 (ms., State Historical Society of Wisconsin).

made by Derleth to Barlow in reference to it in 1934 is of supreme interest: "According to the mythology as I understand it it is briefly this: the Ancient or Old Ones ruled the universes—from their authority revolted the evil Cthulhu, Hastur the Unspeakable, etc., who in turn spawned the Tcho-Tcho people and other cult like creatures."[2] This, in essence, is the "Derleth Mythos." Virtually all the elements are here, chiefly the good-vs.-evil scenario (the "Ancient or Old Ones" become the "Elder Gods" in later tales) and the "revolt" of Cthulhu, etc. The notion of the gods as elementals is already faintly present in "The Thing That Walked on the Wind."

Derleth put the seal on his disfigurement of Lovecraft's mythos in "The Return of Hastur," begun in 1932 but put aside and not finished until April 1937. It was published in *Weird Tales* for March 1939 after being initially rejected by Wright. Some correspondence between Derleth and Clark Ashton Smith concerning the tale is highly revealing. Even before reading the story, Smith—responding to Derleth's attempts to systematise the mythos—commented:

> As to classifying the Old Ones, I suppose that Cthulhu can be classed both as a survival on earth and a water-dweller, and Tsathoggua is a subterranean survival. Azathoth, referred to somewhere as "the primal nuclear chaos," is the ancestor of the whole crew but still dwells in outer and ultra-dimensional space, together with Yog-Sothoth, and the demon piper Nyarlathotep, who attends the throne of Azathoth. I shouldn't class any of the Old Ones as *evil*: they are plainly beyond all limitary human conceptions of either ill or good. (Letter to Derleth, 13 April 1937; *Selected Letters* 287)

Smith is clearly responding to Derleth's attempt to shoehorn the mythos entities into elementals. Then, a little later, Smith writes: "A deduction relating the Cthulhu mythos to the Christian mythos would indeed be interesting; and of course the unconscious, element in such creation is really the all-important one. However, there seems to be no reference to expulsion of Cthulhu and his companions in 'The Call'" (letter to Derleth, 21 April 1937; *Selected Letters* 291). Here again Smith is trying to steer Derleth on to the right track, since he knew Lovecraft repudiated Christianity.

Then, after reading "The Return of Hastur," Smith writes: "One reaction, confirmed rather than diminished by the second reading, is that you have tried to work in too much of the Lovecraft mythology and have not assimilated it into the natural body of the story" (letter to Derleth, 28 April 1937; *Selected Letters* 294). Derleth was very fond of making huge catalogues of

---

[2] August Derleth to R.H. Barlow, 15 June 1934 (ms, John Hay Library).

mythos entities and terms in his tales, as if their mere citation would serve to create horror, he also hammered home his conception of the mythos in story after story, since he had evidently come to the conclusion—one that some politicians of today have also discovered—that if one repeats something often enough, no matter how false, people begin to believe it. Smith's strictures had absolutely no effect on Derleth, who assumed that his views were self-evidently correct and was seeking only commendation and support for them.

It would have been bad enough for Derleth to expound his conception of the Mythos in his own fiction—for it could conceivably have been assumed that this was his (legitimate or illegitimate) elaboration upon Lovecraft's ideals. But Derleth went much further than this: in article after article he attributed his views to Lovecraft, and this is where he stands most culpable. In this way Derleth impeded the proper understanding of Lovecraft for thirty years, since he was looked upon as the "authority" on Lovecraft and as his appointed spokesman. The first published article in which Derleth propounded his views was in "H. P. Lovecraft, Outsider," published in an obscure little magazine, *River,* for June 1937. By this time Derleth had conveniently found the fictitious "All my stories . . ." quotation supplied by Farnese, which he would use repeatedly to bolster his conception of the mythos. The critical passage in this article is as follows:

> After a time there became apparent in his tales a curious coherence, a myth-pattern so convincing that after its early appearance, the readers of Lovecraft's stories began to explore libraries and museums for certain imaginary titles of Lovecraft's own creation, so powerful that many another writer, with Lovecraft's permission, availed himself of facets of the mythos for his own use. Bit by bit it grew, and finally its outlines became distinct, and it was given a name: the Cthulhu Mythology: because it was in *The Call of Cthulhu* that the myth pattern first became apparent. (88)

The disingenuousness of the passive voice here ("it was given a name") is evident: it was Derleth who had given the mythos this name. Later, citing Farnese's "All my stories . . ." fabrication, Derleth commented that this formula is "remarkable for the fact that though it sprang from the mind of a professed religious unbeliever, it is basically similar to the Christian mythos, particularly in regard to the expulsion of Satan from Eden and the power of evil."

The charade continued. In "A Master of the Macabre" (*Reading and Collecting,* August 1937), an article that began as a review of the Visionary

DISSECTING CTHULHU

Press *Shadow over Innsmouth* (1936) but awkwardly turned into a memorial tribute, Derleth cites both the fake "All my stories..." quotation and the real one ("All my tales are based on the fundamental premise that common human laws and interests and emotions have no validity or significance in the vast cosmos-at-large"), which, as any intelligent person should have been able to tell, directly contradicts the fake one!

As for Derleth's own "Mythos" fiction—whether it be the deceitful "posthumous collaborations" with Lovecraft or his own tales, included in *The Mask of Cthulhu* (1958) and *The Trail of Cthulhu* (1962)—the less said of it the better. It may sound odd to say so, but Derleth really had no genuine feel for the weird. All his work in this domain is either very conventional (tales of ghosts, haunted houses, etc.) or clumsy pastiche. Many of these Lovecraft-inspired tales are, in addition, poor not in their deviation from Lovecraft's own conceptions (some later work that so deviates is highly meritorious, as we shall see), but in the basic craft of fiction writing; they are written carelessly and hastily, with very poor, ham-fisted attempts to imitate Lovecraft's style (Derleth frequently maintained that Lovecraft's prose was very easy to mimic!), clumsy development, laughable attempts at verisimilitude by long catalogues of esoteric terms, and flamboyant conclusions in which good triumphs in the nick of time over evil (in the final tale of the "novel" *The Trail of Cthulhu*, Cthulhu ends up being nuked!). These tales really are subject to the very flaws that critics have falsely attributed to Lovecraft—verbosity, artificiality, excessive histrionics, and the like.

Derleth tries as much as possible to sound like Lovecraft but fails pitiably. For some bizarre reason, he set nearly all his "Cthulhu Mythos" tales in New England, which he had never seen, and as a result is totally unconvincing in his atmosphere. He attempts to mimic Lovecraft's archaistic prose when presenting old documents but produces comical errors. He is fond of pomposities such as the following: "I have come out of the sky to watch and prevent horror from being spawned again on this earth. I cannot fail; I must succeed" (*Trail of Cthulhu* 70). But it is too painful to make a catalogue of Derleth's shortcomings; they are now all too apparent for all to see.

It is also too painful to examine the utter mediocrity of most subsequent "additions" to Lovecraft's mythos, whether it be such pulp hacks as Hugh B. Cave or such modern hacks as Brian Lumley. Only in the rarest instances have some writers actually said something of their own using Lovecraft's idiom: Ramsey Campbell ("Cold Print," "The Franklyn Paragraphs"), Colin Wilson (*The Mind Parasites*, "The Return of the Lloigor"), Karl Edward Wagner ("Sticks"), T. E. D. Klein ("Black Man with a Horn"), Thomas Li-

THE CTHULHU MYTHOS: LOVECRAFT VS. DERLETH

gotti ("The Last Teast of Harlequin"), and a very few others. James Turner, August Derleth's successor at Arkham House, has been attempting to point the way to a "new" conception of the Mythos with his revised version of *Tales of the Cthulhu Mythos* (1990) and the recent *Cthulhu 2000* (1995), but one wonders how many are listening. The spate of "Mythos fiction" will no doubt continue, and no doubt find the Gehenna of mediocrity it so richly deserves.

As for me, I'll stick to the real McCoy and just keep rereading Lovecraft.

Works Cited

Derleth, August. "H. P. Lovecraft, Outsider." *River* 1, No. 3 (June 1937): 88–89.

———. *The Trail of Cthulhu.* 1962. New York: Beagle, 1971.

Schultz, David E. "From Microcosm to Macrocosm: The Growth of Lovecraft's Cosmic Vision." in *An Epicure in the Terrible: A Centennial Anthology of Essays in Honor of H. P. Lovecraft,* ed. David E. Schultz and S. T. Joshi. Rutherford, NJ: Fairleigh Dickinson University Press, 1991. 199–219.

Smith, Clark Ashton. *Selected Letters of Clark Ashton Smith.* Ed. David E. Schultz and Scott Connors. Sauk City, WI: Arkham House, 2003.

[*Mythos Tales and Others* No. 1 (1996): 76–87]

Toward a Reader-Response Approach to the Lovecraft Mythos

By Steven J. Mariconda

I. The Lovecraft Mythos: The Great Not-To-Be-Named

Over the past six decades, readers and critics alike have discussed and written about the Lovecraft Mythos more than any other aspect of the author's work. Despite this, the Mythos remains the most poorly understood facet of Lovecraft's oeuvre. Opinions about its meaning and importance vary wildly. A numerically large contingent of readers and a particularly vehement set of critics believe it is the most significant thing about Lovecraft. They spend much time not merely categorizing Loveraft's Mythos entities, but also inventing their own entities, writing stories about them, participating in role-playing games that involve them, reading comic books about them, watching movies that feature them, trading electronic mail about them, making jokes about them, and even believing in their literal existence. Mainstream reference works, forced by space constraints to convey Lovecraft's legacy in a few sentences, often mention the Mythos as the centerpiece of his fiction. Arrayed against this Mythos-focused faction are the leading Lovecraft scholars—including such notables as S. T. Joshi and David E. Schultz—who see the Mythos simply as background elements which Lovecraft drew upon to add highlights to his cosmic montage. These latter scholars have amassed such a Promethean understanding of Lovecraft through primary research that it is striking to note how well the Mythos-focused contingent has flourished in the face of their arguments.

Despite the inordinate scrutiny given it since Lovecraft's death in 1937, the Mythos has succeeded in evading explication or even definition. One indication of this is the still-ongoing attempt at taxonomy that was begun half a century ago. It is instructive to compare the attempt by Francis T. Laney (1942) to encompass and define Mythos entities with similar efforts by Bernadette Bosky (1982), Robert M. Price (1983, 1991b), and others. There are basic disagements about what to include and what to exclude. Among those elements that are included, there is a basic inability to find a cornmon definition of meaning or even basic attributes.

A good example of the latter is the entity called Nyarlathotep. Price describes this entity as "variously depicted but seems in general to be a messenger or harbinger of Azathoth, almost an antichrist who brings fatal knowledge of the end of all things to those unwise enough to summon him or seek him out. He may appear in human or monstrous form" (Price 1991b, 252). The use of so many qualifiers in this brief passage by Price—the scholar who more than anyone has specialized in the Mythos—is instructive. Of the same entity, Laney says: "The noxious Nyarlathotep, a mad, faceless god, forever howls blindly in the darkness, though somewhat lulled by the monotonous piping of two amorphous idiot flute players. He is also known as a mighty messenger, and bringer of strange joy to Yuggoth. Father of the million favored ones is another of his titles" (Laney 30). Given the small and well-bounded set of source material required to create such a definition, the lack of congruence between the two attempts is striking. And neither writer addresses Nyarlathotep's role in "The Whisperer in Darkness" (1930), where Lovecraft implies the entity is a crablike being who has donned a mask and robe to participate in a rather cosmic practical joke on an unsuspecting human being.

It is more convenient for systematizers to ignore such things, and ignore them they do. Examples abound. Shub-Niggurath is said to be "friendly to man" in "Out of the Aeons" (*HM* 273), but Price instead cites Lovecraft's joke letter to an adolescent fan and soberly instructs us that Shub-Niggurath is a "cloud-like entity" (Price 1991b, 252). Yog-Sothoth, clearly inimical to the human race in "The Dunwich Horror," is shown to be benign in "Through the Gates of the Silver Key." Unable to codify this type of discrepancy, taxonomer can only ignore it. Characterizations of Cthulhu, likewise, focus on the tentacled devil-god of "The Call of Cthulhu," but never, ever refer to the "spirit of universal harmony anciently symbolised as the octopus-headed god who had brought all men down from the stars" (*HM* 136). Nigguratl-Yig (in "The Electric Executiononer"), though apparently derived from Yig ("The Curse of Yig" and others) and Shub-Niggurath ("The Whisperer in Darkness" and others), is likewise too bothersome to deal with. Yet Price and Will Murray have built a miniature critical cottage industry around Nug and Yeb, drawing most of their information on these entities (mentioned in Heald's "Out of the Aeons," de Castro's "The Last Test," and Zealia Bishop's "The Mound") from joking allusions in private correspondence (Price 1985a, 44).

Equally unsuccessful are attempts to decide which Lovecraft stories contribute to or belong to the Mythos. Assessments range from three of them (including one story that mentions no entities [Murray 1986, 30]) to all of them (Mosig 4). These attempts have led to some especially futile attempts at sub-distinguishing among "Yog-Sothoth Cycle of Myth," "Arkham Cycle," and other types of tales. Similarly confounding is the question of where the Mythos begins and ends. Some commentators have gone back to before Lovecraft was born, drafting the hapless Ambrose Bierce (we can only wish we might read the cynic's response to being drafted). Most of these same pundits agree the Mythos is still being supplemented by contemporary writers (mostly adolescents who enjoy creating odd-sounding names).

Mythos-oriented commentators have jumped through logical hoops to explain their inability to codify the Mythos. In the case of specific entities, they simply ignore information that doesn't fit. Sometimes they come up with situation-specific band-aids, as when they simply throw up their hands and label the inscrutable Nyarlathotep a shape-shifter. On a broader level, Murray remarks blithely that "a creative writer is not going to let the fact that he said something in print in one story hold him back from revising that concept in a later story, to make it better, to push it in another direction" (Murray 1984, 18). And, of course, the easiest out of all: that real myth patterns are inconsistent across various accounts, so Lovecraft must have made these rationally irreconcilable characterizations on purpose.

The work of a single scholar, Robert M. Price, serves to show that interpretative issues regarding the Mythos are impossible to pin down. Why does Price, who is one of the brightest critics in the field—he possesses multiple Ph.D.s in religious studies—find it so difficult to explain the Mythos? The body of material he has to work with is relatively small, has well-defined boundries, and is rich in easily accessible source material. At first, Price suggested that Lovecraft originally conceived the Mythos entities as gods and subsequently transformed them to alien beings (Price 1986); he later rescinded this and concluded that they were always aliens (Price 1991a, 21). Despite this change of position, Price later published a genealogy of

Mythos entities, an approach that has no meaning (a genealogy of aliens?) under his current exegesis (Price 1993b, 30).

Similarly, Price has been unsuccessful in enumerating which tales do and do not "belong" to the Mythos. In his paper "H. P. Lovecraft and the Cthulhu Mythos," whose stated object is "to bring increased clarity to the Cthulhu Mythos debate," he proposed three myth cycles: the Dunsanian cycle, the Arkham cycle, and the Cthulhu cycle. After noting that "a piece of lore may be transferred between [sic] the three cycles," he concludes: "The stories draw on various bodies of lore indiscriminately, but that does not mean we cannot discriminate between the bodies of lore" (5). Price dodges the obvious question: if lore is interchangeable and used indiscriminately, why bother to set up the dichotomy? Price later reversed himself and posited that all Lovecraft stories draw from a large single body of lore (Panel Discussion 28); still later, he claimed that the stories themselves rather than the lore should be considered the Mythos (Price 1993a, 19). The various genealogies of Mythos entities Price has published mutate from appearance to appearance; at the conclusion of the most recent effort, which includes entities mentioned in no Lovecraft story or letter, he concludes sheepishly: "In compiling this genealogy I have rejected pervious attempts, thinking it better to start fresh" (Price 1993b, 30).

All this indicates that the Mythos escapes categorization and explication. Critic Stanley Fish, citing a commentary on Milton, speaks of a similar situation: a set of interpretative issues that cannot be agreed upon by diverse editors, even though—as with Price's theories—"every position taken is supported wholly by convincing evidence." Fish concludes that

> these are problems that apparently cannot be solved, at least not by the methods traditionally brought to bear on them. What I would like to argue is that they are not *meant* to be solved, but to be experienced (they signify), and that consequently any procedure that attempts to determine which of a number of readings is correct will necessarily fail. What this means is that the commentators and editors have been asking the wrong questions and that a new set of questions based on a new set of assumptions must be formulated. (Fish 1980a, 164–65)

Later in this article I would like to suggest a few new assumptions under which we might henceforth consider the Mythos.

Not only has the Mythos escaped categorization and explication, it has even escaped naming. Derleth began during Lovecraft's lifetime by proposing "The Mythology of Hastur," which Lovecraft politely shrugged off. After Lovecraft's death, Derleth used "Cthulhu Mythology" and, more widely, "Cthulhu Mythos." Later, after Derleth died and scholars began to distinguish between Lovecraft's apparent intent as indicated in his tales and letters and Derleth's obsfuscations, other names were proposed for part or all of it. Tierney offered the "Derleth Mythos"; Mosig, the "Yog-Sothoth Cycle of Myth"; and Burleson and Joshi, the "Lovecraft Mythos." Other names are to be expected in the future.

As mentioned, Lovecraft himself refused to give it a name. Mythos-oriented scholars have not interepreted this fact to mean that whatever the Mythos is, it is not something of a nature that can or should be named. This, in turn, calls to mind something mentioned in a Lovecraft story but never commented upon by Mythos-oriented critics: the *Magnum Innominandum*, the Great-Not-To-Be-Named. Perhaps this is what the Mythos should be called.

In conclusion, a survey of Mythos-related criticism reveals that the Cthulhu Mythos cannot be defined or bounded. The meaning of the Lovecraft Mythos is that it is beyond meaning. Not only can it not be explicated on a rational level, it cannot even be named.

II. Yet Another Interpretation: The Mythos as Symbol

Most Mythos criticism has taken the entities Lovecraft uses to be literal beings. One of the new set of assumptions I propose is that Lovecraft considered these entities to be symbolic rather than representative. A symbol combines a literal referent with a cluster of abstract or suggestive aspects. With this approach, literal catalogues of the attributes of various entities ("Cthulhu is large octopoid creature who smells real bad and likes to eat boats for lunch") would be superseded by attempts to understand the complex of emotional meanings associated with the entities. To date, no critic has done extensive study of the Mythos as symbol.[1]

Lovecraft left some clues that he created the Mythos because he needed his own, more powerful and aesthetically refined set of symbols than traditional myth and folklore. He often attributed the idea for a personal myth cycle to Lord Dunsany,[2] who he said "weaves a strangely potent fantastic

---

[1] On specific entities, Donald R. Burleson has done some work in this area; for example, he sees Cthulhu as "most significant . . . for his effects in absence," concluding that Cthulhu is "an allegorization of the textually necessary absence of a center" (81). Derleth made some feeble and unsuccessful efforts to tie the Lovecraft Mythos to the Christian Mythos. Others have made general statements about what the Mythos as a whole is meant to symbolize.

[2] "Regarding the solemnly cited myth cycle of Cthulhu, Yog-Sothoth, R'lyeh, Nyarlathotep, Nug, Yeb, Shub-Niggurath, etc., etc.,—let me confess that this is a synthetic concoction of my own, like the populous and varied pantheon of Lord Dunsany's Pegāna" (HPL to R. E. Howard, 14 August 1930; *SL* 3.166).

beauty which has its roots in primitive myth and folklore" (*SL* 2.227). Taken to task by a colleague about his use of a personal myth cycle, Lovecraft defended himself this way:

> I really agree that Yog-Sothoth is basically an immature conception, & unfitted for really serious literature. The fact is, I have never approached really serious literature as yet. But I consider the use of actual folk myths as even more childish than the use of new artificial myths, since in employing the former one is forced to retain many blatant puerilities & contradictions of experience which could be subtilised or smoothed over if the supernaturalism were modelled to order for the given case. The only permanently artistic use of Yog-Sothothery, I think, is in symbolic or associative phantasy of the frankly poetic type; in which fixed dream-patterns of the natural organism are given embodiment & crystallization. (*SL* 3.293)

The impetus for this "symbolic phantasy" came from Lovecraft's enchantment with the natural world. He wrote to composer Harold Farnese about how he tried to effect or embody his iinaginative impulses:

> In my own efforts to crystallise this spaceward outreaching, I try to utilize as many as possible of the elements which have, under earlier mental and emotional conditions, given man a symbolic feeling of the unreal, the ethereal, & the mystical— choosing those least attacked by realistic mental and emotional conditions of the present. Darkness—sunset—dreams— mists—fever—madness—the tomb—the hills—the sea—the sky—the wind—all these, & many other things have seemed to me to retain a certain imaginative potency despite our actual scientific analyses of them. Accordingly I have tried to weave them into a kind of shadowy phantasmagoria which may have the same sort of vague coherence as a cycle of traditional myth or legend—with nebulous backgrounds of Elder Forces & trans-galactic entities which lurk about this infinitesimal planet, (& of course about others as well), establishing outposts thereon, & occasionally brushing aside other accidental forms of life (like human beings) in order to take up full habitation. This is essentially the sort of notion prevalent in most racial mythologies—but an artificial mythology can become subtler & more plausible than a natural one, because it can recognize & adapt itself to the information and moods of the present. The best artificial mythology, of course, is Lord Dunsany's elaborate & consistently developed pantheon of Pegāna's gods. (*SL* 4.70ff)

Here Lovecraft makes what must be the clearest *précis* in print about the genesis and function of the Mythos. It is a set of simple steps.

> 1. Lovecraft sought a means to embody his imaginative impulses.
> 2. To do this, he identified those elements of reality which powerfully symbolize the unreal.
> 3. Having identified these elements, he created a "phantasmagoria" (a constantly shifting complex succession of things seen or imagined, or, literally, an assembly of phantasies) with the "vague coherence" of a cycle of traditional myth or legend.[3]

The passage cited above is, to my mind, by far the most important piece of primary information about the Mythos we have, even more so than the widely cited and discussed "All my stories" passage from a 1927 letter to *Weird Tales* editor Farnsworth Wright. The recommendation that we approach the Mythos as a set of symbols that are beyond "meaning" rather than literal representations of scary monsters with odd-sounding names is consistent with traditional approaches to myth itself. D. H. Lawrence put it this way:

> Myth is descriptive narrative using images. But myth is never an argument, it never has a didactic or moral purpose, you can draw no conclusion from it. Myth is an attempt to narrate a whole human experience, of which the purpose is too deep, going too deep in the blood and soul, for mental explanation or description And the images of myth are symbols. They don't "mean something." They stand for units of human feeling, human experience. A complex of emotional experience is a symbol. And the power of a symbol is to arouse the deep emotional self, and the dynamic self, beyond comprehension. Many ages of accumulated experience still throb within a symbol. And we throb in response. (Lawrence 31)

These "units of human experience" will tend to vary from one human to another, based on their respective life experiences. Henri Peyre, in a well-known book on symbolism, puts it this way:

---

[3] Lovecraft makes similar statements elsewhere, for example: "The fact is, I rather prefer purely original weird concepts as opposed to those derived from genuine folklore. Authentic folk-beliefs are likely to be insipid, ill-proportioned, freakish, and in general far less aesthetically effective than concepts formed by an author with a specific artistic purpose in mind" (HPL to E. H. Price, 29 May 1935; *SL* 4.169).

[A symbol] is a sign that as such demands deciphering This sign represents or evokes in a concrete manner what is innate within it, the thing signified and more or less hidden. The two meanings, one concrete and the other ulterior and perhaps profound, are fused into a single entity in the symbol. The meaning beneath appearances is not necessarily a single one; the symbol is not a riddle within which human ingeniousness (that of an artist, a priest, a legislator, or a prophet) . . . has been pleased to enclose a certain meaning which would otherwise be too clear. . . . Within the symbol there is therefore a polyvalence, a multiplicity of meanings, certain ones addressed to all, others to the initiated alone. . . . Each person, on beholding a sign or symbol, may according to his turn of mind (concrete, esthetic, oneiric, metaphysical, artistic) extract from it the meaning that is most enriching for him or her. (Peyre 8)

The notion that each person—in our scenario, each reader of Lovecraft—will extract a different meaning from the Mythos leads me to my next assumption: that the Mythos is most productivitely examined from the perspective of the reader's response to it.

III. The Weird Tales Mythos

For the bulk of his writing career, the majority of Lovecraft's fiction was submitted to and ultimately published in *Weird Tales* magazine. In considering the Lovecraft Mythos, *Weird Tales* is important for two reasons. Firstly, the very fact that *Weird Tales* was Lovecraft's primary fictional market shaped the manner in which the Mythos developed. Secondly, from the reader-response perspective (which will be further examined in section IV), the readership of *Weird Tales* was the first community of readers to experience the unfolding of the Mythos as it happened. As such, their experience of it is of historical interest.

In this section, I wish to examine how *Weird Tales* itself, and the circumstances of Lovecraft's perception of the magazine as his primary market, shaped the way the Mythos came to life. We can identify three factors which contributed to the development of the Mythos in *Weird Tales*.

First, Lovecraft knew that he would submit most if not all of what he wrote to *Weird Tales*. Lovecraft knew that editor Farnsworth Wright was generally inclined to accept his work (this was particularly true prior to 1930). In *Weird Tales*, Lovecraft knew that he had a captive audience. He took advantage of this well-defined forum, which offered a fairly well-bounded set of fairly faithful readers, as a place in which to create a new universe.[4]

Secondly, starting in the mid-1920s, Lovecraft ghostwrote stories which he often knew were intended for *Weird Tales* but which would be published under other names (Adolphe de Castro, Hazel Heald, Zealia Bishop). This ability to put tales in front of the same readers of his signed tales broadened Lovecraft's "power base" and enhanced his ability to make the Mythos seem real. He realized that by using the Mythos in tales signed by others, he could add credibility to the Mythos and create among the reader community a unique set of sensations—awe, puzzlement, perhaps thrills—unachievable by any set of tales signed by a single author.

Thirdly, Lovecraft was in touch by mail with other major *Weird Tales* contributors. He could thus encourage their use of his Mythos properties and ask permission to use theirs. Again, Lovecraft's use of elements coined by such *Weird Tales* titans as Robert E. Howard and Clark Ashton Smith—writers highly regarded by the readership—leveraged the effectiveness of the Mythos in ways unavailable to any author operating autonomously, even one publishing tales under other names.

Why did Lovecraft undertake the use the Mythos in ghostwritten tales and encourage its use by writers who published in the magazine? Two reasons: the sheer fun of it, and the ability to lend realism to his creation. "It rather amuses the different writers to use one another's synthetic demons & imaginary books in their stories. This pooling of resources tends to build up quite a pseudo-convincing background of dark mythology, legendry, & bibliography," he wrote to a correspondent in 1934. He adds disingenuously: "of course none of us has the least wish actually to mislead readers" (*SL* 4.346). This was, in fact, his exact objective.[5]

Let us consider briefly the creative processes that may possibly have taken place during the period of roughly 1925–35, when Lovecraft created the Mythos using *Weird Tales*. A table that shows a chronology of the writing and publication of Lovecraft's stories is useful to examine how his use of the Mythos in a tale being written for *Weird Tales* may have been

---

[4] Cf. Lovecraft's own loyalty to early pulps *All-Story* and the *Argosy*. Lovecraft claimed to have read every issue of the former magazine published between 1905 and 1914 ("To the All Story Weekly," *MW* 496). He was also a prominent part of the Argosy's community of readers, and was at one point something of a celebrity feature in its letter column (see de Camp 76–80). His sense of the continuity and community of the Weird Tales readership was undoubtedly fostered by these experiences.

[5] There are many similar passages in *Selected Letters,* for example: "For the fun of building up a convincing cycle of synthetic folklore, all our gang frequently allude to the pet demons of others. . . . Thus our black pantheon acquires an extensive publicity and pseudo-authoritativeness it would otherwise not get. . . . All this gives it a sort of air of verisimilitude" (HPL to W. F. Anger, 14 Aug. 1934; *SL* 5.16).

affected by his knowledge that other tales had been or were to be published in *Weird Tales* (see Appendix). There is little activity in the Mythos prior to 1926, primarily sporadic use of Abdul Alhazred and the *Necronomicon*. The inflection point for the development of the Mythos seems to have been "The Call of Cthulhu"—not the writing of the story, but its placement in *Weird Tales*.

As mentioned, Lovecraft's power over the *Weird Tales* readership was factorially increased by a fortuitous circumstance: his ghostwriting of horror tales for others' *Weird Tales* placements. Sometime in 1927, subsequent to the writing of "The Call of Cthulhu," Lovecraft revised Adolphe de Castro's "The Last Test" (item 54). Lovecraft, who was particularly bored with the revision of this tale, dropped some Mythos names into the story as expletives in a speech of one of the characters, without detail or explanation. It appears that Lovecraft knew that "Call" was to be published in *Weird Tales* (item 56) and that de Castro planned to submit his tale to *Weird Tales* as well. He therefore saw an opportunity to create some unusual reactions among the *Weird Tales* readership. He admitted as much in a letter:

> The reason for its echoes in Dr. de Castro's work is that the latter gentleman is a revision-client of mine—into whose tales I have stuck these glancing references for sheer fun. If any other clients of mine get work placed in W.T., you will perhaps find a still-wider spread of the cult of Azathoth, Cthulhu, and the Great Old Ones! (*SL* 3.166)

Lovecraft implies a cause-and-effect relationship between use of Mythos names in revision tales and their anticipated placement in *Weird Tales*.

We can see a similar relationship between Lovecraft's use of the Mythos in certain tales and his knowledge of stories that had been accepted for publication or already published in the magazine. As Lovecraft was writing "The Dunwich Horror" in the summer of 1928 (item 60), he was aware that "The Last Test" was to be published in *Weird Tales* (item 61) and that he planned to submit "Dunwich" to *Weird Tales* as well. He thus seeded the story with six Mythos names. In writing "The Curse of Yig" sometime in 1928 for Zealia Bishop (item 58), Lovecraft refrained from loading on the Mythos names. This may be because he did not know if Bishop planned to submit the tale to *Weird Tales*. However, once "The Curse of Yig" was published in *Weird Tales* in November 1929 (item 66), Lovecraft knew that the next story he wrote for Bishop was likely to be published there as well. He thus loaded "The Mound" (item 67) with over a dozen Mythos names. As it happened, this story was rejected by editor Farnsworth Wright.

Of course, Lovecraft also measured the Mythos element in his signed offerings by the knowledge of what *Weird Tales* readers had previously seen. He wrote the *Fungi from Yuggoth* sonnet cycle with *Weird Tales* primarily in mind, mentioning four Mythos names in four separate sonnets (items 68–77).

The use of Mythos elements in "The Whisperer in Darkness" proves that Lovecraft had an eye on the reactions of the *Weird Tales* readers to his ongoing creation. Here we see a very different approach to use of Mythos names than in any of the previous signed fiction. Over two dozen names appear, and for the first time Lovecraft aggressively pulls from no less than five other writers (Howard, Dunsany, Bierce, Long, Chambers), past and present, for names. What caused this shift? A letter from a *Weird Tales* reader published in March 1930 clearly provides the answer. One N. J. O'Neail wrote to the letter column, "The Eyrie":

> I was very much interested in tracing the apparent connection between the characters of Kathulos, in Robert E. Howard's "Skull-Face," and that of Cthulhu, in Mr. Lovecraft's "The Call of Cthulhu." Can you inform me whether there is any legend or tradition surrounding that character? And also Yog-Sothoth? Mr. Lovecraft links the latter up with Cthulhu in "The Dunwich Horror" and Adolphe de Castro also refers to Yog-Sothoth in "The Last Test." Both these stories also contain references to Abdul Alhazred the mad Arab, and his *Necronomicon*. I am sure this is a subject in which many readers besides myself would be interested; something which could be reviewed in a series of articles similar to those [on common folk beliefs] written by Alvin E Harlow. (Joshi/Michaud 31)

O'Neail's letter appears to have had a profound effect upon the manner in which Lovecraft subsequently developed the Mythos. As it happened, Lovecraft was just beginning his correspondence with Robert E. Howard— who is mentioned by O'Neail's letter—when the letter was printed. Five months later Lovecraft wrote Howard:

> [Frank Belknap] Long has alluded to the *Necronomicon* in some things of his—in fact, I think it is rather good fun to have this artificial mythology given an air of verisimilitude by wide citation. I ought, though, to write Mr. O'Neail and disabuse him of the idea that there is a large blind spot in his mythological erudition! (*SL* 3.166)

The manner in which and extent to which Lovecraft used Mythos names in "The Whisperer in Darkness" (item 83)—including a tip of the hat to both O'Neail and his new correspondent Howard by his use of the latter's "Kathulos"—shows that he was sensitive to the effect of his work on the readership. The effect upon a *Weird Tales* reader of encountering sixteen Mythos names created by six authors strung together in an independent clause leads us to the consideration of a reader-response approach to the Cthulhu Mythos.

IV. Toward a Reader-Response Approach to the Lovecraft Mythos

As mentioned at the outset of this paper, one of the most remarkable things about the Mythos is that no two scholars can seem to agree upon what it is. Even the single scholar who specializes in it cannot seem to choose among several theories he has successively proposed and discarded. Critic Stanley Fish, writing of texts in general and the phenomenon of multiple conclusions drawn from exactly the same evidence, remarks: "[these critical analyses] assume that meaning is embedded in the artifact [and so] will always point in as many directions as their are interpreters." Not only will it prove something, it will prove everything. The text will not accept these interpretations and remains determinedly evasive (Fish 1980a, 166). Fish's assessment of how differing groups choose those interpretative strategies which prove their critical stance is reminiscent of the factionalism of to-day's Mythos criticism, with Robert M. Price accusing others of a critical heterodoxy even as he creates one of his own. Giving the example of Augustine's "rule of faith" for interpreting the Scriptures to find God's love for us throughout, even if it involves figurative interpretation, Fish continues:

> Interpretive communities are made up of those who share interpretive strategies not for reading (in the conventional sense) but for writing texts, for constituting their properties and assigning their intentions. In other words these strategies exist prior to the act of reading and therefore determine the shape of what is read rather than, as is usually assumed, the other way around. . . . [I]f a community believes in the existence of only one text, then the single strategy its members employ will be forever writing it. The first community will accuse the members of the second of being reductive, and they in turn will call their accusers superficial. The assumption of each community will be that the other is not correctly perceiving the "true text," but the truth will be that each perceives the text (or texts) its interpretive strategies demand and call into being. (Fish 1980a, 182)

On the basis of the evasiveness of the Lovecraft Mythos and its inability to yield to any critical faction, I would therefore propose a reader response approach to its meaning. Fish explains the reader-response approach this way:

> The concept is simply the rigorous and disinterested asking of the question, what does this word, phrase, sentence, paragraph, chapter, novel, play, poem, *do?*; and the execution involves *an analysis of the developing responses of the reader in relation to the words as they succeed one another in time.* . . . The category of response includes any and all of the activities provoked by a string of words: the projection of syntactical and/or lexical probabilities; their subsequent occurrence or non-occurrence; attitudes toward persons, or things, or ideas referred to; the reversal or questioning of those attitudes; and much more. . . . [T]he analyst . . . in his observations must take into account all that has happened (in the reader's mind) at previous moments, each of which was in turn its subject to the accumulating pressures of its predecessors. . . . [I]n an utterance of any length . . . the report of what happens to the reader is always a report of what has happened to that point [and] includes the reader's set toward future experiences but not those experiences. (Fish 1980b, 73–74)

Thus, it is the experience of an utterance—or of a sequence of utterances, or paragraphs, or stories—that is its meaning.

No one has yet considered exactly what the reaction of a reader might be as he or she encounters the name Cthulhu or Yog-Sothoth for the first time. Under the reader-response approach, we would focus on instances in the experience in reading Lovecraft when attention is compelled because an expectation has been fulfilled or disappointed by the appearance of an unpredictable element such as a Mythos name (Fish 1980b, 94). One approach of particular interest would be to concentrate on a very specific interpretative community: the readership of *Weird Tales* as the Mythos was experienced for the first time.[6] Discarding the auctorial intent upon which the earlier parts of this essay are based, we would instead concentrate on how a typical reader would react to Mythos-related cues found

[6] Of course, there are a number of interpretative communities with which one might conduct a reader-response analysis in mind, for example, Lovecraft critics who have read the stories dozens of times. But the *Weird Tales* readership was the first such community to experience the Mythos. And, if we fall back to auctorial intent, it is apparent from Lovecraft's letters and the contents lists for prospective story collections he drew up near the end of his life that he never expected any interpretative community to reread his stories with the idea of collating the Mythos.

in stories appearing in *Weird Tales* bylined by Lovecraft or otherwise. The reader's activities would be at the center of the analyses, since they reflect the meaning—the experience—of the Mythos. The meaning they have is a consequence of making and revising assumptions, rendering and regretting judgments, coming to and abandoning conclusions, giving and withdrawing approval, specifying causes, asking questions, supplying answers, and solving puzzles (Fish 1980b, 172).

While conducting this exegesis is beyond the scope of this paper, it is likely that we would conclude that the Lovecraft Mythos means the reversal of expectations, the refusal of reality to adhere to preconceived schemas. Meanwhile, we can touch on some of the ideas that the reader-response approach to the Lovecraft Mythos implies.

When considering reader response to the Mythos, we might first consider what the reader experiences when he or she encounters a Mythos name in a story for the first time. Lovecraft said he created his Mythos names to evoke Arabic, Hebraic, Oriental, Celtic, and non-human sources:

> [A]s to those artificial names of unearthly places and gods and persons and entities—there are different ways of coining them. To a large extent they are designed to suggest—either closely or remotely—certain names in actual history or folklore which have weird or sinister associations with them. Thus "Yuggoth" has a sort of Arabic or Hebraic cast, to suggest certain words passed down from antiquity in the magical formulae contained in Moorish and Jewish manuscripts. Other synthetic names like "Nug" and "Yeb" suggest the dark and mysterious tone of Tartar or Thibetan folklore. Dunsany is the greatest of all name-coiners, and he seems to have three distinct models— the Oriental (either Assyrian or Babylonian, or Hebrew from the Bible), the classical (from Homer mostly), and the Celtic (from the Arthurian cycle, etc.). . . . I myself sometimes follow Dunsany's plan, but I also have a way strictly my own—which I use for devising non-human names, as of the localities and inhabitants of other planets. . . . The sounds ought not to follow any human language-pattern, and ought not to be derived from—or adapted to—the human speech-equipment at all. In other words, the whole design ought to be alien to both the ideas and the tongue of mankind—a series of sounds of different origins and associations, and capable only in part of reproduction by the human throat and palate and mouth. Just how far, and in what direction, such a sound-system ought to differ from human speech, must of course depend on how far and in what direction the imaginary users are represented as

differing. . . . Usually my stories assume that the non-human sounds were known to certain human scholars in elder days, and recorded in secret manuscripts like the Necronomicon, the Pnakotic Manuscripts, etc. In that case I likewise assume that the . . . ancient authors of these manuscripts gave the non-human names an unconscious twist in the direction of their own respective languages—as always occurs when scholars and writers encounter an utterly alien nomenclature and try to represent it to their own people. (HPL to Duane Rimel, 14 February 1934, *SL* 4.386ff)

He went on to remark that it is certainly advantageous now and then to introduce a coined word that has been shaped with great care from just the right associational sources (*SL* 4.386ff).

Aside from the reaction of a *Weird Tales* reader to a specific instance of Mythos nomenclature, we must consider how the Lovecraft Mythos appeared to a *Weird Tales* reader as it developed over the decade following 1925. This approach looks at the experience of the Mythos, and its resulting meaning to a reader, not at a point in time but over a time series. Studying the chronological publication information in the Appendix gives a sense of how the Lovecraft Mythos would have unfolded to a hypothetical *Weird Tales* reader.[7] For example, readers who read Lovecraft's sonnet "Nyarlathotep" (pub. Jan. 1930) would have last seen the name in a de Castro tale, "The Last Test" (pub. Nov. 1928), and perhaps dinily recall its prior appearance in "The Rats in the Walls" (pub. March 1924). As Wolfgang Iser, another pioneer of the reader-response approach, comments:

> Whatever we have read sinks into our memory and is foreshortened. It may later be evoked again and set against a different background with the result that the reader is enabled to develop hitherto unforeseeable connections. The memory evoked, however, can never reassume its original shape, for this would mean that memory and perception were identical, which is manifestly not so. The new background brings to light new aspects of what we had committed to memory; conversely these, in turn, shed their light on the new background, thus arousing more complex anticipations. Thus, the reader, in establishing these inter-relations between past, present, and future, actually causes the text to reveal its potential multiplicity of connections. (54)

---

[7] For this exercise to be meaningful, the Appendix would have to be fleshed out with stories written by others—Robert E. Howard, Clark Ashton Smith, Frank Belknap Long, etc.—published in *Weird Tales*.

Of course, not every reader of *Weird Tales* would have read every issue. Any single reader might have missed issues, skipped stories, and so on. But the implied reader for a reader-response analysis of the Lovecraft Mythos among the interpretative community of *Weird Tales* readers would likely have seen some combination of tales signed by Lovecraft, ghostwritten by Lovecraft, and written by Lovecraft's correspondents.

How can we characterize the interpretative community of *Weird Tales* readers? Lovecraft, speaking of coining Mythos names, realized that they were a heterogeneous group, remarking: "It really is a perplexing question to determine just what will strike the sensible reader right, & what will impress him as childish & meaningless stage paraphernalia. No two readers, of course, are alike, so one must use his own judgement about how wide a circle to aim at" (*SL* 4.70f). So who was the circle of readers—or to use the reader-response term, the implied reader—Lovecraft aimed at? Without doing any primary research, we can take Lovecraft's word for it: the bulk of *Weird Tales* readers were "crude and unimaginative illiterates" (*SL* 4.53). Elsewhere he was more expansive if no less harsh:

> [Pulp magazine editors] aim to please the very lowest grade of readers, probably because these constitute a large numerical majority. When you glance at the advertisements in these magazines . . . you can see what a hopelessly vulgar and stupid rabble comprise the bulk of the clientele. These yaps and nitwits probably can't grasp anything even remotely approaching subtlety. (*Uncollected Letters* 34)

Elsewhere he called *Weird Tales* readers "zippy morons" and suggested to Frank Long that his sense of these implied readers had affected his use of Mythos names: "It ruins one's style to have a publick of tame-souled half-wits hanging over one's head as one writes" (*SL* 2.79). However, despite all this there is evidence that Lovecraft believed that there was another, more intelligent implied reader of *Weird Tales*. He contrasts a small group of elite readers with what he termed "the Eyrie-bombarding proletariat": "It seems to me that there is little doubt but that *Weird Tales* is bought and read by large numbers of persons infinitely above the pulp-hound level—persons who relish Machen and Blackwood and M. R. James, and who would welcome a periodical of the Machen-Blackwood-James degree of maturity and fastidiousness if such were published" (*SL* 5.322). The response of this more literate section of the *Weird Tales* readership must have reacted in quite a different way than the "zippy morons" to this infamous passage to "The Whisperer in Darkness":

> I found myself faced by names and terms that I had heard
> elsewhere in the most hideous of connexions—Yuggoth, Great
> Cthulhu, Tsathoggua, Yog-Sothoth, R'lyeh, Nyarlathotep,
> Azathoth, Hastur, Yian, Leng, the Lake of Hali, Bethmoora,
> the Yellow Sign, L'mur-Kathulos, Bran, and the Magnum
> Innominandum—and was drawn back through nameless aeons
> and inconceivable dimensions to worlds of elder, outer entity at
> which the crazed author of the *Necronomicon* had only guessed
> in the vaguest way. (*DH* 223)

Readers familiar with Dunsany ("Bethmoora"), Bierce ("Hali"), and
Chambers ("the Yellow Sign") would have a much different experience of
this passage—one of amusement, no doubt—than that of N. J. O'Neail,
who had written in perplexity a few months before about the possible relation of Cthulhu and Kathulos.

The original meaning of the Lovecraft Mythos, then, lies in an examination of the way in which the *Weird Tales* readership—its original interpretative community—experienced it. Each successive interpretative community, including modern-day Lovecraft scholars and Mythos fans, will have
a slightly different experience of it; thus, for them, it will have a slightly
different meaning. The reader-response approach is a useful one to take in
examoning the Mythos, for it has tenaciously evaded explication, definition, and even naming. Without realizing it, a spectator at the 1986 World
Fantasy Convention panel discussion on "What Is the Lovecraft Mythos?"
perhaps came closest to the spirit of the reader-response approach. Speaking of the Mythos and her first reading of the tales, she remarked: "I think
that's the magic of Lovecraft. I can still remember reading my first story; I
didn't understand who the creatures were, and the names were strange to
me, but that's what made it exciting" (Panel Discussion 24).

Works Cited

Bosky, Bernadette. "In Search of a Mythos Genealogy." *Crypt of Cthulhu*
No. 8 (Michaelmas 1982): 16–22.

Burleson, Donald R. *Lovecraft: Disturbing the Universe*. Lexington: University Press of Kentucky, 1990.

de Camp, L. Sprague. *Lovecraft: A Biography*. Garden City, NY: Doubleday,
1975.

Fish, Stanley E. "Interpreting the Variorum." In *Reader-Response Criticism: From Formalism to Post-Structuralism,* ed. Jane Tompkins. Baltimore: Johns Hopkins Univeristy Press, 1980. 164–84. Cited in the text as Fish 1980a.

Fish, Stanley E. "Literature in the Reader: Affective Stylistics." In *Reader-Response Criticism: From Formalism to Post-Structuralism,* ed. Jane Tompkins. Baltimore: Johns Hopkins University Press, 1980. 70–99. Cited in the text as Fish 1980b.

Iser, Wolfgang. "The Reading Process: A Phenomenological Approach." In *Reader-Response Criticism: From Formalism to Post-Structuralism,* ed. Jane Tompkins. Baltimore: Johns Hopkins University Press, 1980. 50–69.

Joshi, S. T., and Marc A. Michaud, ed. *H. P. Lovecraft in "The Eyrie."* West Warwick, RI: Necronomicon Press, 1979.

Laney, Francis T. "The Cthulhu Mythology." *Acolyte* 1, No. 2 (Winter 1942); rpt. *Crypt of Cthulhu* No. 35 (Hallowmas 1985): 28–34.

Lawrence, D. H. "The Dragon of the Apocalypse." In *Literary Symbolism,* ed. Maurice Beebe. Belmont, CA: Wadsworth Publishing Co., 1960. 31–32.

Lovecraft, H. P. *Uncollected Letters.* Ed. S. T. Joshi. West Warwick, RI: Necronomicon Press, 1986.

Mosig, Dirk W. "Innsmouth and the Lovecraft *Oeuvre:* A Holistic Approach." *Nyctalops* No. 14 (March 1978): 3, 5.

Murray, Will. "The Dunwich Chimera and Others." *Lovecraft Studies* No. 8 (Spring 1984): 10–24.

———. "An Uncompromising Look at the Cthulhu Mythos." *Lovecraft Studies* No. 12 (Spring 1986): 26–31.

———. "Lovecraft and the Pulp Magazine Tradition." In *An Epicure in the Terrible: A Centennial Anthology of Essays in Honor of H. P. Lovecraft,* ed. David E. Schultz and S. T. Joshi. Rutherford, NJ: Fairleigh Dickinson University Press, 1991. 101–31.

Peyre, Henri. *What Is Symbolism?* Trans. Emmett Parker. University: University of Alabama Press, 1982.

Price, Robert M. "A Lovecraft Taxonomy." *Crypt of Cthulhu* No. 12 (Eastertide 1983): 17–19.

———. "Demythologizing Cthulhu." *Lovecraft Studies* No. 8 (Spring 1984): 3–9.

———. "The Revision Mythos." *Lovecraft Studies* No. 11 (Fall 1985): 43–50. Cited in the text as Price 1985a.

———. "H. P. Lovecraft and the Cthulhu Mythos." *Crypt of Cthulhu* No. 35 (Hallowmas 1985): 3–10. Cited in the text as Price 1985b.

————. "The Last Vestige of the Derleth Mythos." *Lovecraft Studies* No. 24 (Spring 1991): 20–21. Cited in the text as Price 1991a.

————. "Lovecraft's 'Artificial Mythology.'" In *An Epicure in the Terrible: A Centennial Anthology of Essays in Honor of H. P. Lovecraft,* ed. David E. Schultz and S. T. Joshi. Rutherford, NJ: Fairleigh Dickinson University Press, 1991. 247–56. Cited in the text as Price 1991b.

————. "What Exactly Is the Cthulhu Mythos?" *NecronomiCon Program Guide.* Boston: Lovecraft Society of New England, August 1993, 17, 19. Cited in the text as Price 1993a.

————. "A Mythos Theogony." *Crypt of Cthulhu* No. 85 (Hallowmas 1993): 28–30. Cited in the text as Price 1993b.

Schultz, David E. "Who Needs the 'Cthulhu Mythos'?" *Lovecraft Studies* No. 13 (Fall 1986): 43–51.

"What Is the Cthulhu Mythos?" (panel discussion). *Lovecraft Studies* No. 14 (Spring 1987): 3–30. Cited in the text as Panel Discussion.

Appendix: Lovecraft Compositions/Publications During *Weird Tales* Period

	Title	M	Y	Act	PP	Elements Used
1	The Rats in the Walls	9	23	wrtg		Nyarlathotep
2	The Unnamable	9	23	wrtg		
3	Ashes (Eddy)		23	wrtg		
4	The Ghost-Eater (Eddy)		23	wrtg		
5	The Loved Dead (Eddy)	?	23	wrtg		
6	The Festival	?	23	wrtg		
7	Dagon	10	23	pub	WT	Alhazred; *Necronomicon*
8	The Horror at Martin's Beach (Greene)	11	23	pub	WT	Dagon
9	Deaf, Dumb and Blind (Eddy)	?	24	wrtg		
10	The Picture in the House	1	24	pub	WT	
11	The Hound	2	24	pub	WT	Alhazred; Long; *Necronomicon*
12	Under the Pyramids (Houdini)	3	24	wrtg		
13	The Rats in the Walls	3	24	pub	WT	Nyarlathotep
14	Ashes	3	24	pub	WT	
15	Arthur Jermyn	4	24	pub	WT'	
16	The Ghost-Eater (Eddy)	4	24	pub	WT	
17	Hypnos	5–7	24	pub	WT	
18	The Loved Dead (Eddy)	5–7	24	pub	WT	
19	Under the Pyramids (Houdini)	5–7	24	pub	WT	
20	The Shunned House	10	24	wrtg		
21	The Festival	1	25	pub	WT	Alhazred; *Necronomicon*
22	The Statement of Randolph Carter	2	25	pub	WT	
23	Deaf, Dumb and Blind (Eddy)	4	25	pub	WT	
24	The Music of Erich Zann	5	25	pub	WT	
25	The Unnamable	7	25	pub	WT	

Appendix: Lovecraft Compositions/Publications During *Weird Tales* Period

	Title	M	Y	Act	PP	Elements Used
26	The Horror at Red Hook	8	25	wrtg		
27	He	8	25	wrtg		
28	In the Vault	9	25	wrtg		
29	The Temple	9	25	pub	WT	
30	In the Vault	11	25	pub	Ty	
31	The Tomb	1	26	pub	WI	
32	The Cats of Ulthar	2	26	pub	WT	
33	Cool Air	3	26	wrtg		
34	The Outsider	4	26	pub	WT	
35	Polaris	5	26	pub	NA	
36	The Moon Bog	6	26	pub	WT	
37	Nyarlathotep	7	26	pub	NA	Nyarlathotep
38	The Call of Cthulhu	Su	26	wrtg		
39	The Terrible Old Man	8	26	pub	WT	
40	He	9	26	pub	WT	
41	The Strange High House in the Mist	9	26	wrtg		Elder Ones
42	Two Black Bottles (Talman)	10	26	wrtg		
43	Pickman's Model		26	wrtg		
44	The Silver Key	?	26	wrtg		
45	The Dream Quest of Unknown Kadath	1	27	wrtg		Azathoth; Elder Ones; Leng; Nyarlathotep
46	The Horror at Red Hook	1	27	pub	WT	
47	The Case of Charles Dexter Ward	3	27	wrtg		Alhazred; *Necronomicon*; Yog-Sothoth
48	The Colour out of Space	3	27	wrtg		
49	The White Ship	3	27	pub	WT	

Appendix: Lovecraft Compositions/Publications During *Weird Tales* Period

	Title	M	Y	Act	PP	Elements Used
50	The Green Meadow	Sp	27	pub	Va	
51	Two Black Bottles (Talman)	8	27	pub	WT	
52	The Colour out of Space	9	27	pub	AS	
53	Picktman's Model	10	27	pub	WT	
54	The Last Test (de Castro)	?	27	wrtg		Alhazred; Irem; Nug; Nyarlathotep; Olathoë; Pnakotic Mss.; Yeb; Yog-Sothoth
55	History of the *Necronomicon*	?	27	wrtg		Alhazred; Cthulhu; *Necronomicon;* Yog-Sothoth
56	The Call of Cthulhu	2	28	pub	WT	Alhazred; Cthulhu; Great Old Ones; Irem; *Necronomicon;* R'lyeh
57	Cool Air	3	28	pub	TM	
58	The Curse of Yig (Bishop)	?	28	wrtg		Yig
59	The Lurking Fear	6	28	pub	WT	
60	The Dunwich Horror	Su	28	wrtg		Alhazred; Cthulhu; *Necronomicon;* Old Ones; Shub-Niggurath; Yog-Sothoth
61	The Last Test (de Castro)	11	28	pub	WT	Alhazred; Irem; Nug; Nyarlathotep; Olathoë; Pnakotic Mss.; Yeb; Yog-Sothoth
62	The Silver Key	1	29	pub	WT	
63	The Dunwich Horror	4	29	pub	WT	Alhazred; Cthulhu; *Necronomicon;* Old Ones; Shub-Niggurath; Yog-Sothoth
64	The Electric Executioner (de Castro)	?	29	wrtg		Cthulhu (Cthulhutl); R'lyeh; Yig
65	The Hound	9	29	pub	WT	Alhazred; Leng; *Necronomicon*
66	The Curse of Yig (Bishop)	11	29	pub	WT	Yig
67	The Mound (Bishop)	1	30	wrtg		Azathoth; Cthulhu (Tulu); gnophkehs; K'n-Yan; Nug; Nyarlathotep; Olathoë; Old Ones; N'Kai; Relex; Shub-Niggurath; Tsathoggua; Yeb; Yig; Yoth
68	The Courtyard (verse)	1	30	wrtg		
69	Hesperia (verse)	1	30	wrtg		

Appendix: Lovecraft Compositions/Publications During *Weird Tales* Period

	Title	M	Y	Act	PP	Elements Used
70	Star-Winds (verse)	1	30	wrtg		Yuggoth
71	Antarktos (verse)	1	30	wrtg		Elder Ones
72	The Bells (verse)	1	30	wrtg		
73	Nyarlathotep (verse)	1	30	wrtg		Nyarlathotep
74	Azathoth (verse)	1	30	wrtg		Azathoth
75	Mirage (verse)	1	30	wrtg		
76	The Elder Pharos (verse)	1	30	wrtg		
77	Alienation (verse)	1	30	wrtg		
78	Recapture	1	30	wrtg		
79	Recapture	5	30	pub	WT	
80	Medusa's Coil (Bishop)	5	30	wrtg		Cthulhu (Clooloo); Elder Ones; Mu; *Necronomicon*; Rlyeh; Shub-Niggurath; Yuggoth
81	The Rats in the Walls	6	30	pub	WT	Nyarlathotep
82	The Electric Executioner (de Castro)	8	30	pub	WT	Cthulhu (Cthulhutl); R'lyeh; Yig
83	The Whisperer in Darkness	9	30	wrtg		Alhazred; Azathoth; Bethmoora; Blk Goat/Woods; Bran; Cthulhu; Hastur; Hnds/Tindalos; K'n-Yan; Lk/Hali; Leng; L'mur-Kathulos; Magnum Innominandum; N'Kai; *Necronomicon*; Pnakotic Mss.; R'lyeh; Shub-Niggurath; Tsathoggua; Yellow Sign; Yig; Yog-Sothoth
84	The Courtyard (verse)	9	30	pub	WT	
85	Star-Winds (verse)	9	30	pub	WT	
86	Hesperia (verse)	10	30	pub	WT	Yuggoth
87	Antarktos (verse)	11	30	pub	WT	Elder Ones
88	The Bells (verse)	12	30	pub	WT	
89	Nyarlathotep (verse)	1	31	pub	WT	Nyarlathotep
90	Azathoth (verse)	1	31	pub	WT	Azathoth

Appendix: Lovecraft Compositions/Publications During *Weird Tales* Period

Title	M	Y	Act	PP	Elements Used
91 Mirage (verse)	2–3	31	pub	WT	
92 The Elder Pharos (verse)	2–3	31	pub	WT	
93 The Outsider	6–7	31	pub	WT	
94 Alienation (verse)	4–5	31	pub	WT	
95 At the Mountains of Madness	3	31	wrtg		Alhazred; Cthulhu; Elder Ones; Great Old Ones; Leng; *Necronomicon*; Olathoë; Old Ones; *Pnakotic Mss.*; R'lyeh; Tsathoggua; Yog-Sothoth
96 The Whisperer in Darkness	8	31	pub	WT	Alhazred; Azathoth; Bethmoora; Blk Goat/Woods; Bran; Cthulhu; Hastur; Hnds/Tindalos; K'n-Yan; Lk/Hali; Leng; L'mur-Kathulos; Magnum Innominandum; N'Kai; *Necronomicon*; *Pnakotic Mss.*; R'lyeh; Shub-Niggurath; Tsathoggua; Yellow Sign; Yig; Yog-Sothoth
97 The Strange High House in the Mist	10	31	pub	WT	Elder Ones
98 The Trap (Whitehead)	12	31	wrtg		
99 The Shadow over Innsmouth		31	wrtg		Cthulhu; Dagon
100 The Dreams in the Witch House	2	32	wrtg		Alhazred; Azathoth; *Black Book*; *Book of Eibon*; *Necronomicon*;
101 The Trap (Whitehead)	3	32	pub	ST	Nyarlathotep; Shub-Niggurath; *Unaussprechlichen Kulten*
102 The Man of Stone (Heald)		32	wrtg		Black Goat; *Book of Eibon*; R'lyeh; Shub-Niggurath; Tsathoggua; Yoth
103 In the Vault	4	32	pub	WT	
104 Winged Death (Heald)	Su	32	wrtg		Cthulhu (Clulu); Tsathoggua (Tsadogwa)
105 The Man of Stone (Heald)	10	32	pub	WS	Black Goat; *Book of Eibon*; R'lyeh; Shub-Niggurath; Tsathoggua; Yoth
106 The Music of Erich Zann	10	32	pub	ES	

Appendix: Lovecraft Compositions/Publications During *Weird Tales* Period

	Title	M	Y	Act	PP	Elements Used
107	The Horror in the Museum (Heald)	10	32	wrt g		Azathoth; *Book of Eibon*; Chaugnar Faugn; Cthulhu; Gnoph-Keh; Leng; *Necronomicon*; Old Ones; Pnakotic Mss.; Rhan-Tegoth; Shub-Niggurath; Tsathoggua; *Unaussprechlichen Kulten*; Yog-Sothoth; Yuggoth
108	The Cats of Ulthar	2	33	pub	WT	
109	Through the Gates of the Silver Key	3	33	wrtg		Alhazred; Cthulhu; Irem; Leng; *Necronomicon*; Pnakotic Mss.; R'lyeh; Tsathoggua; Yian-Ho; Yog-Sothoth; Yuggoth
110	Out of the Aeons (Heald)	?	33	wrtg		Alhazred; Black Book; *Book of Eibon*; Elder Ones; Ghatanothoa; Leng; *Unaussprechlichen Kulten* (*Nameless Cults*); Mu; *Necronomicon*; Nug; Pnakotic Mss.; Shub-Niggurath; Tsathoggua; Yeb; Yig; Yuggoth
111	The Dreams in the Witch House	7	33	pub	WT	Alhazred; Azathoth; *Black Book*; *Book of Eibon*; *Necronomicon*; Nyarlathotep; Shub-Niggurath; *Unaussprechlichen Kulten*
112	The Horror in the Museum (Heald)	7	33	pub	WT	Azathoth; *Book of Eibon*; Chaugnar Faugn; Cthulhu; Gnoph-Keh; Leng; *Necronomicon*; Old Ones; Pnakotic Mss.; Rhan-Tegoth; Shub-Niggurath; Tsathoggua; *Unaussprechlichen Kulten*; Yog-Sothoth; Yuggoth
113	The Thing on the Doorstep	8	33	wrtg		Alhazred; Azathoth; *Book of Eibon*; *Necronomicon*; Shub-Niggurath; *Unaussprechlichen Kulten*
114	The Festival	10	33	pub	WT	Alhazred; *Necronomicon*
115	The Other Gods	11	33	pub	FF	
116	The Horror in the Burying Ground (Heald)	7	33	wrtg		
117	Polaris	2	34	pub	FF	
118	Winged Death (Heald)	3	34	pub	WT	
119	Celephaïs	5	34	pub	MT	Cthulhu (Clulu); Tsathoggua (Tsadogwa)

Appendix: Lovecraft Compositions/Publications During *Weird Tales* Period

	Title	M	Y	Act	PP	Elements Used
120	From Beyond	6	34	pub	FF	
121	Through the Gates of the Silver Key	7	34	pub	WT	Alhazred; Cthulhu; Irem; Leng; *Necronomicon*; Pnakotic Mss.; R'lyeh; Tsathoggua; Yian-Ho; Yog-Sothoth; Yuggoth
122	Beyond the Wall of Sleep	10	34	pub	FF	
123	The Other Gods	10	34	pub	TSS	
124	The Music of Erich Zann	11	34	pub	WT	
125	"Till A' the Seas" (Barlow)	1	35	wrtg		
126	The Shadow out of Time	3	35	wrtg		Alhazred; *Book of Eibon; Cultes de Goules; De Vermis Mysteriis; Necronomicon;* Old Ones; Nyarlathotep; Pnakotic Mss.; Tsathoggua; *Unaussprechlichen Kulten*
127	The Doom that Came to Sarnath	3–4	35	pub	MT	
128	Out of the Aeons (Heald)	4	35	pub	WT	Alhazred; *Black Book; Book of Eibon;* Elder Ones; Ghatanothoa; Leng; *Unaussprechlichen Kulten (Nameless Cults);* Mu; *Necronomicon;* Nug; Pnakotic Mss.; Shub-Niggurath; Tsathoggua; Yeb; Yig; Yuggoth
129	Arthur Jermyn	5	35	pub	WT	
130	The Quest of Iranon	7–8	35	pub	Ga	
131	The Challenge from Beyond	8	35	wrtg		Eltdown Shards
132	The Challenge from Beyond	9	35	pub	FM	Eltdown Shards
133	The Disinterment (Rimel)	2	35	wrtg		
134	The Diary of Alonzo Typer (Lumley)	10	35	wrtg		*Book of Dzyan; Book of Eibon (Livre d'Eibon); De Vermis Mysteriis;* Pnakotic Mss.; Shub-Niggurath; Yian-Ho
135	The Haunter of the Dark	11	35	wrtg		Azathoth; *Book of Dzyan; Book of Eibon (Liber Ivonis); Cultes des Goules; De Vermis Mysteriis; Necronomicon;* Nyarlathotep; Old Ones; Pnakotic Mss.; *Unaussprechlichen Kulten;* Yog-Sothoth; Yuggoth

Key to PP (place of publication) codes:

AS	*Amazing Stories*	ST	*Strange Tales of Mystery and Terror*
ES	*Evening Standard* (London)	TM	*Tales of Magic and Mystery*
FF	*Fantasy Fan*	TSS	*True Supernatural Stories*
FM	*Fantasy Magazine*	Va	*Vagrant*
GA	*Galleon*	WS	*Wonder Stories*
MT	*Marvel Tales*	WT	*Weird Tales*
NA	*National Amateur*		

II. The Books

Genres in the Lovecraftian Library

By Robert M. Price

As all readers know too well, one of the staples of Lovecraftian fiction, whether actually penned by HPL or by his acolytes, is the "mouldy hidden manuscript." Lovecraft himself invented several, and thus opened a floodgate for similar efforts by his imitators. Leaving aside questions about the propriety or effectiveness of this ever-burgeoning library of "rare" and "secret" texts, the present essay seeks merely to draw a few boundaries within the cluttered terrain. In light of recent developments, Lin Carter's glossary "H. P. Lovecraft: The Books" could stand some updating. But our task is even more modest than this. For we want simply to describe the principal genres of occult-related literature now loading the sagging shelves of the Mythos.

Grimoires

First, as might be expected, prominent among our texts are grimoires, books containing recipes and prescriptions for spells. Real books of this kind include *The Sixth and Seventh Books of Moses*, *The True Grimoire*, and *The Great Grimoire*. From the Arkham archives, we might select Ludvig Prinn's *De Vermis Mysteriis* (Robert Bloch). Depending on the connotation of "worm," the title might mean either "secrets of the grave" or "secrets of the Dragon." Dragon would denote either Satanism (cf. Revelation 12:9) or alchemy, of which the dragon is the symbol. If "secrets of the Dragon" is intended, we would have a parallel to the modern European grimoire *The Fiery Dragon*.

Cultes des Goules by Comte d'Erlette might be a grimoire, providing that the French "cult" is taken as meaning "worship," the title then being understood as "The Worship of the Ghouls." Otherwise, see our next category below. By the way, Eddy C. Bertin gives the comte's personal name as "François-Honoré Balfour."

There is, surprisingly, similar ambiguity in the case of the chief Mythos book, the *Necronomicon*. Only in Lovecraft's later stories does the book of Abdul Alhazred appear as a grimoire. In earlier tales, especially "The Hound," the notorious tome is of quite a different nature (again, see below). Other Mythos grimoires include Lumley's *Cthäat Aquadingen* and Michael S. Warnes's *Black Tome of Alsophocus*.

Demonologies

Before Lovecraft made the *Necronomicon* into a grimoire, he was explicit that it fell under the rubric of a "demonology," i.e., a text like the medieval *Malleus Malifecarum*, a guidebook to heretical beliefs, to be used in suppressing them. In "The Hound," reference is made to "the old Arab daemonologist" Abdul Alhazred (*D* 174). He hates and fears the horrors he relates. Note his distaste for wizards in the passage quoted in "The Festival." Interestingly, though HPL himself turned the book into a grimoire in later years, his followers (Derleth, Carter, et al.) persisted in seeing Alhazred's tome as a demonology.

Returning to d'Erlette's *Cultes des Goules*, it too is likely to be a demonology if "cultes" denotes "cults" (thus, "Ghoulish Cults"), as in Kenneth Grant's *Cults of the Shadow* or in the *Unaussprechlichen Kulten* of Friedrich Wilhelm von Junzt. The latter is, of course, one of the foundational volumes in the Cthulhu Mythos. It was invented by Robert E. Howard. Incidentally, Von Junzt's first name as given above is supplied by Lovecraft. As for the name of the volume itself, it is most often, but incorrectly, translated as "Nameless Cults." But "unaussprechlichen" denotes "unspeakable" not in the sense of "unknown," but rather in the sense of "indescribable" or "unmentionable" (cf. Ephesians 5:12: "It is shameful even to speak of what is done in secret"). Howard dubbed the book simply *Nameless Cults* with no supposed German original, but August Derleth supplied "Unaussprechlichen." E. Hoffmann Price, I believe, pointed out the lack of precise equivalency, but Derleth's version had an irresistible ring of ominous Teutonic erudition, so *Unaussprechlichen Kulten* it stayed. Eddy C. Bertin introduced a thinly veiled duplicate of Von Junzt's work in his story "Darkness, My Name Is." It is Kazaj Heinz Vogel's *Of the Damned, or: A Treatise About the Hideous Cults of the Old*. Both heresiologists were eighteenth-century Germans.

Probably another demonology is *The Confessions of Clithanus the Monk* (August Derleth, "The Passing of Eric Holme," "Something from Out There," "The Horror from the Depths"). It would seem to embody the penitential and/or devotional musings of a converted warlock. Though it is said to contain at least one spell summoning a sea-monster, Clithanus may have included it in the course of refuting and denouncing his former beliefs, much as St. Augustine described Manichaeanism in his lengthy repudiation of it in his own *Confessions.* Finally, Rev. Ward Phillips's *Thaumaturgical Prodigies in the New English Canaan* is also a work of this kind, being modeled on Cotton Mather's *Magnalia.*

Scriptures

Our third category is that of occult scriptures, those books like *Aradia: The Gospel of the Witches; The Satanic Bible;* or *The Book of Shadows,* which are used in occult or pagan liturgy. They would correspond to the prayer books, missals, and lectionaries of traditional religions. Cthulhu-cult lore includes scriptures such as Ramsey Campbell's *Revelations of Glaaki,* Derleth's *Dhol Chants,* and Carter's *Rituals of Yhe.* We might also note HPL's *Seven Cryptical Books of Hsan,* which seem analogous to the divination manual *I Ching.*

Non-Human Chronicles

Fourth in our list are prehistoric or extraterrestrial records. The foremost examples are Lovecraft's Pnakotic Manusctipts, Richard F. Searight's Eltdown Shards, and Clark Ashton Smith's *The Book of Eibon.* Regarding the last named, one may question whether it rightfully belongs to the Cthulhu Mythos at all. In a mood of extravagant expansiveness, however, HPL adopted Smith's Hyperborean stories lock, stock, and barrel into the Mythos, mentioning Eibon and "toadlike Tsathoggua" nearly as often as his own scriptures and demons. Ah well, no use crying over spilt slime.

Other survivals from nonhuman times and climes include Duane Rimel's *Chronicle of Nath,* Henry Kuttner's *Book of Iod,* Derleth's *Celaeno Fragments* and *R'lyeh Text,* Lumley's *G'harne Fragments,* and Carter's *Zanthu Tablets* and *Ponape Scripture.* The last volume is, down to the very palm-fronds it is printed on, a take-off on the already fictitious *Stanzas of Dzyan* or *Book of Dzyan* trumpeted by Madame Blavatsky and the Theosophists.

Monographs

We come next to consider a whole raft of anthropological treatises, beginning with two by Derleth's Professor Laban Shrewsbury: *Investigations into the Myth-Patterns of Latter-Day Primitives, with Especial Reference to the 'R'Iyeh Text'* and *Cthulhu in the Necronomicon.* These monographs were probably based on real-life works of scholarship like Margaret Murray's *The Witch-Cult in Western Europe* and Sir James Frazer's *The Golden Bough*, and crank volumes like W. Scott-Eliot's *The Story of Atlantis and The Lost Lemuria*, all mentioned by Lovecraft.

Lin Carter contributed a shelf full of titles of this kind. His archaeologist Harold Hadley Copeland single-handedly produced *Prehistory in the Pacific: A Preliminary Investigation with Reference to the Myth-Patterns of Southeast Asia*, and *Polynesian Mythology, with a Note on the Cthulhu Legend-Cycle*, and *The Prehistoric Pacific in the Light of the 'Ponape Scripture,'* and finally *The Civilization of Mu, a Reconstruction in the Light of Recent Discoveries, with A Synoptic Comparison of the 'R'lyeh Text' and the 'Ponape Scripture.'* Shrewsbury should have sued him. (Carter also embellished Lovecraft's brief mention of Gottfried Mülder, who wrote *The Secret Mysteries of Asia, with a Commentary on the 'Ghorl Nigral.'*) In view of all this, it seems nearly miraculous that Brian Lumley's Sir Amery Wendy-Smith did not pen a tome with a title like *Seismological Surveys of Mid-African Myth-Patterns, with Particular Reference to the 'G'harne Fragments.'* Now don't go getting ideas.

Lumley also borrowed *Unter Zee Kulten, Hydrophinnae,* and *Dwellers in the Depths* from Carl Jacobi's neglected Cthulhu Mythos tale "The Aquarium."

Inspired Poetry

Our next group of writings is constituted by the works of decadent poets. This is actually one of the oldest of the Mythos genres. The most famous example is Justin Geoffrey's *People of the Monolith* (in Robert E. Howard's "The Black Stone," and Howard-and-Derleth's "The House in the Oaks"). This notion of a too-sensitive artist driven to madness (though not delusion) by his visions of ultra-telluric horrors actually comes from HPL's "The Nameless City." There Abdul Alhazred, in his earliest appearance, is called "the mad poet" (*D* 98). Asleep at the site of the buried city of intelligent dinosaurs, Alhazred wakes up in a cold sweat and sings this famous couplet:

> That is not dead which can eternal lie,
> And with strange aeons, even death may die.

Similarly, Justin Geoffrey awakens after a bad night's sleep at the ancient shrine of toadlike Gol-Goroth, and composes these lines:

DISSECTING CTHULHU

They say foul things of Old Times still lurk
In dark forgotten corners of the world,
And gates still gape to loose on certain nights,
Shapes pent in Hell.

The musical compositions of Erich Zann and the pictures of Richard Upton Pickman derive from similar inspiration, as does *Azathoth and Other Horrors* by Lovecraft's poet Edward Pickman Derby (in "The Thing on the Doorstep"). We might also mention the disturbed sculptor Henry Anthony Wilcox (in "The Call of Cthulhu") and the demented writer Robert Blake ("The Haunter of the Dark").

Fritz Leiber in "The Terror from the Depths" introduces his own mad poet, who is, like him, a German. He is Georg Reister Fischer, author of *The Tunneler Below*. Lumley's poetess is Ariel Prescott (*Visions from Yaddith*). Lin Carter serves as the literary agent for poets Edgar Henquist Gordon (*Night Gaunts*) and Wilbur Nathaniel Hoag (*Dreams from R'lyeh*) and prose writers Phillip Howard ("The House of the Worm" and "The Defilers"), and Amadaeus Carson (*Black God of Madness*), the latter pair being spin-offs from HPL's "Robert Blake," a fictional surrogate of his pal Robert Bloch. One may speculate that this genre of "inspired fiction" might have promised some welcome relief from the overuse of crumbling grimoires and chronicles in Mythos stories. But has it perhaps already been done to death? We know we're in trouble when Lumley actually has a character leaf through one of Lin Carter's works side-by-side with the *Necronomicon*!

Variant Versions

In his segment of "The Challenge from Beyond," Lovecraft explained how certain recently unearthed Paleolithic inscribed shards which mystified scholars were dubiously translated by eccentric ecclesiastic Arthur Brooke Winters-Hall under the title *The Eltdown Shards*. This version was rejected by respectable scholars, since the clergyman's renderings seemed much too fulsome to represent the scanty and fragmentary originals. Yet, of course, the revelations of the Eltdown Shards as translated by Winters-Hall prove eerily accurate, implying perhaps that he had access to arcane sources of information parallel to those contained in the shards themselves. Thus Lovecraft inaugurated another genre of occult literature, the variant version, a new recension of an ancient text which (perhaps mediumistically) augments the secrets of the original.

A more recent example is Lumley's *Original Notes on the Necronomicon* by occultist Joachim Feery. Lumley has characters call the work an "often-fanciful reconstruction" of Alhazred's text, containing pericopae unattested in any known manuscripts. We should probably so understand Bertin's "*Liyuhh*, the almost unknown German translation, or rather adaptation and analysis of the *R'lyeh Text*." Such tendentious recensions of older texts are hardly uncommon. Many grimoires have reached their present form by such an evolutionary process of redaction. Eldon J. Epp has also studied the theological slant of the famous "Western Text" of Luke-Acts in the New Testament. The "variant version," then, is a clever and innovative departure in Mythos lore, though its very attractiveness as a literary device will probably soon lead to its exhaustion. Would that new Mythos writers would imitate the originality of the creators of the several genres, rather than slavishly copying the specific products of that originality.

[*Crypt of Cthulhu* 1, No. 3 (Candlemas 1982): 14–17]

Higher Criticism and the *Necronomicon*

By Robert M. Price

One of the greatest controversies in the history of Western religion was occasioned by the application of "higher criticism" to the Bible. This Promethean use of literary and historical criticism prompted some to declare a great apostasy throughout Christendom, and others to herald the greatest religious advance since the Reformation. What was the issue? Hadn't the Bible always been the object of study, and thus of historical and literary analysis? Indeed it had, but scholars such as Julius Wellhausen, David Friedrich Strauss, and Rudolf Bultmann dared suggest that "things that you're liable to read in the Bible ain't necessarily so." The trouble was that the "Word of God" was now to be treated like any other human literature, and thus as open to disconfirmation of historical reports, ascriptions of authorship, etc. Did Moses really write Genesis? Did the whale swallow Jonah? Did Jesus speak all the words attributed to him in the Fourth Gospel? Well perhaps, even probably, *not.* Pseudonymy and secondary material, then, were discovered in the scriptures. What has all this to do with the *Necronomicon* of Abdul Alhazred? The fabled grimoire has been deemed a "Bible" of sorts in its own right, and this article will show the utility of "higher" or "biblical criticism" as a model for understanding the *Necronomicon* in Lovecraft's fiction and subsequent literature in the Cthulhu cycle.[1]

Our first observation concerns a threefold division into which biblical

---

[1] Incidentally, "higher criticism" is distinguished from "lower criticism," the scrutiny of the history of the text's transmission with a view to establishing a critical text. In the case of the *Necronomicon,* Lovecraft himself outlined a history of textual transmission, admittedly incomplete. Mark Owings has since updated the textual history. See his "The Existing Copies—a Bibliography," in Mark Owings, ed., *The Necronomicon: A Study* (Baltimore: Mirage Associates, 1967), n.p. The lack of extant copies makes the identification of interpolations and transcriptional errors impossible in more than a general sense.

scholars divide ancient materials: the "canonical," the "apocryphal," and the "pseuepigraphical." The first named refers to the classical texts of a tradition, which shape further developments and provide the criteria for the legitimacy of such developments. The canonical texts form the standard against which subsequent works may be measured as having "fallen away" or, alternatively, as being "faithful representations," etc. At the same time, the "canon" also usually implies the definitive collection of materials by an important author. *Vis-à-vis* the Bible, the canon refers to the collection of 66 books (39 in the Old Testament, 27 in the New), believed (at one time) to have been authored by various prophets and apostles. In this context, the actual derivation of the term "canon" is most clearly meaningful, for canon means "rule" or "ruler" against which things are measured. Relative to the *Necronomicon,* the canon would refer to the original, uninterpolated work of Alhazred, but since (as some readers may need to be reminded!) we are after all dealing with fiction, our "canonical" category properly refers to the *Necronomicon* as conceived and "quoted" by Lovecraft himself, as opposed to the use made of it by subsequent writers.

The reference to later imitative writers introduces our second category, the apocryphal. Literally the word means "secret writings," but the point is not really that they are esoteric (as Lin Carter seems to imagine in "Zoth-Ommog" when he speaks of "the sinister nightmarish tone of certain volumes of the Biblical apocrypha" [157]). Rather, the idea is that such texts are "deutero-canonical," i.e., secondary but not completely alien to the canon. Thus "apocrypha" refers in the first instance to the set of historical and sapiential books including I and II Maccabees, Sirach, the Wisdom of Solomon, Tobit, and Judith. But the term is also used to refer to other texts such as the "infancy gospels" (e.g., Thomas, Pseudo-Matthew) which contain famous folktales such as that of the child Jesus bringing clay birds to life. For our purposes, the apocryphal additions to the canonical *Necronomicon* will include the quotations and summaries of its contents by Cthulhu Mythos writers such as August Derleth, Clark Ashton Smith, and Lin Carter.

The category of works the farthest distant from the original canonical collection is comprised by "pseudepigraphical" or pseudonymous books. These bear the name of an ancient author so as either to win a hearing for the book which the real writer's signature would never command (e.g., I Enoch, IV Ezra), or to pull the wool over someone's eyes (e.g., the Acts of Paul, the Book of Mormon). Into this class fall ancient works as well as modern hoaxes purporting to be the writings of biblical worthies. How, the reader may wonder, can the rubric of pseudepigrapha be applied to the study of the *Necronomicon*, which is an admitted work of fiction? The aptness of the category lies in the fact that recently at least two works have appeared on the market purporting to be the *Necronomicon*, as if it had been discovered to be no mere device of Lovecraft's fiction. But a detailed evaluation of these claims will follow below. First, we must give some attention to just how the various pieces of Lovecraftiana we have mentioned fit into the threefold pattern outlined here.

Returning to Lovecraft's canonical *Necronomicon*, we should note first his portrait of the Mad Arab Abdul Alhazred. This figure is described first of all as a religious renegade, an "indifferent Moslem" ("History of the *Necronomicon*" [1927], *MW* 52). This phrase seems to imply that Alhazred had made no formal repudiation of Islam, which would have been an unnecessarily dangerous thing to do in his day. Rather, it was that he also "worship[ed] unknown entities whom he called Yog-Sothoth and Cthulhu" (*MW* 52). In view of' the veil of secrecy which historically surrounded the Cthulhu cult, we should probably not take this statement (presumably deriving from Alhazred's twelfth-century biographer Ibn Khallikan) to imply that the Mad Arab publicly advocated or practiced such worship. Lin Carter also interprets Lovecraft's words in this manner: "he *secretly* worshiped dark gods" ("H. P. Lovecraft: The Books" 226; emphasis mine). It is probably only the reading of the *Necronomicon* itself which yields information of Alhazred's heresy. At any rate, it is to be understood that Abdul Alhazred, according to Lovecraft, was a sorcerer. As we will see, this point comes to be ignored or confused in Mythos material subsequent to Lovecraft.

As to the Mythos itself, it is no surprise that Lovecraft was reticent as to details. And clearly the singular eeriness of his stories derives largely from this modesty. He knew that the imagination of the reader can supply more horror than any explicit descriptions by the writer, so long as the latter, shall we say, draws the proper blanks for the reader to fill in. In particular, Lovecraft never revealed much about the Great old Ones. There was no primordial "fall of the angels" or "war in Heaven," in which the "Old Ones" revolted against the "Elder Gods" such as we find in subsequent Mythos tales. Instead, the two terms, obviously synonymous, referred to the same entities. And the resulting horror was all the greater, since the reader was left both to conclude that earth's original Lords were sub-human yet super-human behemoths, and to wonder how and why they did not currently rule.

Interestingly, in Lovecraft's *Necronomicon*, we are informed that Yog-Sothoth "knows where the Old Ones broke through of old, and where they shall break through again." And "Great Cthulhu is their cousin, yet can he espy them only dimly" (*DH* 170). In other words, neither of the "entities" worshipped by Alhazred were among the Great Old Ones! They might better be compared with the "spawn of Cthulhu," the Deep Ones and other ever-proliferating races of sub-human servitors of the Old Ones in Derleth's Mythos tales. (Keep in mind that Lovecraft's Deep Ones in "The Shadow over Innsmouth" were atavistic degenerates like those in "The Lurking Fear" or "The Festival.") A significant scene in "The Call of Cthulhu" provides an analogue to Cthulhu's own role. Dispersed cultists in the Louisiana bayou were discovered to have kept and venerated "a huge, formless white polypous thing with luminous eyes"(*DH* 137). Similarly we may infer that Cthulhu himself was hardly one of the old ones, but rather some sort of a demon, loosely associated with them.

Shub-Niggurath is patently a character of the same kind, being simply a variant on the medieval symbol of devil-worship, the satanic satyr. In Nyarlathotep we have a much more interesting fragment of the mythology provided by Lovecraft, and presumably by Alhazred. This character appears in the Lovecraft canon as the familiar spirit of the Shining Trapezohedron in "The Haunter of the Dark," in which role he is called an "avatar of Nyarlathotep." He also appears as an itinerant mystagogue in the early tale "Nyarlathotep," and as an apocalyptic "Antichrist" figure in the "Nyarlathotep" stanza of *Fungi from Yuggoth*. Together these images suggest a sort of evil version of the Hindu conception of Vishnu as a savior repeatedly incarnating to deliver his people. And as Vishnu will one day return as Kalki, the messianic righter of wrongs, so will Nyarlathotep arise for the last time in Egypt to "blow earth's dust away."[2] But even Nyarlathotep is supposed to be the messenger of the Old Ones, and not one of them. Finally, Lovecraft does note the existence of Azathoth, the mindless nuclear chaos unstably pulsating at the center of reality, and we may assume that Azathoth is, at last, one of the Old Ones.

So much for the canonical Alhazred (and his alter ego Lovecraft). What of the apocrypha? The secondary Mythos authors have begun to adapt the image of the Mad Arab, so that he is a repentant sorcerer, having learned his lesson at last. This is implied in Derleth's *Necronomicon* quotation appearing in *The Lurker at the Threshold*, where it is said that Alhazred opened the portal of the Old Ones at the ruins of Irem. Yet Alhazred goes on to characterize the anticipated return of the Old Ones as "that Evill," which the Elder Gods will intervene to try to stop. Carter makes all this explicit in an "extract" from the *Necronomicon*, his short story "The City of Pillars." There the Mad Arab recounts the ill-fated trip

---

[2] Robert Bloch has taken up this hanging thread in creative, if overexplicit, ways in "The Shadow from the Steeple" and *Strange Eons*.

to Irem in order not to advocate magic but to warn against it. Likewise, he is presented as having once been a visionary of the beyond in the "Abdul Alhazred" stanza of Carter's *Dreams from R'lyeh*. Yet in "Zoth-Ommog," Alhazred has become nothing but a demonologist, a pious outsider who catalogues the beliefs and practices of heretics and wizards (174–78). The *Malleus Maleficarum* and the *Demonolatry* of Nicholas Remigius are real examples of the kind of work the *Necronomicon* has become in this story. Gerald W. Page's "Preface to the *Necronomicon*" presents Alhazred as a reformed sorcerer-turned-demonologist. Here, then, we have a major departure from Lovecraft's *Necronomicon*.

But there are even more important deviations concerning the Mythos itself. Lovecraft's imitators could not leave well enough alone. Where Lovecraft was silent, his well-meaning acolytes could not stop talking. And as the Taoist epigram has it, regarding the esoteric realm, "Those who know don't say; those who say don't know." In new passages of Alhazred, we suddenly find full-blown cosmogonies. The pages of the *Necronomicon* according to Derleth and Carter fairly swarm with Great Old Ones, now including Cthulhu and Yog-Sothoth, as well as innumerable others including Smith's Tsathoggua, Derleth's Cthugha, Ithaqua, Lloigor, Zhar, etc. Lin Carter has his narrator in "Zoth-Ommog" understate the case: "Let it suffice to say that the great old ones grew numerous."[3] One almost needs a scorecard to keep them straight. And, sure enough, one is provided; Derleth already in *The Lurker at the Threshold* adds "a revolt of the angels" myth modeled on the biblical fall of Satan (Rev. 12:7–9) and the Greek myth of the Olympians vs. the Titans. The Old Ones are for the first time distinguished from the "Elder Gods" against whom they rose, and by whom they were imprisoned.

It is evident that much of the evocative effect of Lovecraft's tantalizing patchiness has been lost with Derleth's and Carter's filling in of the gaps. But it is not only the explicitness that dispels the Lovecraft magic, but also the robbing from the Mythos of its secret and alien character. Much of the eerie charm of "The Call of Cthulhu" was due to the fact that the degenerate Cthulhu worship had somehow escaped the notice of anthropologists and comparative religion scholars. The implications were disturbing. Lovecraft was able to draw precisely this contrast by juxtaposing the *Necronomicon* alongside real works of arcana such as Frazer's *Golden Bough* and Murray's *Witch-Cult in Western Europe*, and by setting stories like "The Dunwich Horror" in the context of New England backwoods

---

[3] One is reminded of how Superman seemed at first to be the "last son of Krypton" but was eventually joined by Supergirl, Krypto, Supermonkey, Superhorse, and countless other ne'er-do-well relatives and refugees from the Phantom Zone.

superstition. The Cthulhu cult, it was implied, is like all this, but, oh my God, the *real thing*. But in the hands of sorcerer's apprentices Derleth and Carter, Great Cthulhu and his kin are thoroughly domesticated. Look more closely in *The Golden Bough* and you will find them after all. For Cthulhu is merely a "water-elemental," and the newcomers Ithaqua and Cthugha are air- and fire-elementals respectively. (This is especially odd in the case of Cthulhu and Cthugha since the prefix "Cth-" must denote earth, or "chthonic," spirits if anything.) So Cthulhu and company had not remained totally underground after all; they had merely used aliases like Quetzalcoatl and the Wendigo. Oh well.

One last note about the apocryphal *Necronomicon* of Derleth, Carter, and others, concerning the literary style of the ancient text. Lovecraft made scant quotes from the tome of Alhazred, realizing that the claims for a book so blasphemous as to drive the reader mad would best be served by leaving it, again, mostly to the imagination. Yet when he granted a brief glimpse of the blasphemous book, it was worth it. An inkling of nightmarish exaltation does accompany the famous passage quoted in "The Dunwich Horror." Clark Ashton Smith is able to match Lovecraft's eerie evocativeness in his quote in "The Nameless Offspring," beginning, "Many and multiform are the dim horrors of Earth, infesting her ways from the prime. They sleep beneath the unturned stone; they rise with the tree from its root. . . ." Both Lovecraft and Smith can convince one that the *Necronomicon* would indeed cost its reader some sleep. Equally important, Smith, Henry Kuttner, and Frank Belknap Long wisely cite the *Necronomicon* as dealing with dark subjects unrelated to the Mythos proper, as in the formula for grisly "resurrection" described in Smith's "The Return of the Sorcerer." This creates the impression that Alhazred dealt with a wide variety of occult subjects, as would likely be the case.

On the other hand, Derleth and Carter associate the *Necronomicon* exclusively with the Cthulhu cult, making it in effect nothing but a "guidebook to the Great Old Ones." Besides this, the style of the *Necronomicon* quotes has suffered. Derleth's passages are cramped in style and crammed in content, as if he were trying to summarize all his stories and Lovecraft's "in twenty-five words or less." The Elder Gods, the Old Ones, the Deep Ones, the Great Race, Yuggoth, etc., etc., reel off at a flying clip, all in one paragraph. His *Necronomicon* need only have been a page or two long! Carter, by contrast, made an innovative step in his "translations" of parts of the text as two short stories, "The City of Pillars" and "The Doom of Yakthoob." But even here, the style is on the level of the dialogue in Marvel Comics' *The Mighty Thor,* with its affected "olde English."

As for the various Mythos stories in which brief quotes appear, Derleth and Carter have been able to copy the pedantic minuteness of detail in Lovecraft's narrative style, but none (or not much) of his substance. In Lovecraft's tales, the plodding detail served to accentuate both the "mustiness and decay" of the setting and the far from mundane character of what was really going on. When he gets to the italicized punchline of the story, the reader is suddenly roused from the drowsiness of the style with a slap in the face by the "awful truth." But there is no awful truth in our "apocryphal," derivative tales. The works of Derleth and Carter proceed tiresomely according to a stereotyped plan. The half-mad protagonist recounts his discovery of blasphemous shenanigans among relatives in New England, which at first he discounts. Later, step by step, he learns the secret which has all along been old stuff to the reader. The pattern was reused a forgivable number of times by Lovecraft himself, but Derleth and Carter have beaten it to death. Very refreshing, by contrast, are Colin Wilson's *The Mind Parasites* and Robert Bloch's *Strange Eons,* which make creative new departures in their use of the Mythos.

If most of the apocryphal additions to the *Necronomicon* show a marked drop in the evocative power of the original fiction, the pseudepigraphical *Necronomicon* makes a greater mistake by no longer claiming to be fiction. The two works to be considered here (though there may be others) are *The Necronomicon* edited by "Simon" and *The Necronomicon: The Book of Dead Names* edited by George Hay. These two books are offered, no doubt, to satisfy the desires of Lovecraft-buffs (including the present writer!) to have a book bearing this title on their shelves, and of the publishers to fill their pockets. On the face of it, the very idea of the suppressed secrets of the ages being published as a mass-market paperback is a bit difficult to take seriously. But we will assume for argument's sake that Hay and Simon are serious in their desire to be taken literally. In this case, the hoaxers have made a couple of serious blunders. As witches of old were imagined to bear the devil's mark somewhere on their bodies, even so forgers of "ancient" documents have traditionally blown their cover by various marks of inauthenticity. One of the classical "dead giveaways" is the failure to supply a manuscript for the scrutiny of scholars. In his fascinating *Famous Biblical Hoaxes,* the late Edgar J. Goodspeed of the University of Chicago repeatedly noted such omissions. Nicholas Notovitch was the "discoverer" of the "Life of St. Issa, Best of the Sons of Men," allegedly a Tibetan biography of Jesus Christ. At first he claimed to have translated the scroll while in a monastic library in Tibet. When no such scroll could be found, he suddenly changed his story; it seemed rather that he had compiled his narrative from brief notes in several disparate works. Needless to say, even these passages remained protected in their original repository—Notovich's imagination. Similarly Ernst Von Der Planitz presented the world with a "critical edition" of the *Letter of Benan*, a reminiscence of an Egyptian physician who had known Jesus during his childhood sojourn in the land of the Pharaohs. Unfortunately, he never presented scholars with his original Coptic manuscript, not even a facsimile, photograph, or transcription. Guess why? Once again, the "Twenty-ninth Chapter of Acts" would have been more plausible (or perhaps less implausible) if the manuscript had not been regrettably "lost" somewhere along the line (Goodspeed 11–12, 55, 65). By contrast, the discoverers and editors of the Nag Hammadi gnostic texts, or of the Dead Sea Scrolls (real ancient texts), had no reticence in making their finds public.

Do the publishers of Alhazred's work "have the goods" to show us? Simon says: "The Editor and the Publisher anticipate that there will be a demand at first for privileged views of the original NECRONCMICON. . . . Let us hasten to state at this point that the original MS. is neither the property of the Editor, nor the Publishers. We were given the right to translate and publish this work . . . but not the right to hold the MS. up to public inspection . . . . Therefore as a matter of policy, we cannot honor any request to see the NECRONOMICON in its original state" (Simon li). In the case of Hay's *Necronomicon,* there is no text at all to deal with, since the work is actually supposed to be the result of decoding an Elizabethan cryptogram. Such evasion does not contribute much to the credibility of either work.

Another feature of "biblical hoaxes" is what one might call the "wink statement," a remark by the "translator" where he tips his hand, as it were. For instance, in the first edition of the *Book of Mormon,* Joseph Smith listed himself not merely as "translator" but as "author," a slip duly corrected in subsequent editions. Kenneth Sylvan Guthrie, "translator" of *The Long-Lost Second Book of Acts,* makes an interesting admission. "If evey [*sic*] word of ours were inspired, would we not be prophets. Having prayer, whose fault is it if we are not?" (flyleaf inscription). In other words, "I wrote this out of whole cloth." And *Necronomicon* editor Hay notes that his book "was designed . . . for men and women of true balance-those who . . . can see the false in the true and the true in the false" (11). Guess what the "false" is?

Another interesting, and suspicious, feature of pseudepigraphical works is their authors' use of phony etymology and lexicography in an effort to simulate scholarship. Joseph Smith in his *Book of Mormon* provides an example, with his imaginary "Reformed Egyptian" alphabet, in which the "golden plates" were inscribed. The energies of Mormon apologists have finally unearthed some similar characters from the Micmac Indian hieroglyphic system, a parallel that is supposed to lend some sort of support to Smith's case (Thomas 30). The same technique has been used to twist the biblical text to diverse ends by eccentrics such as Herbert W. Armstrong, who supports his dogma that the English are the Lost Tribes of Israel ("Saxons" = "Isaac's Sons"; "British" = "Berith-Ish," or "man of the covenant") (Martin 299). Hal Lindsey finds the U.S.S.R. predicted in Ezekiel ("Rosh" = "Russia"; "Meshech" = "Moscow"; "Tubal" = "Tobolsk") (52–54). See also the etymological illusions of John M. Allegro, who tries to associate early Christianity with a hallucinogenic mushroom cult [the "stumbling block" of the cross (I Corinthians 1:23) = "bolt mushroom" because of a doubtful Aramaic play on words] (48–49).

Fantastic lexical gaffs abound in our two texts. First of all, Hay translates "Necronomicon" as "The Bock of Dead Names." This translation is almost certainly, as well as blatantly, mistaken. Simon is more clever than Hay, but no more convincing, in his attempt to link the Cthulhu Mythos with the Sumerian-Babylonian myth cycle. Cthulhu can perhaps be made roughly equivalent to "Kutulu" ("man of the underworld"), but the equation of "Azathoth" with "Azag-thoth" or "Lord of Magicians" (actually "Enchanter Thoth") raises a bit of a problem, since "Thoth" represents the wrong (viz. Egyptian) mythology! "Nyarlathotep" must present the same embarrassment to this theory. Similarly the Sumerian "Ishniggarab" is made the root of "Shub-Niggurath," but the latter is plainly derived from the Latin niger ("black"), i.e. "black goat of the woods."

Let us turn at this point to the criteria already employed in the earlier discussion, the "canonical" and "apocryphal" *Necronomica*. How is Abdul Alhazred portrayed in the two pseudepigraphs? Hay recalled his Lovecraft better than did Derleth, for the Mad Arab is once again an out-and-out sorcerer, not a warner against sorcery. The "fragments" of the *Necronomicon* edited by Hay are all concerned with the rites to summon the Old Ones. Simon, by contrast, has made Alhazred into an opponent of "Kutulu," "Azag-thoth," et al. He relates the secrets of their rituals only so that the reader may be forewarned and forearmed. Of course, this completely contradicts Lovecraft's conception of Alhazred, as does the religious setting in which the Mad Arab is placed. Whereas Lovecraft made him a Muslim (albeit an "indifferent" one), Simon has him worshipping Marduk and Anu! Perhaps we are to understand this glaring anachronism as evidence of Alhazred's prowess in time travel!

What of the Mythos itself? Both Hay and Simon have followed Derleth's lead in importing the secondary "revolt in heaven" motif into the *Necronomicon*. Hay's version is straight Derleth, "Elder Gods," "Elder

Sign" and all. Simon connects the myth with the destruction of Tiamat (the chaos dragon) by Marduk. This is doubly confused, since, as Simon himself points out, this myth has the gods revolting against the monster-titans, reversing the order of Derleth's myth. Also, Simon seems at first to identify Cthulhu with Tiamat, then to distinguish him as her male counterpart. At any rate, the use of this mythology indicates the secondary character of the work in two ways, since it depends on Derleth's apocryphal additions to Lovecraft's simpler version, and it continues Derleth's misguided domestication of the Old Ones by co-opting them in terms of real historical myth-cycles (in this case, the Sumerian-Babylonian; Robert Turner, writing in Hay's volume, identifies the Mythos with Madame Blavatsky's myths).

As for the Old Ones themselves, we find Hay including Cthulhu and Yog-Sothoth in their number, contra Lovecraft. He wisely eliminates most of the vast horde, retaining only six: the two just named plus Shub-Niggurath, Azathoth, Nyarlathotep, and Hastur. Apparently, Hay has thought to cover himself by limiting himself to those actually named first in Lovecraft stories (e.g., he has eliminated even Tsathoggua, mentioned by Lovecraft in "The Whisperer in Darkness," but created previously by Clark Ashton Smith). But he has slipped in retaining Hastur the Unspeakable. As Lin Carter correctly notes, Lovecraft had first mentioned Hastur, along with the place names Hali and Carcosa (all lifted from Ambrose Bierce), in "The Whisperer in Darkness," but with no explanation. It was Derleth who (along with Mark Schorer in "The Lair of the Star-Spawn") made a "Great Old One" of Hastur (*Look Behind the Cthulhu Mythos* 99). Yet according to Hay, he appears as a deity already in the *Necronomicon* itself. Hay also has Alhazred obediently parroting Derleth's interminable list of sub-human servitor races including the "abominable [or better, unpronounceable] Tcho-Tcho." Simon behaves himself on this score, though he does mistakenly include Derleth's "Elder Gods."

Finally, what of the style of the two *Necronomica*? It must be admitted that both have some ring of authenticity as magical grimoires. But this is not saying much, since such texts usually are about as stimulating as cookbooks or automotive manuals. Simon does show a bit of stylistic flair at times, but dips too often into transparent science fiction, as when Alhazred recounts seeing a priest of Cthulhu melt like the witch in *The Wizard of Oz!* But all told, we must raise against the authenticity of these texts the same complaint aimed earlier at Derleth and Carter: Is *this* the book that drove its readers mad? If the "blasphemous" book of Lovecraft would deprive one of sleep, those of Hay and Simon might well cure insomnia.

But the plodding pedantry of the books raises one last question. Could these texts have been seriously intended for occult use? This possibility is suggested by the recent composition and use of liturgies such as the "Ceremony of the Nine Angles" and "The Call to Cthulhu" by Satanist fanatics.[4] Rumor has it that Simon's *Necronomicon* (or perhaps some third version) has been written, or at least is used, by such a group.

Our study has sought to demonstrate the utility of biblical "higher criticism" in evaluating developments in the fictional tradition of Lovecraft's *Necronomicon*. We saw that the categories of "canonical," "apocryphal," and "pseudepigraphical" provided helpful rubrics for tracing the decline of literary imagination from Lovecraft through the imitators to the forgers. Not only did the *Necronomicon* and its occult mythology grow more mundane in the process, but soon even the acknowledgment of fiction was lost. And various criteria of "biblical hoaxes" allowed the identification of two current *Necronomica* as frauds. If the loss of literary imagination is to be construed as a sign of the creeping influence of the Old Ones, then perhaps their hour is at hand at last.

Works Cited

Allegro, John M. *The Sacred Mushroom and the Cross*. New York: Bantam, 1971.

Carter, Lin. "H. P. Lovecraft: The Books." In *The Shuttered Room and Other Pieces*, ed. August Derleth. Sauk City, WI: Arkham House, 1959. 212–49.

———. *Lovecraft: A Look Behind the Cthulhu Mythos*. New York: Ballantine, 1972.

———. "Zoth-Ommog." In *The Disciples of Cthulhu*, ed. Edward P. Berglund. New York: DAW, 1976. 141–93.

Goodspeed, Edgar J. *Famous Biblical Hoaxes*. Grand Rapids, MI: Baker Book House, 1956.

Guthrie, Kenneth Sylvan, trans. *The Long-Lost Second Book of Acts*. New York: Theosophical Publishing Co., 1904.

Hay, George, ed. *The Necronomicon: The Book of Dead Names*. Jersey, UK: Neville Spearman, 1978.

Lindsey, Hal, with C. C. Carlson. *The Late Great Planet Earth*. New York: Bantam, 1976.

---

[4] In Anton Szandor LaVey, *The Satanic Rituals* (New York: Avon, 1972), pp. 179–201. Incidentally, in view of LaVey's fine literary style, as evidenced here and in his earlier work *The Satanic Bible*, it is a shame that he did not try his hand at a pseudepigraphical *Necronomicon*. Unlike the attempts of Simon and Hay, it would very likely have come close to the eerie evocativeness of Lovecraft's and Smith's *Necronomicon* passages.

Martin, Walter R. *The Kingdom of the Cults.* Minneapolis: Bethany Fellowship, 1968.

Simon, ed. *The Necronomicon.* New York: Avon, 1980.

Thomas, Mark. "Scholarship and the Future of the Book of Mormon." *Sunstone* (May–June 1980): 24-29.

[*Lovecraft Studies* No. 6 (Spring 1982): 3–13]

The Lurker at the Threshold of Interpretation: Hoax *Necronomicons* and Paratextual Noise

By Dan Clore

If the Necronomicon legend continues to grow, people will end up believing it and accusing me of faking when I point out the true origin of the thing!
—H. P. Lovecraft (cited in Harms and Gonce 47)

Tho-ag in Zhi-gyu slept seven Khorlo. Zodmanas zhiba. All Nyug bosom. Konch-hog not; Thyan-Kam not; Lha-Chohan not; Tenbrel Chugnyi not; Dharmakaya ceased; Tgen-chang not become; Barnang and Ssa in Ngovonyidj; alone Tho-og Yinsin in night of Sun-chan and Yong-grub (Parinishpanna), &c., &c..
—The Book of Dzyan

There Is No Religion Higher Than Truth.
—Theosophical Society motto

Nothing is true. Everything is permitted.
—Last words of Hassan i Sabbah

THE LURKER AT THE THRESHOLD OF INTERPRETATION

The publication of hoax editions of the *Necronomicon*—a fictional work used as a prop in the weird fiction of Howard Phillips Lovecraft and other writers—may seem a simple matter. On closer examination this may no longer appear to be the case. It is not merely a question of the self-denying hoax—for the hoax versions are all either admitted spoofs, or indicate their nature as hoax by internal evidence—it is not merely that a hoax must not present itself as a hoax, in order for it to actually function as a hoax. Instead, the subject opens up onto a field that Gérard Genette has termed the *paratext:* roughly, the manner in which one text influences the interpretation of another text. The paratext may be a *peritext,* which appears alongside the text (examples include the title, author's name, preface, introduction, and so forth); or it may be an *epitext,* which appears in a physical location not directly connected to the text. Genette explains that "More than a boundary or a sealed border, the paratext is, rather, a *threshold,* or—a word Borges used apropos of a preface—a 'vestibule' that offers the world at large the possibility of either stepping inside or turning back" (2). Where the epitext is concerned, moreover, the paratext displays a "potential for indefinite diffusion" (346) as more and more texts become mutually relevant and interconnected. It is evidently this problematic which study of the hoax *Necronomicons* provides data for.

Before attempting to tackle the hoax editions of the *Necronomicon* themselves, it should be informative to observe how the subject is prefigured in Lovecraft's own work. Lovecraft saw the weird tale as itself necessarily similar to a hoax—in a letter to Clark Ashton Smith dated October 17, 1930, he says:

> My own rule is that no weird story can truly produce terror unless it is devised with all the care & verisimilitude of an actual *hoax.* The author must forget all about "short story technique", & build up a stark, simple account, full of homely corroborative details, just as if he were actually trying to "put across" a deception in real life—a deception clever enough to make adults believe it. My own attitude in writing is always that of the hoax-weaver. One part of my mind tries to concoct something realistic & coherent enough to fool the rest of my mind & make me swallow the marvel as the late Camille Flammarion used to swallow the ghost & revenant yarns unloaded on him by fakers & neurotics. For the time being I try to forget formal literature, & simply devise a lie as carefully as a crooked witness prepares a line of testimony with cross-examining lawyers in his mind. . . . This ideal became a conscious one with me about the 'Cthulhu' period . . . (*SL* 3.193)

In short, the weird tale is devised as a hoax but it is not presented as one, which effectively means that it is merely devised to be *like* a hoax. The difference comes from the concrete speech-act that sets the text adrift in the world. A hoax that is presented as a hoax, that presents itself as a hoax, is no longer a hoax, but while an actual hoax is not presented as a hoax, neither is a work of fiction presented as a hoax—but in the latter case this precondition for the hoax prevents it from functioning as a hoax. But then the "care & verisimilitude of an actual hoax" may create the suspicion in the reader that the tale is a fictionalized version of real events, and in effect an inverse hoax presenting reality as fiction rather than the other way around.

The possibility that such a fiction may be taken for reality is not all that remote, considering that even a seasoned "skeptic" like James Randi has included entries in his *Encyclopedia of Claims, Frauds, and Hoaxes of the Occult and Supernatural* which appear to take the historical existence of the *Necronomicon* as a mediaeval grimoire as uncontested fact [110–11, 159]. He may, on the other hand, have intended these entries tongue-in-cheek, as the book does contain the occasional witticism, such as an entry on "Martinet Jardinier," which is actually a spoof based on Martin Gardner. If so, these dry attempts at humor are remarkably out of place in something apparently intended as a serious reference work. Likewise, it is interesting to note that the Cthulhu Mythos genre would later incorporate the idea that Lovecraft had disguised fact as fiction as one of its abiding clichés. An interesting example occurs in Robert Shea and Robert Anton Wilson's *Illuminatus!* Trilogy, in which a character inquires of Lovecraft "In 'The Case of Charles Dexter Ward' you quote a formula from Eliphas Levi's *History of Magic*. But you don't quote it in full. Why not?" and Lovecraft responds that "One doesn't have to believe in Santa Claus to recognize that people will exchange presents at Christmas time. One doesn't have to believe in Yog-Sothoth, the Eater of Souls, to realize how people will act who do hold that belief. It is not my intent, in any of my writings, to provide information that will lead even one unbalanced reader to try experiments that will result in the loss of human life'" (331-32). In fact, Lovecraft employed even more caution than this passage implies, as he never published *The Case of Charles Dexter Ward* in any form. One can only wonder where his visitor had managed to acquire a copy. Elsewhere in the trilogy a scholar researching Lovecraft and other weird fiction writers explicitly states our theme:

> The usual hoax: fiction presented as fact. This hoax described here opposite to this: fact presented as fiction (296; italics in original).

To complete the cycle, all we need is a work of fiction that describes these prior works of fiction, which describe Lovecraft as presenting fact in the guise of fiction, as themselves presenting fact in the guise of fiction—by someone who believes that this is in fact true.

This ambivalent fiction-presented as fact vs. fact-presented-as-fiction status is put into play in "The Haunter in the Dark." The tale is told from the viewpoint of an anonymous narrator, who devotes the majority of the story to a paraphrase of the diary of Robert Blake, a young fantaisiste, and most of the rest to paraphrases of supplementary accounts from other witnesses and newspaper stories. The narrator, however, does not accept Blake's word for the events he describes. He begins with the assertion that "Cautious investigators will hesitate to challenge the common belief that Robert Blake was killed by lightning, or by some profound nervous shock derived from an electrical discharge" and that "the entries in his diary are clearly the result of a fantastic imagination aroused by certain local super-stitions and by certain old matters he had uncovered" (*DH* 92). But "his death may have nipped in the bud some stupendous hoax destined to have a literary reflection" (*DH* 93)—note already the connection between the weird tale and the hoax. The narrator informs us that "the newspapers have given the tangible details from the sceptical angle"—which the narrator clearly accepts as the true account of events—"leaving for others the draw-ing of the picture as Robert Blake saw it—or thought he saw it—or pre-tended to see it" (*DH* 93). He therefore follows the latter course, despite his own rejection of the conclusion implied in it. The tale is thus constructed on ironic grounds: what the narrator presents as a hoax, the reader must assume instead to be true in the fictional world of the text, or the tale will not be an effective weird story. In short, Lovecraft has concocted a hoax (after his usual fashion) to present as fiction instead of an "actual" hoax, but then has the narrator argue that it is in fact a hoax destined for use in the construction of a work of fiction.

"The Haunter of the Dark", however, also opens up the field in another direction. In the story, the protagonist Robert Blake discovers a typical library of forbidden tomes: "He had himself read many of them—a Latin version of the abhorred *Necronomicon,* the infamous *Cultes des Goules* of Comte d'Erlette, the sinister *Liber Ivonis,* the *Unaussprechlichen Kulten* of von Junzt, and old Ludvig Prinn's hellish *De Vermis Mystertis.* But there were others he had known merely by reputation or not at all—the Pnakotic Manuscripts, the *Book of Dzyan,* and a crumbling volume in wholly iden-tifiable characters yet with certain symbols and diagrams shudderingly recognisable to the occult student" (*DH* 100). Now, most of these are the fictional inventions of members of the Lovecraft circle, but the *Book of*

Dzyan is another matter.

If Robert Blake had desired to read the *Book of Dzyan* (more properly, the *Stanzas of Dzyan*), he needed to look no further than H. P. Blavatsky's massive two-volume opus *The Secret Doctrine,* which contains both a translation of these Stanzas and select translations from the traditional commentaries on them, and is itself comprised of Blavatsky's own lengthy commentaries. Blavatsky describes the book: "An Archaic Manuscript—a collection of palm leaves made impermeable to water, fire, and air, by some specific unknown process—is before the writer's eyes" (I 1) written in a language known as Senzar, which ultimately derives from "the inhabitants of lost Atlantis" (I xliii)—an unlikely story that is not helped by wild tales of secret subterranean galleries deep in Central Asian regions unvisited by Westerners, containing libraries left over from lost civilizations. (Some of these legendary cavern libraries have since been discovered and excavated.) The term *Dzyan* itself seems to have been invented by Madame Blavatsky, and derives from a Sanskrit root that refers to meditation and by extension to the enlightenment that results from the practice of meditation. The same root gives the Japanese term *zen.*

Contemporary research has shown that Blavatsky did in fact have contact with teachers of many different religious groups—Rosicrucian, Sufi, Druze, Hindu, and both Hinayana and Mahayana Buddhist. The books she refers to and sometimes presents purported translations of—the *Chaldean Book of Numbers,* the *Book of the Golden Precepts,* and the *Book of Dzyan* itself—reveal genuine lore from Sufi, Mahayana Buddhist, and other traditions, though the precise source texts cannot be identified. These traditional teachings have been recognized by such authorities as D. T. Suzuki, the famous exponent of Zen; Lama Kazi Dawa-Samdup, who translated the famous version of the Tibetan Book of the Dead edited by W. Y. Evan-Wentz; and the ninth Panchen (or Tashi) Lama, who sponsored an edition of *The Voice of the Silence* in 1927. It seems that she was simultaneously charged with giving these groups' secrets to the world and at the same with time concealing her connection with them. In some cases, this may have been for mundane political reasons: a number of the figures she was involved with in India were actively fighting against British colonial rule and presumably would not wish to draw further attention to themselves from the authorities. The cover story referring to Tibetan Mahatmas—safely located in a country which was then closed to the West—provided the necessary blind to put authorities off the track. (Perhaps it is a significant coincidence in this connection to note that the first appearance of the *Necronomicon* in Lovecraft's fiction, which occurs in "The Hound," refers to its information on "the ghastly soul-symbol of the corpse-eating cult of inaccessible Leng, in Central Asia" [*D* 174]—where Leng is a fictional doublet of Tibet.)

Aleister Crowley provides yet another view of Blavatsky's work. In a commentary on *The Voice of the Silence*, Crowley—who was acquainted with Hinayana, but not Mahayana, Buddhism, and frequently takes issue with perfectly correct statements about Mahayana teachings—opines of the work that "it is better than 'genuine,' being, like *The Chymical Marriage of Christian Rosencreutz*, the forgery of a great adept" (236). In Crowley's view, then, a hoax may in fact be the genuine article. Crowley also describes his own "Liber Trigrammaton" as "An account of the Cosmic process: corresponding to the stanzas of Dzyan in another system."

The most probable source for the *Book of Dzyan* itself has recently been identified. In an article Blavatsky said that the book "is the first volume of the Commentaries upon the seven secret folios of *Kiu-te*, and a Glossary of the public works of the same name" (cited in Pratt). This work, in its own turn, has created more confusion, but the matter becomes settled when it is realized that *kiu-te* is a rough phonetic rendering for a Tibetan title correctly transliterated as *rGyud-sde*. This title refers to the Kanjur and the Tanjur, a massive set of some 325 volumes, copies of which were held by at least two of Blavatsky's contacts in the region. Indeed, Blavatsky herself refers to these works in the introduction to *The Secret Doctrine* (xxvii), though she does not claim them as her source for the *Book of Dzyan*. Nonetheless, the precise text in the Kanjur and Tanjur from which the *Book of Dzyan* derives has not been identified, and most likely has been withdrawn from public circulation.

An entire procession of cults and obscure religious sects has followed Blavatsky's lead, copying their doctrines from her and from one another while simultaneously denying their true sources and instead attributing their second- and third-hand revelations to further contact with the Hidden Masters of the Great White Brotherhood. This process has been called "genealogical dissociation" (Johnson 1995, 158) and has continued through groups more or less in the classical Theosophical mold, such as Guy Ballard's I AM or Elizabeth Clare Prophet's Church Universal and Triumphant, and also into more up-to-date models in the form of the flying saucer contactee cults that replace the Hidden Masters in their Himalayan hideaways with Space Brothers winging in their cosmic wisdom from Venus or the Pleiades. J. Gordon Melton has noted that the flying saucer is practically the only new element of the story—many of the older tales had the element of interplanetary travel already, such as Blavatsky's Hidden Masters originating in the distant past when the Lords of Flame traveled to earth from Venus—and that even this element is often absent from current contact accounts, leaving them almost indistinguishable from nineteenth-century accounts (7; cf. also Stupple).

But this is all by way of a digression.

While the construction of a weird tale *like* a hoax does not itself involve the construction of the tale *as* a hoax, there are two senses in which Lovecraft's fiction can truly be said to indulge in hoaxing. The first involves the use of the various paraphernalia of the Lovecraft Mythos—the invented gods and forbidden tomes shared by the contributors to the Mythos. It is perhaps significant that this technique seems to have first occurred to Lovecraft as the result of an interesting example of paratextual noise: a letter writer to *Weird Tales* named N. J. O'Neail inquired whether there wasn't some connection between Lovecraft's Cthulhu and Kathulos, who had appeared in Robert E. Howard's novel *Skull-Face;* he also noticed the presence of Cthulhu and Yog-Sothoth in a story by Adolphe de Castro, a Lovecraft revision client (cited by Mariconda 35). Lovecraft writes to Howard, in a letter dated August 14, 1930, that "[Frank Belknap] Long has alluded to the *Necronomicon* in some things of his—in fact, I think it is rather good fun to have this artificial mythology given an air of verisimilitude by wide citation" (*SL* 3.166). He explains the strategy further in a letter to William Frederick Anger, dated August 14,1934:

> For the fun of building up a convincing cycle of synthetic folklore, all of our gang frequently allude to the pet daemons of the others—thus Smith uses my Yog-Sothoth, while I use his Tsathoggua. Also, I sometimes insert a devil or two of my own in the tales I revise or ghostwrite for professional clients. Thus our black pantheon acquires an extensive publicity & pseudo-authoritativeness it would not otherwise get. We never, however, try to put it across as an actual hoax; but always carefully explain to enquirers that it is 100% fiction. In order to avoid ambiguity in my references to the *Necronomicon* I have drawn up a brief synopsis of its history...All this gives it a sort of air of verisimilitude. (*SL* 5.16)

And in another letter, to Margaret Sylvester, dated January 13, 1934, he says:

> Regarding the *Necronomicon*—I must confess that this monstrous & abhorred volume is merely a figment of my own imagination! Inventing horrible books is quite a pastime among devotees of the weird, & ... many of the regular *W.T.* contributors have such things to their credit—or discredit. It rather amuses

the different writers to use one another's synthetic demons &
imaginary books in their stories—so that Clark Ashton Smith
often speaks of my *Necronomicon* while I refer to his *Book of
Eibon* . . . & so on. This pooling of resources tends to build up
quite a pseudo-convincing background of dark mythology,
legendry, & bibliography—though of course none of us has the
least wish actually to mislead readers. (*SL* 4.346; ellipses as in
original)

The reader will note Lovecraft's disingenuous disavowal of the intention of misleading readers, even though the strategy he outlines relies on
doing precisely that. It should be noted that the strategy involves more
than merely disseminating elements of the Mythos into multiple texts; in
addition, many are altered in the process. In some cases this transformation
reaches absurd heights, as in "The Mound," in which loathsome Cthulhu
appears as "Great Tulu, a spirit of universal harmony anciently symbolised
as the octopus-headed god who had brought all men down from the stars"
(*HM* 136). This creates the impression, amongst naive readers, that author
A and author B are not borrowing from each other—*or even from the same
source*—but are instead borrowing from sources which had in turn borrowed from earlier sources, which in turn were ultimately derived from a
single ur-source and which reveal the traces of evolution over time, much
as the variant versions of real myths do. In short, the transformation of the
elements of the Mythos not only does not detract from the air of verisimilitude through the inconsistency, but adds to the air of verisimilitude by
operating on another level. Since Lovecraft never codified his conceptions
but instead continually added new ones while reconceptualizing the old
(so that, for example, supernatural beings become extra-dimensional or
ultra-terrestrial creatures more akin to the alien races of science fiction
than to traditional supernatural monsters), this strategy provided greater
room for his creativity.

It is noteworthy that one example of an earlier writer whose inventions
were put to use by Lovecraft comes in Arthur Machen, for Lovecraft says,
in the letter to Robert E. Howard cited above, that "Long and I often debate
about the real folklore basis of Machen's nightmare witch-cult hints—'Aklo
letters', 'Voorish domes', 'Dols', 'Green and Scarlet Ceremonies', etc., etc."
(*SL* 3.167). In "The Haunter of the Dark," for example, Blake deciphers a
text "in the dark Aklo language used by certain cults of evil antiquity, and
known to him in a halting way through previous researches" (*DH* 106).
Howard's Kathulos, which apparently first began the whole business, itself
appears in a laundry-list of Mythos names derived from Lovecraft, other

members of the Lovecraft circle, Lovecraft revision clients, and precursor writers such as Ambrose Bierce and Robert W. Chambers, names which the narrator had "heard elsewhere in the most hideous of connexions," in the form "L'mur-Kathulos," which likely adds a reference to the lost continent Lemuria (*DH* 223).

The second sense in which Lovecraft can be said to have truly indulged in hoaxing incorporates and intensifies the first. This refers to Lovecraft's revisions, which, as mentioned in the letters cited above, frequently include references to the Mythos elements created by Lovecraft and other members of his circle. It should be noted as well that to refer to these works as "revisions" is often a bit of an exaggeration: Lovecraft frequently discarded anything his revision clients chanced to produce and simply wrote a new tale, almost purely of his own devising, to be sold as the client's work. The Lovecraft Mythos was not only disseminated through the work of many authors, but Lovecraft himself *was* many of those authors. The later publication of these stories under Lovecraft's own name—which he would be unlikely to approve of, both as a matter of professional courtesy to his revision clients and out of (sometimes justified) concern over the aesthetic quality of these tales—destroys the paratextual effect intended by the author.

All of which brings us by a rather circuitous route to actual *Necronomicon* hoaxes. We will not deal here with such matters as the various spoof sale ads for whatever edition of the *Necronomicon,* nor with the card catalogue entries that a number of university libraries (Yale, UC Berkeley, etc.) have sported at various times, nor with the entries in assorted bibliographies, etc. etc. etc. Here we will deal only with actual editions of texts that purport to present the *Necronomicon* itself. Unfortunately, no Pierre Menard has arisen to rewrite the mad Arab's text in the way that Menard reproduced that of Cid Hamete Benengeli. Instead, we have three main editions (there are others)—the de Camp-Scithers, the Wilson-Hay-Langford-Turner, and the Simon *Necronomicons.* Of these, the first two are admitted spoofs. Each of the three presents within itself the denial of its own authenticity as the work of the mad Arab, as we shall see below. These hoax *Necronomicons* frequently display an utter lack of verisimilitude where a little research would have provided a much more convincing story: the Hay-Wilson-Langford-Turner *Necronomicon,* for example, spins a cock-and-bull story about Lovecraft's father obtaining the *Necronomicon* through his contacts in Egyptian Masonry and passing the book on to his son before going insane; in fact, while Lovecraft's father was not a Mason, his maternal grandfather, Whipple Phillips, not only belonged to the Masons but had himself founded a Masonic lodge. Clearly it was during little

Howard's formative years, when grandfather Whipple took on the role of father to him after driving his real father insane, that the elderly gentleman introduced him to the Book of Hell.

Lovecraft himself considered writing a hoax *Necronomicon*. In a letter to James Blish and William Miller dated May 13, 1936, he says:

> If anyone were to try to write the *Necronomicon*, it would disappoint all those who have shuddered at cryptic references to it. The most one could do—and I may try that some time—is to "translate" isolated chapters of the mad Arab's monstrous tome. . . . A collected series of such extracts might later be offered as an abridged and expurgated *Necronomicon*—although I am opposed to serious hoaxes, since they really confuse and retard the sincere student of folklore. I feel quite guilty every time I hear of someone's having spent valuable time looking up the *Necronomicon* at public libraries. (*Uncollected Letters* 37–38)

Perhaps it is unfortunate that Lovecraft himself did not close the field to further hoax editions; perhaps it is fortunate that the open-endedness of his enterprise remained unsullied.

Colin Wilson, in his "The *Necronomicon:* The Origin of a Spoof," regarding the Hay-Wilson-Langford-Turner *Necronomicon*, fulminates against Gerald Suster for daring to accuse the producers of the volume of "commercial opportunism," and he himself informs us that the book denies its own authenticity: "In fact, anyone with the slightest knowledge of Latin will instantly recognize it for a fake—it is subtitled 'The book of dead names'—when the word 'necronomicon' actually means the book of dead laws" (88). In fact, anyone with the slightest knowledge of Latin will instantly recognize that the word *necronomicon* is not Latin but Greek, and Wilson's translation is no more accurate than the (inaccurate) translation included as the spoof's subtitle.

He does, however, hit the nail on the head regarding the De Camp-Scithers volume when he discusses the stories produced for the Wilson-Hay-Turner-Langford spoof before he had become involved in the project (the original idea was to present stories *about* the *Necronomicon*, not a hoax text of the *Necronomicon* itself):

> It was awful. The writers all seemed to have the idea that all they had to do was to imitate the basic Lovecraft formula. And this formula, as we all know, is deceptively straightforward. The writer explains that he is cringing in a garret in Arkham—or

Innsmouth—committing his awful story to paper by the light of a guttering candle. Six months ago, in the library of Miskatonic University, he came across an ancient manuscript written in mediaeval German. . . . He ignored the advice of the doddery old librarian, and proceeded to practise its magic spells in the hills behind Arkham. Even the violent death of the old librarian failed to deflect him from his foolishness. And now, too late, he realises that he has unleashed the Thing on the inhabitants of Massachusetts . . . even as he writes, he can hear an ominous creaking on the stairs, as if an oversized elephant is trying to tiptoe on its hind feet. . . . But even as the door cracks open, he continues to write: "I can hear its hoarse breathing, and smell its loathsome graveyard stench. . . . Aaaargh! . . ." (88; ellipses in original)

But this "basic Lovecraft formula" never appears in Lovecraft's work. It is in fact a cliché-plot that derives from the work of Lovecraft's less creative imitators—and those who in turn have imitated the imitators rather than the original, having found in them an example of "how to do it." In short, the imitation has eclipsed the original, becoming not only a model for the method of imitation but for the material to be imitated as well. While the elements described by Wilson do exist in many Lovecraft tales, the formula abstracts them from the novel conceptions at the heart of each tale, all of which contain some unique and innovative subject. Just such a story introduces the de Camp-Scithers *Necronomicon,* explaining why the publishers have left the text in its original Arabic rather than provide a translation. It seems that the first translator that L. Sprague de Camp had hired disappeared without a trace; the second was heard screaming, whereupon his locked study was found empty; the third disappeared, spatters of his blood remaining on the walls, floor, and ceiling of his room (de Camp 125–26). In short, de Camp has done nothing with "the basic Lovecraft formula" except to apply triplification to it after the manner described by Vladimir Propp in his study of Russian folktales. The Simon *Necronomicon* provides us with a similarly suspicious tale of a mysterious appearing/disappearing manuscript, though it mercifully refrains from splattering its translators on the walls and ceiling.

There is another way in which the internal evidence of the texts presented as the *Necronomicon* denies that they are the *Necronomicon* that Lovecraft wrote of: they embody, not the Lovecraft Mythos, but the Derleth Mythos—for the authors themselves had fallen victim to hoaxing, conscious or otherwise.

The Simon *Necronomicon* describes Lovecraft's mythology as follows:

> Lovecraft developed a kind of Christian Myth of the struggle
> between opposing forces of Light and Darkness, between God
> and Satan, in the Cthulhu Mythos. . . . Basically, there are two
> "sets" of gods in the mythos: the Elder Gods, about whom not
> much is revealed, save that they are a stellar Race that occasionally
> comes to the rescue of man, and which corresponds to the
> Christian "Light"; and the Ancient Ones, about which much is
> told, sometimes in great detail, who correspond to "Darkness".
> These latter are the Evil Gods who wish nothing but ill for the
> Race of Man, and who constantly strive to break into our world
> through a Gate or Door that leads from the Outside, In. (Simon
> xiv)

In Robert Turner's commentary on the Hay-Wilson-Langford-Turner
Necronomicon (Turner is the author of the actual text presented as an
extract from the *Necronomicon*), he likewise accepts the Derleth Mythos
of cosmic good guy Elder Gods vs. evil Old Ones, although he uses the
fact to argue that Lovecraft had borrowed his cosmology from the *Book of
Dzyan* (!). But this whole scenario never appears in Lovecraft's work: it is
the invention of August Derleth.

Derleth was able to insinuate his own concepts, which were frequently at
great variance with those of Lovecraft, into common conceptions of Lovecraft's work in two ways. First, he was the publisher of Lovecraft's texts in
book form, and provided them with introductions, giving his ideas greater
influence on the reader's experience then they would otherwise have (he
also spread these interpretations far and wide in magazine articles). Derleth tells us, for example, that "As Lovecraft conceived the deities or forces
of his Mythos, there were, initially, the Elder Gods . . . these Elder Gods
were benign deities, representing the forces of good, and existed peacefully
at or near Betelgeuse in the constellation Orion, very rarely stirring forth
to intervene in the unceasing struggle between the powers of evil and the
races of Earth. These powers of evil were variously known as the Great Old
Ones or the Ancient Ones" (introduction to *Tales of the Cthulhu Mythos,*
viii). This is all very unlike Lovecraft, in whose work the Elder Gods never
appear (but perhaps this is merely a limit case showing how "rarely" they
stir forth—never), and there is no unified pantheon of Great Old Ones.
Indeed, the term "Ancient Ones" only appears in one story, "Through the
Gates of the Silver Key," and this says of the protagonist: "He wondered at
the vast conceit of those who had babbled of the *malignant* Ancient Ones,
as if They could pause from their everlasting dreams to wreak a wrath
upon mankind. As well, he thought, might a mammoth pause to visit

frantic vengeance on an angleworm" (*MM* 433–34). Derleth's work, on the other hand, is filled with recaps of his basic cosmic good guys vs. bad guys scenario. Derleth further tells us that "To supplement this remarkable creation [the *Necronomicon*], Lovecraft added . . . the *R'lyeh Text*" (x). In fact, Lovecraft never referred to the *R'lyeh Text*, as it was invented by August Derleth after Lovecraft's death.

In these paratexts to Lovecraft's work, Derleth provided not only summaries of these ideas, but support for them in the form of an alleged quotation from one of Lovecraft's letters. This, the infamous "black magic" quotation ("All my stories, unconnected as they may be, are based on the fundamental lore or legend that this world was inhabited at one time by another race who, in practicing black magic, lost their foothold and were expelled, yet live on outside ever ready to take possession of this earth again"), supports not only the expulsions and imprisonment of the Old Ones—a key element of Derleth's good vs. evil scenario—but also affirms that Lovecraft's stories are all based on a shared myth. In this case Derleth was the victim of yet another hoax, albeit both hoaxster and victim most likely believed in it in good faith. The actual author of the passage allegedly cited from a Lovecraft letter is one Harold Farnese, who gave the passage in a letter to August Derleth as a direct quotation from his correspondence with Lovecraft. Farnese, it appears, had little grasp of what Lovecraft was doing in his fiction, and simply projected his own concerns with black magic onto Lovecraft, and then presented a paraphrase from memory as a direct quotation which Derleth then seized upon, as it fortuitously coincided with his own ideas about the Cthulhu Mythos, however much it might contradict Lovecraft's own words (Schultz 1990).

Second, Derleth presented many of his own works as "posthumous collaborations" with Lovecraft. Often based on a single sentence from Lovecraft's commonplace book (in which he kept notes of ideas for future stories), for practical purposes these can be considered the work of Derleth alone. Derleth was relatively forthcoming about the nature of this practice in, for example, his pamphlet *Some Notes on H. P. Lovecraft*, in which he describes the actual Lovecraftian material on which the stories were based, noting that only three of them "contain very much Lovecraft prose" (x)—which itself is a bit of exaggeration, it would be more accurate to say that only three of them "contain *any* Lovecraft prose"—and he gives the actual prose fragments he worked with. As he says: "The rest of the stories grew out of jotting left by Lovecraft, insufficient in most cases to give any sure form to plot" (x)—which may in fact be viewed as a similar exaggeration. Nevertheless, the practice allowed Derleth to insinuate his own work in the minds of readers into the Lovecraft corpus, as the stories appeared under both of their names, implying genuine dual authorship, or even under Lovecraft's name alone. The most insidious example of this appears to be the current editions of *The Lurker at the Threshold* and *The Watchers out of Time* published by Carroll & Graf, which contain only Lovecraft's name on the front cover, spine, and title page, and on the back cover give "H. P. Lovecraft with August Derleth." (Thus the Carroll & Graf edition of *The Watchers out of Time* may cause some confusion amongst unwary readers, as it ends with the note that the title story was *"Unfinished at the time of August Derleth's death, July 4, 1971."*) The old hoaxster, who published his own work under the names of others in order to create singular paratextual effects through cross-comparison, now has another's work published under his own name, displacing the earlier paratextual effects with new ones, erasing and writing over his conceptions like a palimpsest. Taken together with the spurious "black magic" quotation, Lovecraft has been doubly erased and overwritten. The whole of this process has the effect of entirely inverting Lovecraft's open-ended, anti-systematic, ceaselessly productive practice into a celebration of him as the inventor and codifier of a closed Mythos that allows breathing room only in so far as newcomers may add additional creatures and entities to fill the slots left vacant by Lovecraft—as for example Derleth's fire-elemental Cthugha: having arbitrarily decided that Lovecraft's creations corresponded to Aristotelian elementals, not even Derleth could cram one into the "fire" slot, and so Cthugha's birth was mandated by the necessity of closing the system.

The title of *The Lurker at the Threshold* opens the field up onto yet another chain of association with similar fiction/reality paradoxes. The term appears to derive from the "Dweller on the Threshold" in Bulwer-Lytton's novel *Zanoni: A Rosicrucian Tale*. Bulwer-Lytton belonged to a Rosicrucian group and embodied a number of their ideas in his fictional works, not only *Zanoni*, but also *A Strange Story* and *The Coming Race* as well. Some of these ideas—such as the "Dweller on the Threshold" and Vril, a sexual energy force through which magick may be performed—were then incorporated into the theories of various later occultists, Blavatsky among them. The Rosicrucians themselves, it should be noted as well, had their origins in a seventeenth-century hoax and only came into existence as this hoax was imitated in real life (Washington 36–40; Borges 70).

While the hoax *Necronomicons* are quite evidently not the fictional work described by Lovecraft, a look at their actual contents may provide some clue as to what they, in fact, are. The Hay-Wilson-Langford-Turner *Necronomicon* contains a rather conventional set of rituals deriving from the common practice of ceremonial magick. As Wilson describes their goal: "the first thing to do was to find someone who really knew something about magic, and persuade him to concoct a book that could have been a perfectly genuine magical manuscript" (89), which they found in the person of Robert Turner. Turner's rituals tend to follow those actually used by ceremonial magickians rather slavishly, with some embellishment in the form of Mythos names and symbols. The Simon *Necronomicon* is likewise utterly conventional in its approach to magick: it mostly consists of ritual récipé texts transcribed from various Mesopotamian sources, Sumerian, Akkadian, Babylonian, and Assyrian, with assorted references to Lovecraftian (and Derlethian) deities tossed in at random. The inclusion of Mythos elements is not at all central to these works, since they could just as well have chosen any other myth-cycle, real or fictional, for the same use: it is yet another form of paratextual noise leading the reader onto a threshold—a threshold to the abyss of interpretation.

We now have the clue that we needed: the Hay-Wilson-Langford-Turner and Simon *Necronomicons* belong to the grimoire genre, the spellbook compilations used by mediaeval wizards. It is a commonplace in the grimoire genre to attribute authorship to the most unlikely sources—Moses, Solomon, Pope Honorius, Pope Leo III, Faust, or occasionally to more likely but nonetheless spurious sources (Cornelius Agrippa, Pietro de Abano). The texts furthermore tend to contain all sorts of anachronisms and otherwise improbable material. Viewed in this light, the misattributed authorship and other problems with the hoax *Necronomicons* mark them as authentic entries in their chosen genre.

And so, after a somewhat lengthy journey through a labyrinth of thresholds, thresholds that do not always lead one out or in as might have been expected at first glance, but instead twist and turn as if they comprised a labyrinth constructed according to some non-Euclidean geometry, we can conclude that the hoax *Necronomicons*—at least the Hay-Wilson-Langford-Turner and Simon versions—falsely claim to be the work of the mad Arab Abdul Alhazred, but in so falsely attributing themselves, they signal their genuine inclusion in the grimoire genre. The misattribution is the mark of their genre, and their very falsity is the condition of their genuineness. The hoax *Necronomicons* are every bit as "authentic" as the *Lesser Key of Solomon* or the *Sixth and Seventh Books of Moses*.

Works Cited

Blavatsky, H. P. *The Secret Doctrine*. Pasadena, CA: Theosophical University Press, 1977. Facsimile of original edition of 1888. 2 vols.

Borges, Jorge Luis. *Collected Fictions.* Translated by Andrew Hurley. New York: Viking, 1998.

Crowley, Aleister, with H.P. Blavatsky, J.F.C. Fuller, and Charles Stanfiel-Jones. *Commentarie on the Holy Books and Other Papers.* New York: Samuel Weiser, Inc., 19996. The Equinox Volume Four, Number One.

de Camp, L. Sprague. Preface to the *Al Azif.* In *The Necronomicon: Selected Stories and Essays Concerning the Blasphemous Tome of the Mad Arab,* ed. Robert M. Price. Oakland: Chaosium,1996.

Derleth, August. *The Lurker at the Threshold.* 1945. New York: Carroll & Graf, 1988. As by H. P. Lovecraft.

———. *Some Notes on H. P. Lovecraft.* 1959. West Warwick, RI: Necronomicon Press, 1982.

———. *The Watchers out of Time.* 1974. New York: Carroll & Graf, 1991. As by H. P. Lovecraft.

———, ed. *Tales of the Cthulhu Mythos.* 1969. New York: Beagle, 1971. 2 vols.

Harms, Daniel, and John Wisdom Gonce, III. *The Necronomicon Files: The Truth Behind the Legend.* Mountain View, CA: Night Shade, 1998.

Genette, Gérard. *Paratexts: Thresholds of Interpretation.* 1987. Translated by Jane E. Lewin. Foreword by Richard Macksey. Cambridge: Cambridge University Press, 1997.

Hay, George, ed. *The Necronomicon: The Book of Dead Names.* 1978. London: Skoob, 1992.

Joshi, S. T. *H. P. Lovecraft: A Life.* West Warwick, RI: Necronomicon Press, 1996.

Johnson, K. Paul. *The Masters Revealed: Madame Blavatsky and the Myth of the Great White Lodge.* Albany: State University of New York Press, 1994.

———. *Initiates of Theosophical Masters.* Albany: State University of New York Press, 1995.

Mariconda, Steven J. "Toward a Reader-Response Approach to the Lovecraft Mythos." In Mariconda's *On the Emergence of "Cthulhu" and Other Observations.* West Warwick, RI: Necronomicon Press, 1995.

Melton, J. Gordon. "The Contactees: A Survey." In *The Gods Have Landed: New Religions from Other Worlds,* ed. James R. Lewis. Albany: State University of New York Press, 1995.

Nethercot, Arthur. *The First Five Lives of Annie Besant.* Chicago: University of Chicago Press, 1960.

Price, Robert M. *H. P. Lovecraft and the Cthulhu Mythos.* Mercer Island, WA: Starmont House, 1990.

Pratt, David. "The Book of Dzyan." World Wide Web document http://ourworld.compuserve.com/homepages/dp5/dzyan.htm

Propp, Vladimir. *Morphology of the Folktale.* 1928. Translated by Lawrence
    Scott. 2nd rev. ed. Austin: University of Texas Press, 1968.

Randi, James. *An Encyclopedia of Claims, Frauds, and Hoaxes of the Occult
    and Supernatural.* New York: St. Martin's Press, 1995.

Schultz, David E. "Notes toward a History of the Cthulhu Mythos." *Crypt
    of Cthulhu* No. 92 (Eastertide 1996): 15–33.

———. "The Origin of Lovecraft's 'Black Magic' Quote." In *The Horror of
    It All: Encrusted Gems from the "Crypt of Cthulhu,"* ed. Robert M. Price.
    Mercer Island, WA: Starmont House, 1990.

Shea, Robert, and Robert Anton Wilson. *The* Illuminatus! Trilogy. New
    York: Dell Publishing Company Co., 1975.

Simon. *The Necronomicon.* 1977. New York: Avon, 1980.

Stupple, David W. "Historical Links between the Occult and Flying Sau-
    cers." *Journal of UFO Studies* N.S. 5.

Washington, Peter. *Madame Blavatsky's Baboon: A History of the Mystics,
    Mediums, and Misfits Who Brought Spiritualism to America.* New York:
    Schocken, 1993.

Wilson, Colin. "The *Necronomicon:* The Origin of a Spoof." In *Black
    Forbidden Things,* ed. Robert M. Price. Mercer Island, WA: Starmont
    House, 1992.

[*Lovecraft Studies* Nos. 42/43 (Autumn 2001): 61–69]

III. The Gods

Demythologizing Cthulhu

By Robert M. Price

A Current Dilemma

Just how seriously did H. P. Lovecraft mean us to take his Cthulhu Mythos? How seriously did he take it himself? Was his use of the "Great Old Ones" and their terrors merely some kind of stage setting, something "he chanced to mould in play"? Or were the blasphemies of the *Necronomicon* actually nightmares haunting Lovecraft, to which his fiction was the nervous response of a "whistler in darkness"? Of late, these theories have made the rounds among fans and scholars of Lovecraft's work. Both alike are unsatisfying. Cthulhu and his cousins are surely more than stylistic accessories. Yet equally certainly, Lovecraft does not seem to have so taken leave of his senses as to have actually given credence to the monsters of his imagination. Perhaps surprisingly, the answer to this dilemma is to be found in the "demythologizing" hermeneutic of New Testament scholar Rudolf Bultmann. To anticipate, Lovecraft's tales of the Great Old Ones are real myths, and thus to be taken seriously but not literally.

Understanding Religious Myth

The debate as to the intent and nature of the Cthulhu cycle strikingly parallels the contest that raged over the miracle stories of the gospels, beginning with Lessing's publication of the *Fragments* of Hermann Samuel Reimarus between 1774 and 1778. For centuries, apologists for the Christian faith had relied on the so-called "proofs from prophecy and miracle" to convince unbelievers. If Jesus could be demonstrated to have fulfilled Old Testament prophecies and to have worked supernatural miracles, then any rational person should acquiesce to his claims to have been the Messiah and the Son of God. Such a convincing case could only be made, of course, as long as all parties assumed that the gospel texts recording his words and deeds were composed by eyewitnesses, and thus contemporaneous with what they described.[1]

Reimarus pointed out numerous indications within the texts that they were not in fact accurate. Among these were the presence of divergent understandings (political vs. spiritual) of the "Kingdom of God" preached by Jesus, and embarrassing contradictions among the resurrection narratives. Reimarus and other rationalist critics after him thus rejected the Christian apologists' claim that the gospels were historically accurate. But they did not think to question the twin claim that the texts were eyewitness accounts. The seemingly inevitable conclusion was that the wonder tales of the gospels were deliberate lies, intended to capture the allegiance of the gullible. Now this would not have been out of the question. Such "pious (or not so pious) frauds" have always been present in religious history. The second-century satirist Lucian chronicles a famous instance in his "*Alexander the Quack Prophet*," wherein one Alexander of Abonuticus establishes a phony oracle, a large snake wearing a mask resembling a human face, and set back from the crowds in the shadows. Alexander collected considerable revenue from the manufactured marvel and even sent out apostles to advertise the new god to more prospective customers! In our own day, the clever hoax-miracles of Reverend Jim Jones provide a parallel. (For instance, the late Jeannie Mills, once an advisor to Jones, recounted to this writer how Jones engineered walking on water!)

Nonetheless, the supernatural stories of Jesus in the New Testament do not seem to fall in this category. David Friedrich Strauss, in his epoch-making *The Life of Jesus Critically Examined* (1835), broke the "hoax or history" deadlock by indicating a third possibility. He simply pointed out that the common assumption of apologists and skeptics, that the gospels were the product of eyewitnesses, was erroneous. Instead, several considerations led to the conclusion that the texts represented the legend-mongering propensity of first- and second-generation religious enthusiasts who had themselves witnessed little or nothing of the activities of their founder. Pious imagination, not cynical deception, was the determinative factor.

But so what? Wasn't the whole enterprise debunked either way? Orthodox apologists thought so, and thus resisted Strauss's conclusion. Strauss himself, on the other hand, was sure that the gospel story of Jesus' incarnation, miracles, and resurrection did enshrine an important truth—the essential unity of humanity and God. This truth, and adjacent ones, were

---

[1] Substantially the same arguments are set forth today in several works, for instance John Warwick Montgomery, *History and Christianity* (Downers Grove, IL: InterVarsity Press, 1974); Josh McDowell, *Evidence That Demands a Verdict* (San Bernardino, CA: Campus Crusade for Christ International, 1973).

presented in the New Testament in pictorial form. The important thing for our purposes is that Strauss had indicated that myth, even if not *literally* true, may be true in an important sense nevertheless. It remained for others to describe more accurately the way in which myth serves to communicate truth. In the present century, the work of two scholars in particular stands out. E. R. Dodds and Rudolf Bultmann moved beyond Strauss, rejecting the "intellectualist bias" present in his view of myth.

Anthropologists James Frazer and Edward Tylor in their theories of the origins of religion from magic and animism, respectively, had imagined primitive man as a kind of early theorist, positing explanations (magic, etc.) for natural phenomena. Even so, Strauss envisioned the early Christians as setting forth philosophical abstractions in mythical terms. Dodds and Bultmann realized instead that myth was an unconscious representation (via externalizing projection) of one's conception of his manner of existence in the world. In his famous essay "New Testament and Mythology," Bultmann argues at length that:

> The real purpose of myth is not to present an objective picture of the world as it is, but to express man's understanding of himself in the world in which he lives. Myth should be interpreted not cosmologically, but anthropologically, or better still, existentially. Myth speaks of the power or the powers which man supposes he experiences as the ground and limit of his world and of his own activity and suffering. (10)

He goes on to describe how the New Testament sees the existence of man as dominated by evil "powers" (demons and evil angels) whose power he can never hope to resist by himself. E. R. Dodds in his *Pagan and Christian in an Age of Anxiety* shows this pessimistic perspective to have been endemic in the Mediterranean world at this time. This perception might have been expressed in terms of disparate religious mythologies or philosophical worldviews, but the underlying sense of guilt, anxiety, and frustration was pretty much the same.

> "The whole world lieth in [the grasp of] the Evil One," says the author of the First Epistle of John; it is "the dominion of fear and terror, the place of distress, with desolation," according to a psalm from Qumran; it is "the totality of wickedness," according to a pagan Hermeticist; for the Gnostic Heracleon it is a desert peopled only by wild beasts; in the Valentinian *Gospel of Truth* it is a realm of nightmare in which "either one flees one knows not where, or else one remains inert in pursuit of one knows not whom." (16)

The key to all these dreary cosmological visions is that "they are very largely an hypostatisation, a dreamlike projection, of their authors' inner experience" (19).

Basically, people found themselves, in their everyday existence, to be at bay—confronted with a snapping pack of disasters including "barbarian invasions, bloody civil wars, recurrent epidemics, galloping inflation and extreme personal insecurity" (Dodds 3–4). Where could they turn for relief? If their subconscious had projected their fears in the form of demonic "powers," it also provided redemptive hope, assuming the form of various salvation schemes. The hope of astrology, oracles, and dream interpretation was that even if one could not divert the blows of Fate, at least one might roll with the punches if he were forewarned. The "mystery cults" of Serapis, Isis, Mithras and others promised actual deliverance from the power of Fate. Gnosticism supplied its adherents with the secret knowledge to slip past the evil *archons* keeping mankind prisoner in this dark vale of tears. And of course Christ was depicted as "having disarmed the powers and authorities triumphing over them by the cross" (Colossians 2:15).

For moderns, the proper response to this mythology is not to reject or subtract it, but rather to "demythologize," i.e., *interpret* it. For, though the myths may be factually untenable, the self-understanding, the view of existence in the world, may still merit our attention. The "demonic powers" may find their counterparts in today's ideologies, slogans, "isms," conventions, propaganda, public opinion, inherited prejudices, orthodoxies, etc. They still hold man prisoner.

So the imaginative pictorial projection of existential self-understanding we find in ancient myths can still be powerful and effective, even when we no longer believe the myths literally (see A. D. Nock, *Conversion: The Old and the New in Religion from Alexander the Great to Augustine of Hippo*).

Bultmann and Lovecraft

Now how does any of this bear on Lovecraft's Cthulhu Mythos? The dilemma with which this article began, it should now be clear, is closely analogous to that which led to the demythologizing of the New Testament. In each case the deadlock was created by the assumption that the myths (of Christ or Cthulhu) must be either dismissed as mere fiction (Christ as a fraud, Lovecraft as a mere storyteller) or taken literally (Christ as a real miracle-worker, Lovecraft as a real occultist). In fact, Lovecraft can be seen as a modern myth-maker, expressing in fictional terms his pessimistic, materialistic worldview. Lovecraft's work can be elucidated in two interesting ways in light of Bultmann's demythologizing program, first by way of analogy, and second by way of contrast.

What might at first seem to be a stark difference between the two men is actually a fascinating similarity. This concerns the manner in which the Christian and Lovecraftian mythologies originated. Bultmann follows Strauss in rejecting the notion that early Christian miracle-stories and supernatural myths were anyone's conscious inventions. But Lovecraft, obviously, artificially created his myths. In view of such a difference, can Bultmann's conceptuality be appropriately used to understand Lovecraft? Yes indeed; remember that for Bultmann the most important thing about myth is what it tells us about the myth-maker's (or the myth-believers') existential self-understanding. And in an era when myths may be accepted only as they are "deliteralized," the only way to create new myths is to create them "artificially," or as already demythologized; they will be wittingly non-literal, but true on a deeper level—true to the myth-maker's experience. And this is what Lovecraft (along with some other recent fantasy writers) has done. Lovecraft is a genuine, though "artificial," maker of myth.

The important point of contrast to Bultmann's conception of myth is that Lovecraft's schema is entirely pessimistic with no redemptive element. A great step forward in understanding the Cthulhu Mythos was the removal of the accretions of August Derleth. Derleth had misread Lovecraft and made the Mythos into a cosmic epic of good vs. evil, of fall and redemption. Lovecraft, by contrast, had depicted a bleak scenario wherein man is in danger of being crushed by cosmic forces whose existence he does not comprehend, and which in turn are indifferent to his welfare. Clearly, Lovecraft's "Great Old Ones" are mythological figures corresponding to the "powers" and "archons" of the Age of Anxiety in Mediterranean religion. Like them, the Old Ones represent blind social and natural forces that toss us about like flotsam and jetsam. But the Cthulhu Mythos leaves mankind at the mercy of the powers. There is no one to save us. Lovecraft would have regarded Derleth's benevolent "Elder Gods" as an instance of childish wish-fulfillment, as he did the Christian story of salvation. Thus Lovecraft's mythology, though a real mythology expressive of his existential self-understanding, disregards Bultmann's stipulation that "myth expresses man's belief that he can be delivered from the forces within the visible world" (11).

In this Lovecraft's mythos would seem to be unique not only in terms of religious myth, but also in the field of fantasy literature. Not only is it to be contrasted with the work of other writers like Robert E. Howard, who do seem to use mythological elements (Crom, Mitra, the Hyborian Age, etc.) simply as exotic stage-setting, but also with others like J. R. R. Tolkien who also craft modern myths. Tolkien's heroic fantasy mythologizes his existential self-understanding whereby the threatening forces of evil (Sauton, Saruman, Smaug) are finally vanquishable by the heroic efforts of the mundane "common man" (Bilbo, Frodo, Sam Gamgee). For the Catholic Tolkien, the aid of a martyred-and-risen savior (Gandalf) may be necessary, but at the end of the day, the portly little bourgeois can triumph. Tolkien's myth is one of optimism, of "eucatastrophe," but Lovecraft's is one of inevitable, and pointless, catastrophe.

The Mythos and the Occult

Finally, the fatalistic and absurdist thrust of the Cthulhu Mythos makes evident the fallacy of the occasional claims that Lovecraft actually believed in his myths, whether he acknowledged it or tried unsuccessfully to repress this belief, as Kenneth Grant, Robert Turner, Colin Wilson, and Ron Goulart have suggested. (Here one thinks of a cute piece of self-parody by Lovecraft: "God! I wonder if there isn't some truth in some of this? What is this my emotions are telling me about Cthulhu? Ya-R'lyeh! Ya-R'lyeh—Cthulhu fhgthagn. . . . . n'ggah . . . . . ggll . . . . . Iä! Iä!" [letter to Frank Belknap Long, November 22, 1930; *SL* 3.234].) Grant and Turner suggest that Lovecraft had unwittingly tapped in on cosmic reality, though he made the mistake of dismissing it as fiction, as if to deny what he knew, deep down, to be the terrible truth. Significantly, Lovecraft almost seems to have foreseen that someone would say this: "Who can disprove any . . . concoction [of the imagination], or say that it is not 'esoterically true' even if its creator did think he invented it in jest or fiction?" (*SL* 3.226). So if anyone wants to maintain that the Cthulhu Mythos is literal truth, there would seem to be no stopping them. But surely this theory runs aground on the fact that the "truth" actually expressed in Lovecraft's fiction (i.e., pessimistic materialism) would seem to be a lot more terrible than that envisioned by occultists like Grant and Turner! Belief in occultism implies an optimistic attempt to escape the kind of absurdist determinism espoused by Lovecraft. It implies that "super nature," like nature, is predictable and manipulable by anyone who knows the proper technique. As Bultmann notes, "Even occultism pretends to be a science" (5; see Eliade 61, Moody 429). Who is the escapist here—the fatalist Lovecraft, or the occultists who would co-opt his popularity in the name of their superstition?

In conclusion it is plain that both those who see Lovecraft's mythology as only a dramatic prop, and those who take the Mythos literally (or believe Lovecraft did), are alike wide of the mark. Modern New Testament scholarship has transcended a similar set of unrealistic assessments of the gospels (as either literal truth or mere hoaxes) by means of demythologizing. Applying this hermeneutical key to the Cthulhu Mythos, Lovecraft's work can be seen to represent *real though artificial* mythology. Thus it is to be taken seriously as an expression of Lovecraft's existential self-understanding, but not literally as an expression of occult belief. And as a pesslmistic myth, Lovecraft's fantasy is seen to be not only unique among religious mythology and fantasy literature, but also completely alien to the worldview of literalistic occultists who would initiate him posthumously into their number.

Did Lovecraft Demythologize?

It remains for us to ask whether Lovecraft himself had anything like demythologizing in mind. As it happens, he did. In fact, the concept enables us to recognize and understand an important development in his writing that can be pinpointed in the year 1929. In short, Lovecraft began at this point to demythologize his own mythos and to hit the reader directly between the eyes with his bleak vision of cosmic isolation. Lovecraft's narrators begin to "spill the beans," explicitly admitting that the shambling monsters of the *Necronomicon* are primitive myths, inadequate allegories for the real horrors of science and its disorienting revelations.

The first intimation of the new approach is found in "The Mound" (1929). Here the gods Tulu (= Cthulhu) and Yig are demythologized in terms reminiscent of Bultmann. "Religion was a leading interest in Tsath, though very few actually believed in the supernatural. . . . Great Tulu [was] a spirit of universal harmony anciently symbolized as the octopus-headed god who had brought all men down from the stars" (*HM* 136). On the other hand, "Yig [was] the principle of life symbolized as the Father of all Serpents" (*HM* 136). Here the truths masked under the names of the Great Old Ones are not so horrifying, but Tulu and Yig are said to be myths symbolizing abstract truths.

In "The Whisperer in Darkness" (1930), we hear of "the monstrous nuclear chaos beyond angled space which the *Necronomicon* had mercifully cloaked under the name of Azathoth" (*DH* 256). Thus the gibbering daemon-sultan of the *Necronomicon* was merely a cipher for the much more frightening revelations of science. In this case it is the advanced science of the Outer Ones, the living fungi from Yuggoth. Extraterrestrials occupy center stage again in *At the Mountains of Madness*, written the very next year (1931). The crinoids of ancient Antarctica "were above all doubt the originals of the fiendish elder myths which things like the Pnakotic Manuscripts and the *Necronomicon* affrightedly hint about. They were the great 'Old Ones' that had filtered down from the stars when earth was young" (*MM* 59). Thus the occult and transcendent Great Old Ones of "The Call of Cthulhu" and "The Dunwich Horror" were simply a race of space aliens. The import of this fact is still supposed to be horrifying, since these creatures had created humanity "as jest or mistake" (MM 22) dim ages ago. Man's cosmic insignificance is once again underscored.

"The Dreams in the Witch House" (1932) was clearly written with the new demythologized outlook in mind. Over-zealous student Walter Gilman penetrates the legends of medieval sorcery and witchcraft to discover that they really cloaked a knowledge of advanced mathematics and physics. The Arkham witch Keziah Mason had mastered interdimensional travel. Gilman follows in her footsteps, reaching an alien plane inhabited by beings identical to the Old Ones of *At the Mountains of Madness* except for their winglessness. Some readers might feel inclined to dispute our interpretation of this tale on the grounds that nowhere else in Lovecraft do we find so much of traditional magic and the supernatural. For instance, Keziah Mason is obviously supposed to have been a casualty of the Salem witch trials. She has a rodent-like familiar (Brown Jenkin) and comports with the satanic "Black Man." She even shuns the crucifix! Yet the narration is clear that the real secret of all this is Keziah's precocious discovery of non-Euclidean calculus. The accoutrements of witchcraft are there simply to say that witchcraft's horror was real after all, but with the reality of science.

The same year (1932), Lovecraft collaborated with E. Hoffmann Price on "Through the Gates of the Silver Key." In it Randolph Carter explores transcendental states of mystical consciousness. Going on to experience the disorientation of the void of "destroyed individuality," he guesses that this "All-in-One and One-in-All" state "was perhaps that which certain secret cults of Earth had whispered of as YOG-SOTHOTH, and which has been a deity under other names . . . yet in a flash the Carter-facet realised how slight and fractional all these conceptions are" (MM 439). Pity poor Henry Armitage who actually believed in a literal Yog-Sothoth!

Finally, in 1934, Lovecraft demythologized the mythos of the Old Ones again in "The Shadow out of Time." There we discover that certain old myths dimly reflected the truth about the Great Race of Yith, another band of extraterrestrials. "In the *Necronomicon* the presence of . . . a cult among human beings was suggested—a cult that sometimes gave aid to minds voyaging down the aeons from the days of the Great Race" (*DH* 389). The context implies that this is not quite what the writer of the *Necronomicon* actually thought was going on. Rather, it is implied, Abdul Alhazred entertained some primitive notion such as that the Old Ones might beget their progeny upon mankind. Again, the dreadful truth is a scientific, not a magical, one. In the same story, it is the discovery of the incredibly ancient

Australian ruins, with their implication of intelligent prehuman life, that terrifies the archaeologist Mackenzie: "These blocks are so ancient they frighten me" (*DH* 405).

Works Cited

Bultmann, Rudolf. "New Testament and Mythology." In *Kerygma and Myth*, ed. Hans Werner Bartsch. New York: Harper & Row, 1961.

Dodds, E. R. *Pagan and Christian in an Age of Anxiety: Some Aspects of Religious Experience from Marcus Aurelius to Constantine.* New York: W. W. Norton, 1970.

Eliade, Mircea. *Occultism, Witchcraft, and Cultural Fashions.* Chicago: University of Chicago Press, 1976.

Moody, Edward J. "Urban Witches." In *Conformity and Conflict: Readings in Cultural Anthropology,* ed. James P. Spradley and David W. McCurdy. Boston: Little, Brown, 1977.

Nock, Arthur Darby. *Conversion: The Old and the New in Religion from Alexander the Great to Augustine of Hippo.* New York: Oxford University Press, 1961.

[*Lovecraft Studies* No. 8 (Spring 1984): 3–9, 24]

The Last Vestige of the Derleth Mythos

By Robert M. Price

H. P. Lovecraft's "artificial mythology" of Cthulhu and Yog-Sothoth, or, as he playfully dubbed it, "Yog-Sothothery," is surely one of his most intriguing and enduring contributions to the field of weird literature. As a student of mythology and theology, I have always been taken with Lovecraft's creation. And now, on Lovecraft's one hundredth birthday, I feel it is time to propose a new way of looking at Lovecraft's mythology.

I first read Lovecraft's tales through the tinted lenses provided by August Derleth in his introductions to various collections of Lovecraft's tales. As readers acquainted with any of the Lovecraft scholarship done in the last fifteen years will know, it was Derleth who systematized "the Mythos," not Lovecraft. HPL scarcely ever brought the mythology out into the forefront as an object of scrutiny in its own right. Instead, he left it lurking ominously and ambiguously in the background. He consciously avoided systematizing the lore of Cthulhu and Yog-Sothoth, Nug and Yeb, because he knew real cycles of folklore and elder myth have been disseminated in many, sometimes contradictory forms through various oral and written channels. A system of Yog-Sothothery would not have served Lovecraft's purposes.

August Derleth was so intrigued with the hints of Lovecraft, who like his own fictional demonologist Abdul Alhazred had only equivocally implied things too terrible for overt disclosure, that Derleth could not rest till he had pulled the plant up by the roots and classified every nodule, killing the plant in the process. He placed Lovecraft's nihilistic, pessimistic schema (humanity doomed, sooner or later, to be Old One fodder) into a dualistic framework of good versus evil. Derleth many times pointed out the (illusory) parallel between "the Cthulhu Mythos" and "the Christian Mythos." The Old Ones (Cthulhu, Azathoth, etc.) he made into devils. For angels Derleth used Lovecraft's phrase the "Elder Gods" in a new way and made of them a benign race of humanity-loving saviors on their far-off Olympus of Betelgeuse. The Old Ones he classified according to the ancient earth-air-fire-water schema. This classification is in one sense faithful to the spirit of Lovecraft, since Lovecraft's elder entities do often seem to be the fictional concretization of the ageless, megalithic hills of New England and the unfathomable mysteries of Antarctica and the oceans. Like Machen's "Little People," Lovecraft's Old Ones are elementals in a sense. But certainly as he explains them in the stories, Cthulhu and the others are extraterrestrials, so to dub them "earth-" or "water-elementals" is absurd in terms of the narrative. Derleth's drastic reinterpretation of what he called "the Cthulhu Mythos" controlled interpretation of Lovecraft's work for years. Its influence is plain, for instance, in the original French edition of Maurice Lévy's *Lovecraft* (the English translation has been purged).

Richard L. Tierney ("The Derleth Mythos"), Lin Carter (*Lovecraft: A Look Behind the "Cthulhu Mythos"*), and Dirk W. Mosig ("H. P. Lovecraft: Myth-Maker") carefully peeled away Derleth's encrustations from HPL's work in the mid-1970s. Of course, most Mythos fiction has continued to use the full-blown Derlethian pantheon; notably the stories and novels of Brian Lumley, Lin Carter, and Richard L. Tierney continued in this vein, ironically, since Carter and Tierney were careful to distance Lovecraft's and Derleth's conceptions from one another in their nonfiction.

As often happens, the reaction to Derleth was an extreme one, obscuring the admittedly slender amount of common ground between Lovecraft and Derleth. I have attempted to show how at several points Derleth's novel conceptions actually resulted from a keen-eyed reading and creative reinterpretation of various details in Lovecraft's stories (see my articles, "The Lovecraft-Derleth Connection," "Obed and Obadiah Marsh," and "The Shadow over Dunwich: A Neglected Subplot in Derleth's *The Lurker at the Threshold*").

I would now like to carry the interpretation of the Lovecraft Mythos (as it is increasingly coming to be known) a step further. The work of Dirk Mosig, alluded to above, made clear the vital insight that Lovecraft's Old Ones symbolized the blind and mechanistic forces of cosmic natural law that already dwarf humanity's significance in the universe-at-large, and which would one day spell our doom. Evolution will eventually pass us by; the cooling of the sun will freeze us: we are merely an ephemeron, cosmic flotsam. We are doomed to fall victim, not to evil enemies who hate us, but rather to impersonal and indifferent forces who will not exempt us from the common fate of all entities: "this, too, shall pass."

It is at this point, I believe, that post-Mosig Lovecraft interpreters, myself included, have recapitulated one of Derleth's errors. Just as Derleth confused what the Old Ones sometimes symbolized in Lovecraft's mind (the ancient sleeping secrets of nature) with what they were supposed to be in narrative terms (extraterrestrial entities), making them "earth-elementals," even so, we post-Derlethians have confused what the Old Ones symbolized (blind cosmic forces transcendent to humanity) with what the narrative makes them. For example, in my article "Demythologizing Cthulhu," I maintained that in earlier Mythos tales (e.g., "The Call of Cthulhu," "The Dunwich Horror"), the Old Ones are transcendent, demonic Powers, not readily objectifiable or personifiable, real gods albeit of a terrible sort. But in later Mythos fiction ("The Whisperer in Darkness," *At the Mountains of Madness,* etc.), I suggested, Lovecraft makes the Old Ones into space aliens pure and simple. The very existence of superhuman, prehuman, posthuman intelligence is the shocker, the shatterer of our belief in our own centrality.

I now see that what I did was, enthused over Mosig's brilliant interpretation, to confuse HPL's underlying philosophy with his narrative intention. In Lovecraft's fiction, I now maintain, there are no deities at all. There is no more a pantheon of Great Old Ones in this sense than there was a pantheon of Elder Gods. In every Mythos tale, it should be clear, Cthulhu, Yog-Sothoth, etc., etc., are beings from outer space. Try to read the tales again, without prior assumptions. I think you'll see what I mean. Brian Lumley is surely not wrong when he makes them into discrete individuals, races of space men, and even natural forces.

I think what first made me realize my error was Peter Cannon's observation in his excellent *H. P. Lovecraft* that the premise of "The Dunwich Horror," that there are invisible and intangible entities lurking between the dimensions we occupy, is borrowed directly from and precisely equal to the premise of "From Beyond." The Old Ones Wizard Whateley sought to unleash were none other than the invisible forms Crawford Tillinghast contacted. Not exactly transcendent gods; more like invisible sharks. This much was fairly clear to the screenwriter of the 1970 movie adaptation of "The Dunwich Horror." When we glimpse the Old Ones who await their return with Wilbur Whateley's help, they are simply horrific individuals on the other side. Lovecraft certainly did not intend body-painted hippies (all the special effects budget of the movie could afford), but he did mean just aliens who wanted our world. Splice the floating ectoplasmic creatures of Stuart Gordon's movie *From Beyond* into the movie *The Dunwich Horror,* and you'll have Lovecraft's meaning.

In short, I am suggesting that it is time to zip away the last vestige of Derlethianism if we wish to understand Lovecraft aright. Since the work of Tierney and Mosig in the 1970s we have gotten rid of one set of un-

Lovecraftian deities, the "Elder Gods." Now let us go all the way and get rid of the equally un-Lovecraftian idea of a group of transcendent gods called the "Great Old Ones." Old Ones there are, to be sure, but let us not share the delusion of their human dupes, like old Castro the Mestizo sailor, that they are gods.

Works Cited

Cannon, Peter. *H. P. Lovecraft.* Boston: Twayne, 1989.

Carter, Lin. *H. P. Lovecraft: A Look Behind the "Cthulhu Mythos."* New York: Ballantine, 1972.

Mosig, Dirk W. "H. P. Lovecraft: Myth-Maker." *Whispers* 3, No. 1 (December 1976): 48–55.

Tierney, Richard L. "The Derleth Mythos." In *HPL,* ed. Meade and Penny Frierson. Birmingham, AL: The Editors, 1972. 53.

[*Lovecraft Studies* No. 24 (Spring 1991): 20–21]

Behind the Mask of Nyarlathotep

By Will Murray

And at last from inner Egypt came
The strange dark One to whom the fellahs bowed;
Silent and lean and cryptically proud,
And wrapped in fabrics red as sunset flame.
Throngs pressed around, frantic for his commands,
But leaving, could not tell what they heard:
While through the nations spread the awestruck word
That wild beasts followed him and licked his hands.

> —"Nyarlathotep" (*AT* 72)

O ne of the most arresting moments in Lovecraft's "The Rats in the Walls" is the inexplicable evocation of Nyarlathotep.

"The Rats in the Walls" was written in 1923, during the first flush of Lovecraft's involvement with *Weird Tales* (although he first tried it on *Argosy* before showing it to editor Edwin Baird) and marks the very first story Lovecraft composed with a pulp market in mind. ("Herbert West— Reanimator" and "The Lurking Fear" were written for *Home Brew*—not, strictly speaking, a pulp.) Nyarlathotep is mentioned late in the story, in a particularly suggestive and portentous manner:

> Then there came a sound from that inky, boundless, farther distance that I thought I knew; and I saw my old black cat dart past me like a winged Egyptian god, straight into the illimitable gulf of the unknown. But I was not far behind, for there was no doubt after another second. It was the eldritch scurrying of those fiend-born rats, always questing for new horrors, and determined to lead me on even unto the grinning caverns of earth's centre where Nyarlathotep, the mad faceless god, howls blindly in the darkness to the piping of two amorphous idiot flute players. (*DH* 44)

131

To 1924 readers of *Weird Tales,* where the story first appeared, the vaguely suggestive name of Nyarlathotep would have evoked only an eerie sensation, not recognition. But as we all know, Nyarlathotep first appeared in the *United Amateur,* November 1920, in a story by the same name.

But that particular Nyarlathotep is no blind faceless god howling in the abyss, but something quite different. The character, in fact, came to Lovecraft in a dream. Writing to Rheinhart Kleiner on December 14, 1920,[1] shortly after the story's first publication, Lovecraft told of a dream in which he received a note from another correspondent, Samuel Loveman, imploring him to catch Nyarlathotep's next lecture.

> I had never heard the name NYARLATHOTEP before, but seemed to understand the allusion. Nyarlathotep was a kind of itinerant showman or lecturer who held forth in publick halls and aroused widepread fear and discussion with his exhibitions. These exhibitions consisted of two parts—first, a horrible—possibly prophetic—cinema reel; and later some extraordinary experiments with scientific and electrical apparatus. (*SL* 1.161)

In the dream Lovecraft did and saw such soul-shocking horrors that he awoke in such a state of agitation he penned "Nyarlathotep," adding a climax to give it a short-story form.

Nyarlathotep is no mere lecturer, however, as Lovecraft makes quite clear:

"Who he was, none could tell, but he was of the old native blood and looked like a Pharaoh. The fellahin knelt when they saw him, and could not say why. He said he had risen up out of the blackness of twenty-seven centuries, and that he had heard messages from places not on this planet." Nowhere else in the story is Nyarlathotep described, except in the terms "swarthy, slender, and sinister" (*MW* 32).

This of course not the first time Lovecraft dreamed up a black figure of horror: his faceless juvenile night-gaunts are infamous for haunting his sleep for many years. Scholars have long wondered at the derivation of the Egyptian name, Nyarlathotep, pointing out that it was subconsciously derived from either Mynarthitep or Alhireth-Hotep—invented names out of Lord Dunsany, whose work Lovecraft had first encountered in 1919. We assume that HPL experienced his weird dream in 1919 or 1920.

It is rarely acknowledged, but Nyarlathotep was Lovecraft's first fictitious god, and the first to appear—if that is the correct term for these fugitive appearances—in more than one Lovecraft story. The Mythos may have

---

[1] The letter is misdated to December 14, 1921, in *SL.*

coalesced with Cthulhu; Arkham and the *Necronomicon* may have been created before him; but Nyarlathotep was the first name in the pantheon. He was also, curiously enough, the central enigmatic figure of Lovecraft's final Mythos story, "The Haunter of the Dark." Or at least an avatar of Nyarlathotep was.

It is striking to note that Nyarlathotep's godlike attributes were not part of Lovecraft's original nightmare, but surface only in the final paragraph, about which Lovecraft later admitted, "I added the macabre conclusion for the sake of climactic effect and literary finish" (*SL* 1.161). As Lovecraft wrote:

> And through this revolting graveyard of the universe the muffled, maddening beating of drums, the thin, monotonous whine of blaphemous flutes from inconconcievable, unlighted chambers beyond Time; the detestable pounding and piping whereunto dance slowly, awkwardly, and absurdly the gigantic, tenebrous ultimate gods—the blind, voiceless, mindless gargoyles whose soul is Nyarlathotep. (*MW* 34)

Presented with this cryptic dream figure, HPL may have simply converted him into a nightmare version of one of Dunsany's often capricious gods—a concept he modified when he wrote "The Rats in the Walls." Whatever compelled him to make Nyarlathotep a faceless god is not clear, but one cannot help but think of the ebony-skinned and featureless night-gaunts which troubled Lovecraft's youthful sleep between 1896 and 1901. Presumably the nightmare Nyarlathotep Lovecraft saw in his sleep possessed a discernible face—although it is not described at all. Paradoxically, when Nyarlathotep reappears in *The Dream-Quest of Unknown Kadath* years later, he is described as having "the young face of an antique Pharaoah" (*MM* 398). It is interesting that when de la Poer's cat flashes by in "Rats," it is described in Egyptian terms, and in most of his appearances Nyarlathotep is linked with a black pit or vortex in the earth.

I do not profess to know what purpose the brief evocation of Nyarlathotep served in "The Rats in the Walls," but I think I do know now what inspired this sinister presence, even if H. P. Lovecraft did not—consciously.

Nyarlathotep was inspired by a tall, slender man who came to America, not out of Egypt, but from Serbia in 1884. Since he bears the same first inital as Nyarlathotep, let us call him "N" and contrast anecdotes of his brilliant career with salient passages from "Nyarlathotep" and the other stories in which the latter appears.

As long as the world left him alone in his Manhattan laboratory to pursue his love affair with electricity, "N" was the happiest man alive. In the waning years of the 1880's and the early 1890's he had enjoyed such a brief period. But when he delivered four blockbusting lectures in America and Europe in 1891–92, he became, in a matter of months, the world's most celebrated scientist, and his private life was never the same again.

Into the lands of civilisation came Nyarlathotep, swarthy, slender, and sinister, always buying strange instruments of glass and metal and combining them into instruments yet stranger. He spoke much of the sciences—of electricity and psychology—and gave exhibitions of power which sent his spectators away speechless, yet which swelled his fame to exceeding magnitude.

A weird, storklike figure on the lecture platform in his white tie and tails, "N" was nearly seven feet tall for he wore thick cork soles during his dangerous demonstrations. As he warmed to his act, his high-pitched, almost falsetto voice would rise in excitement. The audience, riveted by the cadenced flow of words, the play of lights and magic, would stare as in a trance. Visitors crowded into the display rooms presided over by the famous "N." Clad in white tie and tails, he stood among a magician's feast of high-frequency equipment, demonstrating one electrical miracle after another. A darkened alcove held tables that glowed with his phosphorescent tubes and lamps. One length of tubing radiated the words, "Welcome, Electricians," which "N" had had laboriously blown letter by letter from the molten glass. . . . Day after day he captivated the curious with his demonstrations illustrating how alternating current worked. On a velvet-covered table small metallic objects—copper balls, metal eggs—were made to spin at great speeds, reversing themselves smoothly at fixed intervals.

And I saw the world battling against blackness; against the waves of destruction from ultimate space; whirling, churning, struggling around the dimming, cooling sun. Then the sparks played amazingly around the heads of spectators, and hair stood up on end whilst shadows more grotesque than I can tell came out and squatted on the heads. And when I, who was colder and more scientific than the rest, mumbled a trembling protest about "imposture" and "static electricity," Nyarlathotep drove us all out.
. . .

He demonstrated the first synchronized electric clock attached to an oscillator and showed his first disruptive discharge coil. The audiences understood little of the science involved, yet were enthralled. And when he seemed to turn himself into a human firestorm by using the apparatus with which he had so often thrilled his laboratory visitors, they cried out in fear and wonder.

A journalist, part of a throng who visited one of "N"'s spectacular public exhibitions, sent this report to his newspaper:

> "N" has been seen receiving through his hands currents at a potential of more than 200,000 volts, vibrating a million times per second, and manifesting themselves in dazzlingly streams of light . . . After such a striking test, which, by the way, no one has displayed a hurried inclination to repeat, "N"'s body and clothing have continued for some time to emit fine glimmers or halos of splintered light.

Both mysterioso figures are associated with wild displays of electricity.

> *. . . what was thrown on a screen in the darkened room prophesied things none but Nyarlathotep dared prophesy, and . . . in the sputter of his sparks there was taken from men that which had never been taken before yet which shewed only in the eyes.*
>
> As to the inadequacy of the scientific terminology of his day—the luminous feathery discharge of electricity in a vacuum tube that he referred to in his lectures as a brush was in fact a beam of electrons and ionized gas molecules. He did not say, "Now I shall describe the cyclotron," for the word was nonexistent; but what he would describe and what he would demonstrate was thought by some who were knowledgable to have been an early ancestor of the atom smasher.

This remarkable man also shared with Nyarlathotep the legend that he was in communication with others planets:

> Another of "N"'s claimed discoveries at Colorado Springs came late one night as he was working at his powerful and sensitive radio receiver . . . Suddenly the inventor became aware of strange rhythmic sounds on the receiver. He could think of no possible explanation for such a regular pattern, unless it were an effort being made to communicate with Earth by living creatures on another planet. Venus or Mars he supposed to be the more likely sources. No one at that time had ever heard of such phenomena as regular sounds from space.

Of course, this has since been determined to be mere background radio waves emitted by the stars themselves. But neither "N" nor the laymen of his day could have guessed that.

Who was this figure of mystery and magic?

Nikola Tesla—the enigmatic inventive genius whose fabulous theories and inexplicable inventions dominated the news between the 1890s and his death in 1943. Tesla is the man who is now acknowledged as the true inventor of radio. He was a pioneer in the fields of computer science, robotics, missile technology, and other advanced concepts. He discovered the principle of alternating current and developed the famous Tesla coil.

Hugo Gernsback, who published *Science and Invention* magazine as well as *Amazing Stories*, in which Lovecraft's "The Colour out of Space" would appear, said of him, "Without a doubt, Nikola Tesla is the world's greatest inventor, not only at present but in all history."

Lovecraft was familiar with Tesla, of course; what person wasn't during Tesla's heyday? And as an interested observer in science, Lovecraft's imagination was undoubtedly fired by near- constant reports of Telsa's grandiose plans, which all too often died for lack of financial backing or absence of vision of the part of those who, like J. P. Morgan, did back him.

At various times Tesla claimed to have invented death rays, a vibratory device capable of ripping the planet earth asunder, seemingly sourceless artificial illumination that would replace incandescent light bulbs, and other marvels which modern science has yet to understand or duplicate.

Oddly, Lovecraft's *Selected Letters* mention Nikola Tesla but twice and then only in passing. One of these references, however, is very suggestive. In a 1932 letter to Maurice Moe, Lovecraft is reminiscing about the year 1900; one of the things he remembers from that year is: "Nikola Tesla reports signals from Mars" (*SL* 4.65). This demonstrates that Lovecraft was familiar with the scientist's activities during his heyday, many years before he incorporated him into his own fiction. Unquestionably, Tesla's work ignited Lovecraft's imagination.

It is a mystery what caused Lovecraft's subconsciousness to take such an intuitive leap that transmuted Nikola Tesla into the masterful Nyarlathotep that night in 1919 or 1920. Tesla was still in the news, but by then in his sixties, his health and wealth dwindling, his most fantastic public pronouncements and discoveries largely behind him.

We may never know, but the cumulative evidence, while circumstantial, is nevertheless compelling.

Note that in the stories in which he appears, Nyarlathotep is a chimerical figure, often assuming different forms—a sardonic pharaoh in *The Dream-Quest of Unknown Kadath*, the Black Man in "The Dreams in the Witch House," and in "The Haunter of the Dark" materializing as "an avatar of Nyarlathotep, who in antique and shadowy Khem even took the form of man" (*DH* 114).

In his recent article, "The Master of Masks," Joel Lane suggests that Nyarlathotep continually pops up in Lovecraft's fiction in obscure guises, not always identified as such. In "Under the Pyramids" he may be Houdini's guide, the Pharaoh-like Abdul Al Reis, and it may have been Nyarlathotep who, all along, was the true face behind the waxen-masked thing calling itself Henry Akeley that held Albert Wilmarth in thrall with stories of the fungi from Yuggoth in "The Whisperer in Darkness," according to Lane.

Lane bases his theory on the line, "And He shall put on the semblance of men, the waxen mask and the robe that hides, and come down from the world of Seven Suns to mock" (*DH* 226).

The identity of "He" is actually clouded in the context of the complete passage from which the quote is taken. He might well be Nyarlathotep, or He could be identical with the "Him in the Gulf . . . Azathoth" (*DH* 226), mentioned earlier in the story. All references to He and Him seem actually to point to Azathoth, with whom Nyarlathotep is often identified. Yet common sense would suggest that Azathoth, who is after all primeval Chaos, would hardly come to earth and take on human form, so the Nyarlathotep theory seems the most probable explanation.

Regardless of that minor uncertainty, it seems clear that Lovecraft's Nyarlathotep is a kind of cosmic shape-shifter, often taking various forms to astonish and confound humanity.

Why not, then, assume the identity of the most bizarre inventor of Lovecraft's era? The many correspondences between the gigantic showmanship of both Nyarlathotep and Nikola Tesla are uncannily close.

Nikola Tesla was by no means a physical twin of Nyarlathotep. He was in fact pale and by all accounts cosmopolitan in bearing, yet a spellbinder on stage. The following florid description best captures Tesla in his prime:

"I saw a tall, slender young man with long arms and fingers, whose rather languid movements veiled extraordinary muscular power," observed Julian Hawthorne, the son of Nathaniel Hawthorne. "His face was oval, broad at the temples, and strong at the lips and chin; with long eyes whose lids were seldom fully lifted, as if he were in a waking dream, seeing visions which could not be revealed to the generality . . . to be with Tesla is to enter a domain of freedom even freer than solitude, because the horizon enlarges so . . ." Yet Waldemar Kaempffert, science editor of the *New York Times*, branded him a "medieval practitioner of black arts . . . as vague as an oriental mystic."

Tesla could be cruel, aloof, compulsive. Occultists were attracted to him and put forth bizarre theories that he was in fact a denizen of the planet Venus who came to earth on a spaceship. He was proclaimed a prophet, a psychic, an uplifter and champion of humanity—extravagant claims Tesla went to some pains to discourage and deny.

This is probably no more than coincidence, but like Nyarlathotep in "The Rats in the Walls," Nikola Tesla is linked with a cat. During his youth in Croatia, Tesla had a cat, "the magnificent Macak, the finest of all cats in the world," according to Tesla.

Tesla was for some reason acutely sensitive to light, and it was through this faculty, and a phenomenon associated with Macek, that Tesla first became interested in electrical activity at the age of three.

"I felt impelled to stroke Macak's back," Tesla wrote of that time. "What I saw was a miracle that made me speechless . . . Macak's back was a sheet of light, and my hand produced a shower of crackling sparks loud enough to be heard all over the place."

When informed by his father that this was electricity, and cautioned by his mother to stop stroking the cat because she feared he'd start a fire, Tesla's mind began racing.

"Is nature a gigantic cat?" Tesla recalled of that formative experience. "If so, who strokes its back? It can only be God, I concluded."

Lovecraft, the passionate cat lover, had he read an account of the novel experience, could hardly have been unimpressed.

Tesla, by the way, was extremely fond of animals and claimed to be to have an understanding, tantamount to silent communion, with a certain pigeon that he befriended and fed. This brings to mind the line from Lovecraft's sonnet "Nyarlathotep," "That wild beasts followed him and licked his hands."

Whatever riotous genius impelled Nikola Tesla to heights of brilliance and folly, he seemed to have made a profound impression on H. P. Lovecraft, and the Cthulhu Mythos is a much richer tapestry for that one riotous nightmare.

Anyone wishing to read more of Nikola Tesla might look into Margaret Chaney's fascinating *Tesla: Man out of Time,* from which the foregoing quotes were extracted.

Works Cited

Chaney, Margaret. *Tesla: Man out of Time.* Englewood Cliffs, NJ: Prentice-Hall, 1981.

Lane, Joel. "The Master of Masks." *Nyctalops* 4, No. 1 (April 1991): 62–66.

[*Lovecraft Studies* No. 25 (Fall 1991): 25–29]

On the Natures of Nug and Yeb

By Will Murray

In the various stories written to order for his revision clients, H. P. Lovecraft created a number of additions to the pantheon of entities in which Yog-Sothoth, Azathoth, and Cthulhu predominated. These secondary entities included Rhan-Tegoth in "The Horror in the Museum" and Ghatanothoa in "Out of the Aeons" (both written with Hazel Heald) and Yig, in "The Curse of Yig" (written with Zealia Bishop). For the most part, these creations are rather well developed with distinct physical properties, but their appearances are limited to Lovecraft's revision work. There are exceptions. The snake-god Yig is mentioned in numerous revisions and then filters into the main body of the Cthulhu Mythos. Shub-Niggurath, first mentioned in "The Last Test" (written with Adolphe de Castro), is mentioned in virtually every Mythos story to follow, but only in passing—never as a physical presence. Otherwise, Lovecraft did not incorporate most of the entities he doubtless created for his clients into his work proper, and they were promptly forgotten. This is a curious fact inasmuch as he willingly absorbed such creations as Clark Ashton Smith's Tsathoggua into the Mythos.

It is not unusual, then, that two of these secondary entities, Nug and Yeb, are relegated to three very brief mentions of various Lovecraft revisions, all of them written between 1927 and 1933. In all these instances, the references in question are so sparse that scant information on the natures of Nug and Yeb is presented. This is in contrast to the fuller characterizations of Yig and the others. Indeed, to read only "The Last Test," "The Mound," and "Out of the Aeons," one would believe Nug and Yeb to be extremely minor creations.

Yet, long after the likes of Rhan-Tegoth and Ghatanothoa were forgotten, even by Lovecraft, the names of Nug and Yeb recur again and again in Lovecraft's letters in such a manner as to suggest strongly that they are an important part of the Mythos, and very close to the surface of Lovecraft's imaginative mind.

Nug and Yeb are first invoked, along with Shub-Niggurath, in Love-craft's revision of Adolphe de Castro's "The Last Test." The reference has no apparent bearing on the story proper. A Dr. Alfred Clarendon, who is a typical Lovecraftian dabbler in forbidden things, is quoted as telling the narrator: "We've both meddled in dangerous things, but you needn't think you know all my resources. How about the Nemesis of Flame? I talked in Yemen with an old man who had come back alive from the Crimson Desert—he had seen Irem, the City of Pillars, and had worshipped at the underground shrines of Nug and Yeb—Iä! Shub-Niggurath!" (*HM* 47).

This is an oblique mention at best. It is not clear whether or not the "Nemesis of Flame" has any connection with Nug and Yeb. The Nemesis of Flame is a strange Tibetan named Surama, who with Dr. Clarendon is spreading the deadly black fever from beyond the earth until an unearthly fire destroys them both. Lovecraft probably picked up the "Nemesis of Flame" from Algernon Blackwood's "The Nemesis of Fire" (a story in *John Silence—Physician Extraordinary*). Interestingly enough, it is a John Silence story about the depredations of an Egyptian fire elemental. Nothing more is said about Nug and Yeb in "The Last Test."

In "The Mound," Panfilo de Zamacona is escorted through the subter-ranean world of K'n-yan, where he sees "the temples of Yig, Tulu, Nug, Yeb, and the Not-to-be-Named-One which lined the road at infrequent inter-vals," and mention is made that "the ceremonies of Nug and Yeb sickened him especially—so much, indeed, that he refrained from describing them in his manuscript" (*HM* 144). As in "The Last Test," the reference to Nug and Yeb is immediately followed by one to Shub-Niggurath, there called "the All-Mother and wife of the Not-to-be-Named-one" (*HM* 144).

This is also the case in "Out of the Aeons." Here mention is made of T'yog, the High Priest of Shub-Niggurath, who "believed that Shub-Niggurath, Nug, and Yeb, as well as Yig the Serpent-god, were ready to take sides with man against the tyranny and presumption of Ghatanothoa." A second mention telescopes the above-named as "Shub-Niggurath and her sons" (*HM* 273–74).

Thus, from Lovecraft's fiction, we are able to glean these simple facts: Nug and Yeb are the sons of Shub-Niggurath, and that they are worshipped in shrines of apparent equal importance with Yig and Tulu (Cthulhu). "Out of the Aeons" makes mention of the fact that in the days of Atlantis, T'yog counted Shub-Niggurath and her sons among the "gods friendly to man" who "could be arrayed against the hostile gods" (*HM* 273). This may or may not be a delusion on his part.

ON THE NATURES OF NUG AND YEB

There is nothing unusual about these references to Nug and Yeb, either in their brevity or absence of description, in and of themselves. Lovecraft, after all, frequently mentions Shub-Niggurath in many, many stories with no other elaboration than the shouted phrase, "The Goat with a Thousand Young!" which is sometimes given as "The Black Goat of the Woods with a Thousand Young!" Her feminine attributes are seldom mentioned. But after publication of these three revisions, further references to Nug and Yeb begin to appear in Lovecraft's correspondence. At first these are only casual mentions in passing.

In a letter to Robert E. Howard dated 14 August 1930, Lovecraft states: "Regarding the solemnly cited myth-cycle of Cthulhu, Yog-Sothoth, R'lyeh, Nyarlathotep, Nug, Yeb, Shub-Niggurath, etc., etc.—let me confess that this is all a synthetic concoction of my own" (SL 3.166). Directly following, he mentions Azathoth, Abdul Alhazred, the *Necronomicon,* his revisions and even Smith's Tsathoggua—in short, just about all the major Mythos entities. It is somewhat surprising to find Nug and Yeb so comfortably ensconced between Nyarlathotep and Shub-Niggurath—especially as not even Yig, the most oft-used and best-delineated of the revision entities, is given a nod. This letter was written only a few months after composition of "The Mound," but three years before "Out of the Aeons." At that time only "The Last Test" had seen print in *Weird Tales,* and that was back in 1928.

The next reference was only a few months later, in a letter to Clark Ashton Smith dated only January 1931. The body of the letter contains nothing relevant; rather, it is Lovecraft's heading and closing that are of interest. The heading reads, as reproduced in *Selected Letters* 3, as follows:

> Shrine of Nng, in The Temple of Infra-
> Red Vapour on The Doomed Nebula
> Zlykariob, in the Hour of the Tor-
> turing of The Worm Bgnghaa-Ythu-
> Yaddith (*SL* 3.247)

The closing is given as:

> Yours for the formula that is not in Olan's Latin Text
> —Ec'h-Pi-El
> Guardian of the Black Flame of Nng & Yeb. (SL 3.247)[1]

Clearly, someone who transcribed that letter misread Lovecraft's handwriting and the reading should be "Nug and Yeb." It is also safe to assume that the reading with which the heading should begin is "Shrine of

[1] ["Olan's" should surely be "Olaus's" (Wormius).—Ed.]

141

Nug." It is fortunate in this case that the two references are in the same letter and that Nug and Yeb are almost always mentioned in the same breath.

Now, admittedly, Lovecraft rather playfully headed or closed off his letters during this period with joking allusions to his work and the work of others, as in:

> Many-columned Arcades of Weed-grown Y'ha-nthlei
> in the Hour of the Unseen Howling (*SL* 4.10)

or:

> Pinnacle of Unknown Kadath
> Hour of the Red Aurora (*SL* 4.341)

but invariably these references accurately reflect the internal integrity of Lovecraft's fiction when they include specific references. But where Nug and Yeb are concerned, these references do more than reflect; they amplify. In another letter to Smith, dated 8 February 1931, Lovecraft closes:

> Yrs for the nether hells of Nyarlathotep
> Ec'h-Pi-El
> Guardian of the Black Fire of Nng & Yeb. (*SL* 3.286)

Another misreading, and now it is "Black Fire" and not "Black Flame" of Nug and Yeb. A year later, Lovecraft closes off another letter to Smith, dated 20 January 1932, with:

> Yours in the adoration of the Black Flame—
> Ec'h-Pi-El (*SL* 4.11)

So far, each of these references is rather minor. However, the one in a letter written to James F. Morton and dated 27 April 1933 is not. In this letter, Lovecraft includes a genealogy of the entities of the Mythos. It is whimsically conceived and carried out—the point is to show Lovecraft's own descent from the Old Ones—but it is significant for a number of more useful reasons.

At the apex of Lovecraft's chart is Azathoth, from whom all the entities listed have descended. From Azathoth arose Nyarlathotep, The Nameless Mist, and Darkness, creating a second generation. The Nameless Mist birthed Yog-Sothoth and Darkness birthed Shub-Niggurath. Yog-Sothoth and Shub-Niggurath then mated (the only sexual union on the chart) to produce Nug and Yeb, who comprise the fourth generation. Cthulhu is immediately descended from Nug, and Tsathoggua is the offspring of Yeb. Lovecraft notes that Cthulhu and Tsathoggua are "first of their respective lines to inhabit this planet" (*SL* 4.183). From Cthulhu and Tsathoggua sprang Shaurash-Ho and Yabou (or possibly Yabon), respectively, from whom other entities not mentioned in the Mythos are descended, including mythical ancestors of Clark Ashton Smith and Lovecraft himself.

Several things are striking about this genealogy, not the least of which is Nug and Yeb's superior placement on the chart with respect to the more famous Cthulhu and Tsathoggua. Then there is the curious absence of Yig, who, as one of Shub-Niggurath's sons, belongs to the fourth generation with Nug and Yeb. But most interesting are the correlations between Lovecraft's chart and the genealogy of the Greek gods, who grew out of Chaos, just as the entities of the Mythos grew out of Azathoth, whom Lovecraft describes as "Ultimate Chaos."

According to Greek mythology, four forces sprang from Chaos: Mother Earth (Gaea), Desire (Eros), Darkness (Erebus), and Night (Nyx) (Reinhold 59–61). Both genealogies contain a force known as Darkness. In the Greek chart, the next generation consists of Air and Day, who are the result of the mating of Darkness and Night, whereupon a number of other forces come into being, all of whom are created asexually, as in Lovecraft's theogony, until Earth and Heaven mate and produce the first generation of actual gods.

Generally, the two genealogies are similar, with Cthulhu and Tsathoggua, as the first of their lines to inhabit the earth, representing the first actual gods. That might mean that Nug and Yeb more or less correspond to either Air and Day, in their unique sexual creation, or to Earth and Heaven. This last supposition draws some strength from the similar genealogy of the Egyptian gods. In that chart, Atum equates to Chaos or Azathoth, from whom the male and female principles of air (Shu and Tefnut) sprang. Shu and Tefnut then produce Earth and Sky, known as Geb and Nut, from whom the main gods, such as Isis, Osiris and others, are generated (Anthes 37). It is probably no coincidence that Nut and Geb, by virtue of changing one letter in each name, become Nug and Yeb. Many of the other Mythos entities bear distinctly Egyptian names.

Are Nug and Yeb derived from Egyptian mythology? In a letter to Duane Rimel dated 14 February 1934 Lovecraft would seem to refute such a suggestion. Referring to the coining of names of his creations, he says: "To a large degree they are designed to suggest—either closely or remotely—certain names in actual history or folklore which have weird or sinister associations connected with them. Thus 'Yuggoth' has a sort of Arabic or Hebraic cast, to suggest certain words passed down from antiquity in the magical formulae contained in Moorish or Jewish manuscripts. Other synthetic names like 'Nug' and 'Yeb' suggest the dark and mysterious tone of

Tartar or Thibetan folklore" (*SL* 4.386).

Again, it is noteworthy that Lovecraft cites these two little-used entities, but that fact aside, this statement does not entirely discount an Egyptian source for Nug and Yeb. For one, the effect of those names, and not their building-blocks, may be what Lovecraft is characterizing as "Thibetan." The homophonic similarities between Nut and Geb and Nug and Yeb are too strong to be easily ignored.

There are further references to Nug and Yeb in Lovecraft's letters. A letter to Robert Barlow, which is dated Second week of February, 1935, is headed:

> Kadath in the Cold Waste—Epiphany
> of Nug. (*SL* 5.93)

Another letter, this one to J. Vernon Shea and dated 13 March 1935, closes:

> Yrs. for the Black Litany of Nug & Yeb—
> Ec'h-Pi-El (*SL* 5.123)

Two other scattered references are similar enough to warrant mention. In a letter to Clark Ashton Smith dated 3 December 1929, Lovecraft expresses his appreciation of Smith's "The Tale of Satampra Zeiros" by exclaiming, "Yug! n'gha k'yun bth'gth R'lyeh gllur ph'ngui Cthulhu yzkaa . . . what an atmosphere!" (*SL* 3.87). Probably Lovecraft is referring to the prophet Yug from Lord Dunsany's *The Gods of Pegāna*.[2] In another letter to Smith, bearing a date of 13 November 1933, the heading bears another possible misreading:

> Pit of Yub.
> Hour of the Squirmers' Emergence
> from the Walls. (*SL* 4.317)

Note that the word "Squirmers" is pluralized, and that the closing is given as:

> Yrs. for the Litany of the Under Pits
> —Ec'h-Pi-El (*SL* 4.317)

It is tenuous at best to link the Squirmers with Nug and Yeb, or their

---

[2] It is worth noting that if you transpose the first letters in Nug and Yeb, the result is Yug and Neb. In "The Outsider" Lovecraft mentions "the rock tombs of Neb" (*DH* 52).

Black Litany with the similar mention above, but the possibility deserves mention. All this, of course, presupposes that Lovecraft kept in mind specific ideas having to do with Nug and Yeb, even though he had ceased using them in his fiction. As improbable as that might seem, the final, and very substantial, mention of these two entities in Lovecraft's published correspondence lends further credence to this assertion.

This letter was written six months before Lovecraft's death, and a full three years after Nug and Yeb had last appeared in "Out of the Aeons." The letter is to Willis Conover and dated 1 September 1936. Tongue-in-cheek, Lovecraft lets Conover in on some hitherto undisclosed information concerning some of the members of the Cthulhu pantheon: "Yog-Sothoth's wife is the hellish cloud-like entity Shub-Niggurath, in whose honour nameless cults hold the rite of the Goad with a Thousand Young. By her he has two monstrous offspring—the evil twins Nug and Yeb" (*SL* 5.303). Later on in the letter, he adds: "As for little Nug and Yeb (only ten feet in diameter when in their average form), they are a bit destructive sometimes, though it's only a playful, good-natured roughness. I like to have the little fellows about (even though they sometimes do dissolve visitors and passersby, and cause occasional troublesome enquiries), for they are basically very friendly and companionable. I imagine they must be somewhat like Howard the ghoul-in temperament, though not in appearance" (*Lovecraft at Last* 93).

Not only does the above add new information on the physical natures of Shub-Niggurath, Nug and Yeb, but, more importantly, it neatly dovetails with all previous mentions of those entities in fiction and correspondence with no apparent contradictions. The conceit that Yog-Sothoth and Shub-Niggurath mated to produce Nug and Yeb is carried through unaltered from the genealogy written over three years previous. There is one ambiguity, however. In all previous mentions of Shub-Niggurath—including many in his letters—Lovecraft almost invariably adds "The Goat with a Thousand Young!" (or one of the variations thereof) to that name, as if Shub-Niggurath *is* the Goat with a Thousand Young. In one letter to Clark Ashton Smith, dated 26 March 1931, he says: "Not yet, despite the outward evidence of silence, hath the aeon-aged blasphemer Ech-Pi-El fallen utterly a victim to Yog-Sothoth & the Goat With a Thousand Young!" (*SL* 3.356). By that phrase, Lovecraft would appear to be referring to Shub-Niggurath, who is never physically described in any Lovecraft fiction. If she is a "hellish cloud-like entity," how can she also be the "Goat with a Thousand Young"? It may be that the goat image is emblematic of Shub-Niggurath's properties as a fertility goddess ("the All-Mother." as Lovecraft calls her in "The Mound" [*HM* 144]) and not to be taken literally. The mention in the letter to Conover about the "rite of the Goat with a Thousand Young" held in Shub-Niggurath's honor appears to support this interpretation.

What, then, do we learn about Nug and Yeb that is new? That they are twins, and therefore probably identical, and not merely siblings. Of them, we also learn that they are "evil" (which is probably more perception than accurate assessment—Lovecraft's entities are beyond good and evil except as we perceive them) and that they average ten feet in diameter. Diameter implies that they are round or oval. Being the offspring of Yog-Sothoth, who is described in "The Horror in the Museum" as "a congeries of iridescent globes" (HM 230), this makes sense. Possibly Nug and Yeb are somewhat amorphous, as well. They might even be shape-shifters, but the implication is that they are identical round entities.[3]

This is a fairly full picture of Nug and Yeb. Curiously full, considering their neglect in the main body of Lovecraft's fiction. Only in "The Shadow out of Time" is there a reference that could be linked with them, and that is the mention of "Nug-Soth, a magician of the dark conquerors of 16,000 A.D" (DH 395). Nug-Soth could have taken part of his name from Nug, whom he may worship. But this is conjecture.

There is also an interesting correlation between Nug and Yeb and one of the descriptions of shoggoths in At the Mountains of Madness; it runs: "They were normally shapeless entities composed of a viscous jelly which looked like an agglutination of bubbles, and each averaged about fifteen feet in diameter when a sphere" (MM 67). This description dovetails with the "congeries of iridescent globes" of Yog-Sothoth. From this we might extrapolate that Yog-Sothoth, the shoggoths, and Nug and Yeb are composed of much the same matter. It is possible that Nug and Yeb possess that bubble-like appearance. It would be stretching things too much to postulate a relationship between the shoggoths and those others, but the suggestion of a connection is there.

It would also be conjecture to attempt to explain so many definite mentions of Nug and Yeb in Lovecraft's letters over an extended period of time. Between 1930 and 1936, there is at least one mention of either of those entities in a letter for every year except 1932 (in which only the Black Flame is mentioned). I am not certain that even Cthulhu is accorded so much consideration. It is almost as if Nug and Yeb had figured in a Lovecraft story in such a way that they assumed great importance in Lovecraft's own mind. This is possible, but not necessarily the case. Shub-Niggurath

---

[3] This stretches credulity, but in Lovecraft's 1923 story "The Rats in the Walls" there is a reference to "those grinning caverns of earth's centre where Nyarlathotep, the mad faceless god, howls blindly in the darkness to the piping of two amorphous idiot flute-players" (DH 44). All later references to these flute-players in other stories do not specify their number. Could they be Nug and Yeb?

was never prominent in the Mythos, although her name is invoked in the majority of stories. It could be, however, that there were more references to Nug and Yeb than in the three revisions and miscellaneous which have come down to us. Possibly in a discarded draft. of a story, an unknown fragment, or even an unpublished revision. For that matter, it is likely that there are other references to Nug and Yeb in letters not printed in the various *Selected Letters*—half the information on them quoted in the letter to Conover was excised from *Selected Letters 5*.

A more likely explanation for Lovecraft's handling of the offspring of Shub-Niggurath is that he had developed them rather clearly in his mind, as he seems to have their mother and other of his creations, in expectation of using them in a future story—which, unfortunately, he never got around to writing. If this is the case—as it surely seems to be—then Lovecraft, at some point, thought out his pantheon of entities in a much more complete and thorough manner than is reflected in any of his published writings. This is something to ponder.

Despite the fuller picture of Nug and Yeb which can be gained from the letters of H. P. Lovecraft, there are many unanswered questions remaining. We do not know their properties, for example. Are they, like Nut and Geb, supposed to represent the earth and the sky? Are they male and female? What is the Black Fire? Is there a connection between it and the Nemesis of Fire mentioned in "The Last Test"? And why were Nug and Yeb worshipped in underground shrines on this planet when they never set foot on it? We will probably never have the answers to these questions. But we do possess enough facts about Nug and Yeb to ensure that they will remain the least known but most tantalizing of all Lovecraft's many creations.

Works Cited

Anthes, Rudolph. "Mythologу.in Ancient Egypt." In *Mythologies of the Ancient World*, ed. Samuel Noah Kramer. Garden City, NY: Doubleday, 1961.

Lovecraft, H. P., and Willis Conover. *Lovecraft at Last*. Arlington, VA: Carrollton-Clark, 1975.

Reinhold, Meyer. *Past and Present: The Continuity of Classical Myths*. Toronto: Hakkert, 1972.

[*Lovecraft Studies* No. 9 (Fall 1984): 52–59]

IV. The Landscape

N.H.

The Modification
of
Coastal Essex County.
Massachusetts
in
H.P. Lovecraft's
"Arkham Cycle"
of Fiction
as Interpreted by
Rbt Martin

150

Arkham Country: In Rescue of the Lost Searchers

By Robert D. Marten

With "In Search of Arkham Country" in the fall of 1986, Will Murray began a series of articles in *Lovecraft Studies* and related publications seeking to demonstrate, in his words, that "everything you know about Lovecraft's Massachusetts is wrong." Do we assume, on Lovecraft's authority; that the fictitious towns of "Arkham." "Kingsport," "Innsmouth," and "Dunwich" derive from (respectively) Salem, Marblehead, Newburyport, and Wilbraham? Then we assume wrong, says Murray. Arkham is really based upon the central Massachusetts hamlet of Oakham, with elements of Franklin County's New Salem thrown in. "Kingsport," we are now informed, is actually coastal Rockport, "Innsmouth" equals Gloucester, and the true original of "Dunwich" can only be the one-time village of Greenwich, now dreaming 'neath the waters of the present-day Quabbin Reservoir.

For Mr. Murray, these "revelations" (which he also terms "findings" and "discoveries") are not subject to doubt. Lovecraft's remarks in letters upon this subject, are, in Murray's words, "strangely qualified," and certain clues in his fiction to alternative interpretations are "compelling" (Murray 1986, 59).

Lest "obvious" similarities Murray sees linking given fictional and actual towns or landmarks, such as "Dunwich"/Greenwich or "Cold Spring Glen"/Coldbrook Springs strike us as no more than happenstance, Murray assures us the resemblances are "not likely to be a coincidence" (ibid., 62). Rather, they are important evidence leading toward Murray's "inescapable conclusion" that Howard Phillips Lovecraft "deliberately misled" us as to the actual whereabouts of the geographical models for his invented locales.

Yes, serene though we've been in the widely held notion of Lovecraft as an hospitable and honest expositor of the method and rationale behind his composition, we are now, in light of "incontrovertible evidence" unearthed in recent "extensive researches," to be "disabused" of this common illusion (Murray 1989, 65).

No fewer than five articles in furtherance of this new view are in print at the time I write. In recent years I note a revision of Jason Eckhardt's excellent little guide to "New England & Adjacent New York," *Off the Ancient Track,* has incorporated elements of the new geographical acceptance. Further, I am now informed of guided tours of "Lovecraft's Rockport" emanating from Lovecraft Conventions held in this region.

Not so fast, please.

I am a Yankee skeptic who has, for many years, found enjoyment in poking out Lovecraft's literary historical, and geographical source material. And, as one who has conducted interested parties through the Lovecraftian settings, I may appreciate, more than some, the value of a carefully planned itinerary in situations where funds or travel time are limited. False steps, backtracking, and blind alleys can be enormously destructive to the Lovecraftian pilgrim's purposes, yet just such pitfalls, I fear, await those who are persuaded to follow in Mr. Murray's footsteps. I have not been so persuaded, and perhaps in showing why I've not been, I may effect the rescue of some of my fellows from needlessly lengthy or costly turnings in the labyrinth.

Anagram-Schmanagram

"It was a common Lovecraftian device," says Murray, "to modify real localities by a letter or two." To bolster this contention, he cites the English town of Ancaster as the basis of the "Anchester" mentioned in "The Rats in the Walls." Neighboring "Exham Priory," likewise, must be patterned on the town of Hexham. The map, however, shows that whereas Hexham is found in the shire of Northumberland, Ancaster lies nearly two hundred kilometers southward in the east midland's Lincolnshire. While this seems at least possible, the orthographic similarity alone apparently is sufficient for Murray to connect these somewhat disparate regions with Lovecraft's fictional setting.

"Anagrammatical transformation," says Murray, may be applied in this manner to the central Massachusetts village of Oakham: "transpose the first two letters, change the *o* to an *r*, and you have . . . Arkham."

By similar manipulations, Murray deciphers the town of "Sefton" in "Herbert West—Reanimator" as Massachusetts' Grafton, which is found in southern Worcester county. Lovecraft's ancient "Kingsport" is identified as Essex county's Rockport, "Aylesbury" as Franklin county's Shutesbury, and, "anagramatically," rustic "Dunwich" can only be Hampshire county's now-flooded Greenwich.

But if a perceived likeness in the sound or appearance of town names is sufficient to identify the original model, how are we to explain the presence of other towns which appear to have anagramatic claims of equal validity? What, for instance, should we make of Sutton, which lies next door to Grafton? Could not Sutton be the original of "Sefton," as easily as Grafton? We might also consider Sheffield in the Berkshires, so long, of course, as we ignore the possibility that Lovecraft had the British Earldom of Sefton in mind when he penned the name.

We are also told that Shutesbury is the "apparent doublet" for "Aylesbury" in "The Dunwich Horror." If so, what of two adjoining towns in northern Essex county named Amesbury and Salisbury? Amesbury makes a near perfect rhyme—and the likeness of Salisbury is more than Hudibrastic: omit the initial letter and we have a simple spelling-variant.

As with Shutesbury, the only thing Rockport has in common with its supposed fictional version is the form of its suffix: Rockport equals "Kingsport." Should we then ignore similarities in prefixes? Massachusetts has a coastal Kingston; so too does Rhode Island, with the surrounding counties of Kingstown—north and south—to boot.

With "Dunwich," we are advised to "follow the example set by Sefton and Grafton . . . we should be looking for a name similar to Dunwich." For Murray, the now-submerged village of Greenwich (which he somehow places in the north central part of the state) fills the bill perfectly: Greenwich, after all, has that -wich suffix, and an n in the prefix besides. Yet if these correspondences are so "anagramatically compelling," how much more so are those between "Dunwich" and the town of Winchendon in the very heart of the "north central" region, where HPL actually placed his fictitious town? We have only to "transpose" a few letters in order to reveal DONNNEWICH, donnnt we?

Ah, but then, just four towns east of Winchendon we find DUNstable!

I remain uncompelled by this game. The suffix forms -port, -ham, -ton, and -wich are by no means uncommon among the names of New England townships. Massachusetts alone has 300-odd corporated place-names from which seekers after surface resemblances may draw wonderfully rash and colorful inferences.

I might, for instance, as a resident of Plymouth, Massachusetts, derive such amusement from the fact that I live in the midst of several towns which have an anagramic likeness to several of the towns in Lovecraft's

Arkham cycle. Coastal Plymouth itself has a *-mouth* suffix, suggesting the possibility of its being what Murray terms a "name-doublet" for Lovecraft's "Innsmouth." To support this, let me point out coastal Wareham, just south of here. If I drop the *w* and substitute *k* for the *e*, then I have "Arkham," which I note in the stories is just south of "Innsmouth." A second adjoining coastal town is Kingston, from which (I now choose to infer) "Kingsport" was obviously derived. And for my neighboring town of "Bolton," it appears I have the choice (among others) of Brockton or Taunton. Surely, if, as Murray supposes, the author sought to draw attention away from his true locations, he could find no more "anagramatically" congenial place to shun than my own neighborhood!

Faraway Street Signs with Same-Sounding Names

In something of a contrast to his anagramic disguise of town names, Lovecraft, according to the current acceptance, was content to utilize street names as he found them. Murray has discovered in Gloucester—the town he equates with "Innsmouth"—at least seven streets having names in common with streets in ill-rumored Innsmouth: Adams, Babson, Church, Federal, Main, Marsh, and Washington. A "Fish Street" is also averred, though I suspect an error here, since no "Fish" appears in the city's street directory.

This bounty of like-named streets might be more impressive if more than half the total—Church, Federal, Main, and Washington—were not found in a large number of towns throughout the country. The similarity is less striking also when we observe that these streets are widely scattered in Gloucester and devoid of the spatial relationships Lovecraft indicates in his narrative, as well as sketch-maps of Innsmouth which the author used in preparing his Innsmouth story.

Again, the game is just a bit too simple: I happen to have been raised in suburban Newton, just west of Boston. In Newton one finds Adams, Bank, Church, Eliot, Payne, River, Washington, Water, and William Streets, for a total of nine in common with "Innsmouth." Mr. Murray, I believe, grew up in Quincy, a suburb just south of Boston. My gazetteer shows Quincy to have Adams, Bates, Elliot, Federal, Main, Marsh, Mill, Payne, River, Rowley, South, State, Washington, and Water, for a grand total of *fourteen* matches with "Innsmouth." Still, I would be surprised if Mr. Murray and I—whatever our differences—could not agree how very little the communities of Quincy and Newton have in common with shadowed "Innsmouth."

Of course Lovecraft's own claim was that his "Innsmouth" was patterned after Newburyport. I think we ought, in simple fairness, to appease those traditionalists who persist—against the prevalent wisdom—in supposing

Newburyport to be "Innsmouth's" model, and tally up *that* city's same-name signage. Here is the list: Adams, Broad, Federal, LaFayette, Marsh, River, State, Washington, and Water. There is one more—sort of. This name is rather uncommon today, and I'd be surprised to find it anywhere along the present-day North Shore; but in the eighteenth century, Newburyport had a broad avenue of this name running from High Street to the Market Square. Today, the way is known as State Street, which Lovecraftians will recall as the route of Joe Sargent's companionable coach in "The Shadow over hinsmouth." But nearly two hundred years ago, the guidebooks say, it was called "Fish Street."

Cold Water

With respect to the handling of names of physical features or landmarks, the matter of "Cold Spring Glen" is little different from the above. It is clear to Murray that Lovecraft must have been familiar with the Oakham region, because this town is "located just four miles south of a place known as Coldbrook Springs." Since Lovecraft's story mentions an area near "Dunwich" named "Cold Spring Glen," we have a similarity which Murray assures us "is not likely to be a coincidence."

Not likely?

If the likeness between fictional "Cold Spring" and "Coldbrook Springs" has to be more than coincidence, then we are at pains to account for the proximity of real places named Cold Spring. Just four miles north of Wilbraham, which the author himself identifies as his model for "Dunwich," is Belchertown, identified on eighteenth-century maps as—you guessed it—"Cold Spring." The name is continued today on street and business signs in this area. I would not claim, however, that even this likeness nails Belchertown as the place that inspired Lovecraft. Just two blocks from the home of my youth in Newton is a fine grove-circled playground, bisected by a quiet brook. Both brook and playground have long been known by the not uncommon name of "Cold Spring." Today I live in Plymouth, about forty miles south of that childhood playground; but you shouldn't be surprised to learn that just a mile north of my home is a brook which maps and local signs proclaim as "Cold Spring."

Dagon Details

I am not at all certain whether it is generally appreciated how deftly and how very lightly Lovecraft touches in his architectural passages. Excepting "The Shunned House," where the author allows himself three paragraphs to describes the Georgian structure of the title, the architectural descriptions are simple and brief—much in keeping with that avoidance of technical jargon which M. R. James advised. Two sentences suffice to describe the mansion of Charles Dexter Ward, and most of the other houses or buildings, including those of Richard Pickman, Nahum Gardner, Henry Akeley, the Whateleys, and "Old Man Marsh," require no more than a single line to portray their salient features accurately.

Ordinarily just enough points of construction or form are sketched in to identify a regional style of building, its overall condition and little more. A good deal, respecting plan and ornamentation, is trusted to the fancy of the mind's eye.

Considering this, it is puzzling when we are so forcibly told that the Legion Memorial Building, a structure in downtown Gloucester, is "absolutely, positively identical to the Order of Dagon Hall" (Murray 1991, 16), which Lovecraft "so painstakingly describes" in "The Shadow over Innsmouth." We can only ask what, in Lovecraft's rather spare description of his "Dagon Hall," warrants this assertion of incontrovertible identity?

The passage in question tells us the hall was "large," that it had pillars, some peeling "once white [and] now grey" paint, and a faded "black and gold sign on the pediment" (*DH* 318)—and *this is all* we are told, in its "painstaking" entirety: large, pillared, peeling, gray, pediment with faded black and gold sign, period. Murray, nevertheless, is prepared to claim Gloucester's "Legion Memorial" is "exactly as Lovecraft described [Dagon Hall]." It is "absolutely clear" to him.

Murray points out the fact that the Legion building has "the Ionic columns." But we find no reference to the Ionic order (as opposed to the Doric or Corinthian orders) in the text. He sees "the black and gold sign . . . indeed over the pediment" (Murray 1988, 13). But indeed, the text has the sign on the pediment. Murray supplies an old drawing which, as it happens, shows the sign he found neither on nor over the pediment: it rests on the frieze.

Incredibly, we are called to witness the present building's paint, which is "indeed, grey and peeling." Are we to suppose that paint which is peeling during Lovecraft's period has persisted in that same peeling state through the intervening half-century? Surely Mr. Murray is pulling our leg.

More is added to this burden. The Legion building has a good many (nearly two dozen) large pillars. These are presented as the "many large pillars Lovecraft described." Yet, Lovecraft did not say "many" pillars, nor "large" pillars. He said only that this hall was "pillared." Murray, apparently, reads Lovecraft's phrase "large pillared hall" as "large-pillared hall," thereby interpreting the pillars rather than the hall as "large." A postscript mentions that the Legion's pillars, pediment, and sign are no older than a

1920 remodeling of the building, which leaves us to imagine how Lovecraft would find a faded and peeling condition less than a decade after this. But all this is by the mark: were Lovecraft, indeed, describing a "rare example of Greek Revival architecture," as Murray terms it, then whether or not a given building fits this description might be germane to the question. This, however, is not the case.

In New England, the pillared hall, like the stately elm, the bandstand, the honor rolls, white-steepled church, and grassy sward, is a staple of the typical village green. Products of the nineteenth-century classical revival, such halls commonly follow Greek or Roman patterns with suitable columns—sometimes of mixed order. When of wood, such buildings are nearly always painted white, and signs that designate the function—be it municipal, ecclesiastical, institutional, or commercial—will often as not follow the traditional form of gold Roman letters on a black ground. Architecturally, Lovecraft could not have added a more typical specimen to his view of Innsmouth's "New Church Green." Since his Dagon Hall possesses no uniquity of design, the case for origination, based as it is upon a supposed *uncommon* similarity, is unsupported.

The irony of this is that the force of Lovecraft's passage is that a common and traditional institution—the Freemason's hall—has been perverted to the exotic uses of an alien cult. A "pillar of the community," so to speak, is now fallen. In "The Dunwich Horror," Lovecraft employs a device we might term "sadly given over" to the situation of a church turned to the use of a mercantile establishment, and likewise Federal Hill's former Free-Will Baptist church is "sadly given over" to the rites of the Starry Wisdom sect; so too this Masonic Temple is "sadly given over" to the Esoteric Order of Dagon's sabbats, thus providing a dramatic architectural symbol of localized societal decay.

Cupola Problems

Similar questions must be raised about an argument that the presence of a First National supermarket in Gloucester is evidence of the origin of the First National grocery in "Innsmouth." We again note an extravagant reading of the text, in the assertion that Lovecraft said the First National "was a prominent landmark" (*DH* 320). All the text supports, of course, is that a First National was there. Through the first half of this century, stores of the First National chain are the ubiquitous "family grocery" along the eastern seaboard. In my Newton boyhood, the First National was a half mile away on Walnut Street, near Center. In Murray's Quincy, it may have been closer—on Beale Street, next to Cox's Hudson dealership.

We are also informed that Gloucester's famous Sargent-Murray-Gilman-Hough house (which Murray simplifies to the "Gilman House") is the original of the dreadful hotel in Innsmouth's "Town Square." This is curious, since the inn in the tale is a rather tall (five floors) commercial structure, whereas Gloucester's antiquarian landmark is but a two-and-one-half-story private dwelling, now (sadly) given over to tourism. The one is seedy and dismal; the other is elegant and charming. Then we must consider the matter of cupolas.

"HPL," says Murray, "spoke of the Gilman House's roof cupolas," and pointing out a row of three dormers on the front pitch of the Gloucester house's roof, which he terms "boxed windows," he allows: ". . . they might be called cupolas."

From what has thus far been demonstrated, I can imagine Mr. Murray calling dormers cupolas. Imagining Lovecraft, the earnest student of colonial architecture, calling a dormer a cupola is more difficult. Freestanding cupolas differ markedly in form and function from dormers that are built into the pitch of a roof. Lovecraft, by the way, speaks not of "cupolas": his hotel has but one cupola—the usual number.

Shadows over Market Square

I find it bewildering that Will Murray's disenchantment with Newburyport begins with his exploration of this town's ancient State Street. Walking this very street, he and a companion are disappointed to find none of those "old brick buildings of State Street" mentioned in the story. Heavens! *They had only to look up!* The entire north half of State (a k a "Fish") Street, from Market Square to the Pleasant Street crossing, is composed of the town's famous steep-roofed brick blocks. These explorers were surrounded by "old brick buildings"!

How did these searchers fail to gain the riverside square at the foot of this street where they would see an open marketplace or "confluence," where as many as six ways and alleys converge? Standing with their backs to the mighty Merrimack, they would have confronted the square's ancient arena of commerce, paven with cobbles, brick and Empire-block, bordered with curving lines of tall brick business structures, with many shop signs in black and gold. Patently, Newburyport's Market Square is accurately described as the point of the narrator's departure from this town. We may also observe that with such a mass of early Federalist construction, this is the only radial brick marketplace in coastal Massachusetts (excepting Boston's North End) which could have inspired Innsmouth's "Town Square."

We don't have to rely entirely upon Lovecraft's claim that his "Innsmouth" was modeled on Newburyport: we have only to reference his descriptions of this town in various letters to identify this town as the model. In one such letter, the author describes the arrival of his motorcoach in "a spacious square lined on every side [with] the quaint brick mercantile buildings of the revolutionary period," as also his stroll through "the maze of picturesque streets . . . with peaked gambrel or flat roofs, massive chimneys [with] chimney pots," glimpsing "flashes of 18th century bye-streets [and] silhouettes of Wren steeples . . ., snatches of glistening harbour [and] antediluvian alleys, tottering wharves" and "stately mansions of old captains of the sea with . . . tall cupolas [to] scan the distant waves . . ." (*Letters to Alfred Galpin* 146–47) in a manner so familiar to readers of "The Shadow over Innsmouth" as to beggar rival comparisons.

Cryptic Charts and Mystic Maps

Much of the newer understanding of Lovecraft's fictional version of Massachusetts seems to rely upon a unique and eccentric reading of the map. The ordinary view of Cape Ann, for instance, is that it is a broad peninsular landmass, projecting eastward from the coast north of Boston. It is further understood, commonly, that this cape physically embraces the towns of Gloucester and Rockport, while including (at least culturally) the towns of Essex and Manchester. The new perception, by contrast, sees Cape Ann not as a great landmass comprised of several towns, but as a point "at the tip" of Gloucester (Murray 1986, 65). Thus, instead of being part of Cape Ann, Gloucester is a town of which Cape Ann is but a part!

With Rockport, we have the same astonishing turnabout: "There is an Andrews Point in Rockport, north of Cape Ann" (ibid.). Possibly, Cape Ann is here confused with famous "Mother Ann," which is (as many a Yankee will tell you) a point of land—a matronly granite profile looking seaward from Gloucester's Eastern Point.

This sizable misapprehension sadly appears to be the basis of Murray's geographical argument for Rockport and Gloucester as Lovecraft's locations for "Kingsport" and "Innsmouth." He quotes the narrator's allusion to "the long line of cliffs that culminate in Kingsport Head and veer off toward Cape Ann" (*DH* 315–16). Apparently, since "Mother Ann" and Cape Ann are conflated, he supposes the narrator's view is eastward across Gloucester and toward the coastal bluffs of Rockport. If Cape Ann were simply another name for "Mother Ann" (which is just south of Gloucester), Murray's reading would make sense; it would also explain why he thinks Andrews Point is north of Cape Ann. The distinction of "Cape" vs. "Mother" Ann collapses the theory, however. Lovecraft's narrator is not looking eastward across Innsmouth toward Kingsport and veering right (south) toward "Cape [Mother] Ann." In fact, the narrator actually looks south across Innsmouth to where the cliffs veer left (eastward) toward the projecting landmass of Cape Ann. "Innsmouth," therefore, cannot be as far south as Cape Ann, and thus Gloucester cannot be its location. Neither can Cape Ann be the location of "Kingsport," since the narrator places the Cape east of this town.

The new geography also attributes significance to Lovecraft's statement in a letter that the cliffs he had in mind when writing "The Strange High House in the Mist" included those at Magnolia (*SL* 3.164). These cliffs, Murray assures us, are "actually in Rockport." Actually, Mr. Murray, any gas-station map will show that Magnolia is nowhere in sight of Rockport, being near the border dividing West Gloucester from Manchester.

Oddly, the objection is made that Newburyport can't be the model for "Innsmouth," because the narrator's bus *leaves* Newburyport, traveling south to reach "Innsmouth." By this mode of reasoning, one can't leave the "model" town behind when traveling to the town created from that model. But why not? Are any physical laws violated? Bones broke? *This is fiction*—the writer does as he pleases! If Lovecraft chooses (as I believe he did) to have his narrator leave Newburyport and go south to the somewhat similar town of "Innsmouth," what's to stop him? Even in the comics I remember that Superman could fly from "Metropolis"—which was modeled on Manhattan—to Manhattan itself quite safely (and without bursting the spheres of "Bizarro" space) because the writers wished him to. Lovecraft described his "hypothetical" towns as "typical but imaginary." Still, nothing forces us to impose the limitations of the typical upon the imaginary.

Quite the same problem arises with another objection to Newburyport, concerning the old coastal Route 1A. The ancient bus rattles down High Street (a segment of 1A) and continues upon this route, crossing Parker River and heading south. In real life, a bus holding to this route would pass through Rowley, then Ipswich and on southward toward Salem. Readers recall, of course, that the bus in the story doesn't hold to this route, but instead forks seaward upon a southeasterly "shore road" toward "Innsmouth." If we, says Murray, were to follow this latter road, which he equates with Route 133, we should wind up in Gloucester, and therefore, "inescapably," Gloucester is "really" Innsmouth.

I have rounded up the usual objections—of reality and fact.

Prior to Rowley—and therefore prior to Ipswich as well—the bus in the story forked left from the main route to the "shore road." Route 133, however, does not appear as a left fork until after both Rowley and Ipswich centers have been passed; nor does Route 133 fit Lovecraft's term "shore" road.

The actual coast, from Newburyport to Rockport, is primarily salt marsh: no such shore road could be built here. That the road to "Innsmouth," like the town itself—and the "line of cliffs" running south of it—could be a writer's pure invention seems never to have been considered.

High time it was.

Compressed Cartography

Will Murray says he has "a very strong, if not explicit, impression" that Arkham and Dunwich are "within short travel distance from one another" (Murray 1991, 15). This "impression" (elsewhere assumed as fact) is based upon supposed resemblances Murray finds between the setting described in "The Dunwich Horror" and the Arkham countryside described in "The Picture in the House," "Herbert West—Reanimator," "The Unnamable," and "The Colour out of Space." The "true seat of Arkham," he believes, was "established and reiterated many times" in Lovecraft's "early" (or pre-1931) fiction, as being not upon the state's North Shore, "but many miles inland in a remote, haunted rural area."

In "The Picture in the House," Murray claims the narrator speaks of "getting lost on the way home to Arkham." Since the locale is described as "backwoods New England," he concludes that Arkham is "many many miles inland." As I read the text, however, I see nothing to suggest that a) the narrator's home is in Arkham; b) the rural house in the story is *in* Arkham, rather than on a road leading *toward* Arkham; or c) that the word "backwoods" is in some way indicative of a "many miles inland" setting. Many ruralities along the Massachusetts coast, in fact, from Cape Ann to Cape Cod, have quite accurately been termed "backwoods" or "backwaters."

In "Herbert West—Reanimator" (which is set in Arkham), Murray finds "several mentions of deserted farmhouses" which persuade him that Arkham must be a rural town. As I read the text, however, I find only several mentions of one deserted farnihouse—"the old Chapman place beyond Meadow Hill" (*D* 136). In his reading of "The Unnamable," Murray finds matter to suggest "a rural farming community, far from the sea," which therefore rules out coastal Salem as the model. Again, my own reading discloses neither distance from nor mention of the sea. Astoundingly, Murray has taken no notice of the fact that by the time he finishes "The Unnamable," Lovecraft has established Arkham as a community having a university, at least two high schools, a hospital, and lighted streets—hardly a "backwater."

With the writing of "The Colour out of Space" in 1927, Lovecraft goes on to specify unequivocally that Arkham, like Salem, is not a mere town, but a corporated city. Arkham, we learn, has at least two daily newspapers and a substantial reservoir project underway. If more is needed, we have in this story mention of "the city water of Arkham," the :city veterinarian from Arkham," and the "city people at Arkham" (*DH* 57, 66, 68).

Of the newspapers cited by name in these stories—the *Arkham Gazette* and the *Arkham Advertiser*—it seems more than coincidental that two of Essex County's foremost papers were the *Salem Gazette* and the *Salem Advertiser*. And while Murray thinks it "ridiculous" that the *Arkham Advertiser* would report Dunwich doings if the towns of Arkham and Dunwich were not close neighbors, the fact is that Salem papers, like those of any other substantial urban center, regularly reported affairs of the state, nation, and world.

Incredibly, the passage in "The Dunwich Horror" where Professor Armitage and company depart from Arkham by motor "Friday morning" to drive to Dunwich, "arriving about one in the afternoon" (*DH* 187), is seen as evidence that the two towns share a tight proximity. Though he admits this means the towns are "at least two" hours apart, Murray suggests "difficult backwoods roads" could account for this length of time. Thus, the towns "may not be terribly far apart as the crow flies." *Flies?* Sorry; but even allowing but two hours, as Mr. Murray does, we're talking *walking* crow here! And isn't Dunwich just off the "Aylesbury Pike," which presumably runs to Arkham? Consider: Massachusetts turnpikes by the 1920s are macadamized. Even at 35 miles per hour, a motor car running from the coast westward on the turnpikes of 1925 can, in two hours, enter the central part of the state where Lovecraft places Dunwich. If Dunwich and Arkham are indeed neighboring towns, then we are pressed to speculate what detours or dawdlings could have transpired to delay the Armitage party for two hours or more on the road between them.

New Age Geography and History

In his second epistle, "In Search of Arkham Country Revisited," Mr. Murray's previous claim that Oakham is the original of "Arkham" prior to 1931 is modified. It seems that soon after his first article appeared, a newspaper travel piece by Ruth E. Gruber disclosed that the little town of New Salem, just west of the present Quabbin Reservoir, was "founded by settlers from [old] Salem itself—just forty years or so after the 1692 witch hunts." While he maintains that Oakham is "obviously" the inspiration for the mythical town's *name*, Murray is now convinced that "Arkham is, in fact, New Salem."

In support of this, Murray tells us of a "tantalizing fact which Lovecraft mentioned in 'The Colour out of Space' . . . [that] Arkham had been settled by *descendants* [my italics] of the Salem witches" (Murray 1989, 67). He is mis-tantalized here: I find no mention of Arkham's founders in the "Colour" tale. Continuing, Murray asserts that the above is "a scrap of background Lovecraft also attached to . . . Dunwich [in] 'The Dunwich Horror.'" "Very significant," we are informed, is "the fact that Lovecraft saw fit to mention it twice."

Twice? Murray's third epistle, "Lovecraft's Arkham Country," expands on this point: "In several of the stories Lovecraft makes the specific and telling reference to the fact that Arkham was settled by descendants of Salem witches who fled west to escape the persecutions" (Murray 1991, 16). Oh?

M'friends, H. P. Lovecraft *did not* mention witch-descendants as founders of Arkham in "several" stories. Nor did he mention it *twice*. Honest, folks, the Providence gentleman *never said this—not even once.*

As I said previously, the topic of founding doesn't arise in "The Colour out of Space," and quite conversely, we have the narrator's exclamation that "most" of the Gardner family's rural Arkham house was built "before 1670" (*DH* 71)—or twenty-two years prior to the witch persecutions.

In "The Dunwich Horror," certainly, we do learn of "two or three armigerous families [who] came from Salem in 1692" (*DH* 157), but this refers wholly to "Dunwich," not "Arkham." Also, the passage suggests that these families were *fugitives* of the witchcraft at the time they came (1692) rather than *descendants* of such fugitives.

Possibly Murray's impression is based on passages in "Through the Gates of the Silver Key," where we learn of the "hills behind crumbling Arkham" having been "settled in 1692 by fugitives from the witchcraft trials in Salem" (*MM* 442). But, again, the reference is to *fugitives,* rather than descendants, and the tale was written nearly two years after the date (1931) when Murray himself says Lovecraft abandoned the inland model for "Arkham" and began using a coastal town instead.

Theorizing that Danvers, rather than Salem proper, is the post-1931 "Arkham," Murray adds the historical puzzler that Danvers is "the true site of the Salem witch trials—although the witch hunt began in Salem" (Murray 1989, 67)—a precise reversal of the facts, since the *accusations* and initial hearings were in Danvers (then called "Salem Village") and the *trials* (and executions) went forward in Salem town.

Of course Danvers was, like Peabody, once a part of Salem. Only the relatively urban part of Salem remains from the old city. I believe a good case can be made that Lovecraft had parts of Danvers and Peabody in mind as he fleshed out his description of Arkham's *countryside* in his "Silver

Key" and "blasted heath" tales. The Rebecca Nurse house in Danvers, for instance, is almost certainly the model for "Goody Fowler's half-rotted cottage" (*MM* 422) in "Through the Gates of the Silver Key."

"The Danvers River," says Murray, "being the only river near Salem, must then be the latter-day Miskatonic River" (Murray 1986, 64). Salem's only nearby river? Urban Salem, in actuality, is flanked, fore and aft, by the North and South Rivers. The proximal relationship of the first of these to downtown Salem has long been likened to that of the "Miskatonic" to "Arkham" in Lovecraft's hand-drawn map of his imaginary town.

Cartography of the Gods

Geographically speaking, if we feel lost in Murray's eccentric version of Essex County, we're far from found in his irregular central Massachusetts. Somehow, he finds it impossible to reconcile that, on the one hand, the text of "The Dunwich Horror" gives the locale of Dunwich as "north central" Massachusetts—which is to say upper Worcester county—while, on the other hand, the author, in various letters, gives a *south* central region as being that which inspired his fictional setting. Murray's response to this disorienting dynamic unfortunately leads to rash attempts to redraw the map.

Lovecraft's identification of Hampden County's Wilbraham, Hampden, and Monson as his models for "Dunwich" is rejected as too southerly. Because the text says "north central," Murray attempts a Lovecraftian survey of this region. Whately he describes as a "focus point" of the Quabbin Reservoir area (Murray 1989, 66). The problem here is that Whately is separated from the Reservoir area by several townships, being situated on the west bank of the Connecticut River, in the center of Franklin County. Murray also places Whately "a little bit west of New Salem," though the map shows an intervention of four townships, about 25 miles of roadway and a major river between them. What is clear is that Whately is not a part of the Quabbin region, nor part of the north central region of the state.

New Salem, seen as the inland prototype of "Arkham," is described as being *west* of now-submerged Greenwich, which Murray supposes the original of "Dunwich" (ibid., 67). Here, the problem is that drowned Greenwich was two towns and several miles *dead south* of New Salem, on the eastern rim of Hampshire County. New Salem itself is on the eastern rim of Franklin County.

Then we have the matter of Greenwich, which, quite contrary to where it is placed on the map supplied with Murray's initial article, is located (by period maps) in the southern half of the state. Pelham, erroneously included among the flooded towns, is, in fact, west of that flood-plain and thrives modestly today.

Shutesbury, which appears to Murray as a "doublet" of Lovecraft's "Aylesbury," is a tiny hamlet which is two towns and a county line (Franklin) northwest of the town Murray labels "Dunwich/Greenwich" and, like New Salem and Pelham, is well west of the reservoir and quite outside the "north central" region.

Oakham, the earlier "Arkham" candidate, is part of "central" Massachusetts, but miles south of the "north central" portion—and several rivers east of the Quabbin Valley's Swift River.

The city of Worcester, an alternative "Aylesbury" candidate, is separated from "Dunwich/Greenwich" by nearly half of Worcester County, and lies even further south than Oakham.

Astoundingly, despite the rejection of Wilbraham, Hampden, and Monson on the basis of their "too remote" distance from the "north central" and Quabbin regions, not one of the proposed new candidates for "Dunwich," "Arkham," or "Aylesbury" is, strictly speaking, to be found in the north central region. One, Greenwich, is among the sunken Quabbin towns, but is too far south and west to be "north central." Also, there is irony in the fact that there was one Quabbin town, the former Dana, which was part of the north central region that is, nonetheless, ignored. The new geography also assumes these were "side-by-side towns" which informed HPL's "original conception of Arkham Country" (Murray 1989, 69). But a glance at the maps shows these supposed early models to be scattered hither, thither, and yon. "Worcester/ Aylesbury" is towns apart from "Oakham/ Arkham," which, in turn, is several towns distant from "Greenwich/Dunwich." This latter is parted from "Shutesbury/Aylesbury" by the intervention of Prescott, which likewise comes between it and "New Salem/Arkham." And the tiny farming hamlet of Bolton—preposterously described as "a factory town just as Lovecraft claims"—is a broad county apart from all the above. Moreover, while Grafton is termed a "neighbor" of Bolton, it is no less than four towns or 25 miles away. In little Massachusetts, that's not neighborly.

Surprisingly, though we find many of the searcher's claims extravagant, they are by no means incautious. Initially, of course, we bought into Lovecraft's claim that Arkham, Kingsport, Innsmouth, and Aylesbury are, respectively, Salem, Marblehead, Newburyport, and the environs east of Springfield. Wrong! "Everything you know about Lovecraft's Massachusetts is wrong!" says Murray. The real locales, without doubt, are Oakham, Rockport, Gloucester, and Worcester.

Pretty heady stuff, this—but before long, cooler heads (or cold feet) prevail: Arkham, he tells us, may, very early on, have been Taunton—and later perhaps became Oakham (in name at least), but more substantially, New Salem—and finally, *old* Salem on the coast, or, more definitely . . . Danvers. That's it . . . *Danvers*. And yes, Kingsport has been said to be Rockport, but, we're cautioned, only *location* was really intended; perhaps Marblehead contributes to Kingsport also. It is steadfastly maintained that Innsmouth is Gloucester, but possibly it is Gloucester with something of Newburyport moved in. Was it said that Aylesbury was Worcester? Let's change that to a probable Shutesbury, for its remarkably similar name— and oh: throw in Amesbury and Shrewsbury just in case. No exaggeration, folks, the above closely follows the evolution of wary assertions through the series of "Arkham Country" papers.

Snipelike, we dart town to town.

The Spectre over Massachusetts

But, you say, what if we compiled unequivocal evidence that none of the newly proposed towns were Lovecraft's model? With nearly two hundred towns in the state, surely Mr. Murray can't cover all the bases?

No? In fact, it is here we begin to appreciate his generous depth of field, as we observe Murray's device to handle every geographical objection. A device which sends whole towns *aloft and gliding forth.*

We are told that Lovecraft had a unique method of choosing locations for his stories. As Murray explains:

> If one takes a map of Massachusetts, and draws a line from the Wilbraham/ Hamden area northward, through the Quabbin Reservoir and connects it with a north central town (let's say Athol, because we know Lovecraft often visited his friend W. Paul Cook there), you would have one side of a rough rectangle in which Arkham might be found. A line running east connects Wilbraham to Grafton, the probable model for Sefton, and Grafton is connected with its northern neighbor, Bolton. Finally, a fourth line connecting Bolton to Athol in the west gives us an area of approximately 500 square miles in which Lovecraft's fictitious town of Arkham should be found.
>
> In almost the exact center of this area, directly east of the Quabbin Reservoir, is the obscure town of Oakham. (Murray 1986, 59)

In a nutshell, then, we are to suppose Lovecraft imagined a box on the map which enclosed certain places he visited and/or fictionalized, such as Athol, Wilbraham, Grafton, and Bolton—and then defined the center of this box and made that town his fictional headquarters. The total area enclosed is about 500 square miles.

Let us set aside the question of whether Lovecraft would adopt the principles of Bermuda Triangle pseudoscience. The only thing above which is important is that part about 500 square miles. This completes one half of the device: a big gameboard. Now observe the construction of the other half—municipal flight:

> Lovecraft's conceptions . . . are fluid and protean (Murray 1986, 66). Lovecraft's places are not fixed—not even in Lovecraft's own mind (Murray 1989, 68). Well, around 1931 certain things started to happen . . . vis-à-vis Arkham and Dunwich: one is that Arkham starts to slide toward the coast. Sometimes it jumps back a little; but usually it's creeping coastward. . . . When the Quabbin project became irreversible . . . that is when Lovecraft begins to slide Arkham toward the coast (Murray 1991, 16). The first story to hint at a coastward shift of Arkham was "The Festival" written in 1923. It is as if Arkham is a phantom city; a spectral thing which hovers near all other seats of Massachusetts horror like some omnipresent malignant entity (Murray 1986, 64–65).

Those who attempt to identify new candidate towns from the Connecticut to the coast on this big gameboard may find their proposed towns have *previously* been hovered over, or at least fly-by'd, by spectral Phantom City!

Oh, these fiery feet of frost!

It has been suggested that one bit of text may support the notion of an inland Arkham: that where the Miskatonic library is said to be closer to Dunwich "geographically" than Harvard's Widener Library in Cambridge (*DH* 169). The map, however, will prove it is the Widener (by one or two miles) which is closer to any given point in the north central part of the state than the location I interpret for Arkham. To be the closer, Arkham would have to be at least as far inland as Topsfield. Quite possibly—as S. T. Joshi recently suggested to me—Lovecraft is stretching a geographical point in order to meet the story's requirement that Wilbur Whateley visit Arkham *prior* to Cambridge. I suspect, however, a simple error may enter in here as well. From what we read in the text and various letters, the author—rightly or wrongly—envisions Dunwich *northwest* of Arkham. He also—trustworthy or not—wants us to imagine Arkham near the coast. Cambridge, we know, is just north of Boston and therefore *south* of Arkham. If we envision the coastline as a roughly vertical line, then logically Dunwich must be closer to Arkham. The problem only arises if we check this against the map, where the coastline is seen to be not vertical, but having a radically westerly course placing Cambridge miles closer to the north central region than we might otherwise imagine. This, I suspect, was Lovecraft's error: his logic here was orderly, but a cartographic premise was faulty.

An Assault upon Common Sense

Allow me to point up a few of the salient problems I have with the new Arkham Country thesis. In order seriously to entertain the proposition that Lovecraft attempted to conceal the true models for his invented towns, we are not only forced to ignore much that is to the contrary, but additionally we must read uncommon significance into seemingly superficial or common resemblances. On the basis of wholly unspecified "discrepancies" and "qualifications" in Lovecraft's remarks, we are asked to discount the author's own identification of his models. We are supposed to believe that the antiquary saved and sacrificed, to the point of fasting, in order to visit and revisit Salem, Marblehead, and Newburyport—the very towns we are told were but a "front" concealing "true" models like Oakham, Rockport, and Gloucester. We must try to envision the Providence gentleman blowing into, let us say, Salem, merely in order to purchase postcards by the pound and dispatch them ink-laden to his multitude of correspondents, thus keeping them off the track of his actual interest. In the absence of any evidence of deed or motivation, I think this is a great deal to ask of us. Is it reasonable to assume—on the basis of nothing—that Lovecraft insinuates bits of historic, geneological, folkloric, and architectural color from Salem into a story, in order to disguise the influence of Oakham? It reminds me of the Arkham folk who "avoid going to Innsmouth whenever they can" and also the folk who "visit Dunwich as seldom as possible."

So little time.

So much to avoid as often, and visit as seldom as schedules permit.

Contradictions of ascertainable fact abound: architecturally, dormers become cupolas, frieze turns pediment, and old brick buildings, block on block, disappear entire. Geographically, a cape encompassing several towns is equated with a headland, bits of Gloucester transubstantiate as landmarks of Rockport, estranged villages are presented as neighbors and erroneously grouped in the Swift River/Quabbin Valley, which is in turn erroneously declared part of north central Massachusetts. And a rocky landmark of Rehoboth slips gneissly into Taunton.

Rescuing the Searchers

Having specified so many objections to another person's interpretation of Lovecraft's fictional geography, I feel some obligation to stick my own neck out, and at least outline my own reckoning of how Lovecraft's New England might be understood.

First off, I don't believe we have to guess where the author places his Essex County towns of Arkham, Kingsport, and Innsmouth; he tells us where. Between his stories and his letters we have sufficient evidence to deduce the fictional town locations. It is in "The Festival" (1923) where we first learn that Kingsport and Arkham are adjoining towns. Kingsport, true to its name, is also established here as fronting upon the Atlantic coast (*D* 209). Next, in the opening of "The Strange High House in the Mist" (1926), we learn that the Miskatonic River, which runs through Arkham, has its estuary immediately north of Kingsport (*D* 277), and a page later we can verify that both towns are in Massachusetts. Here, too, we learn downtown Arkham is "leagues" up the navigable river and west of Kingsport (*D* 280).

Then, in "The Shadow over Innsmouth" (1931), enough information is added to place all three of these seaport towns. First, Innsmouth is part of Essex County (*DH* 310). The story's narrator views this town spread below him in a coastal valley, just south of Plum Island Sound (*DH* 315–16). In the same passage we find the (fictional) Manuxet River channeling through Innsmouth to where it "joins the sea just north of the long line of cliff s that culminate in Kingsport Head and veer off toward Cape Ann" (*DH* 315–16). The "Strange High House" of the earlier tale is seen distantly from this (clearly northern) vantage point. The skyline of Arkham, we note, is not mentioned, since we can assume it is "leagues" westward and upriver, as has been previously established. Lovecraft also describes "old carriage roads" that stretch "inland" toward Rowley and Ipswich (*DH* 316), from which we may reasonably infer that the centers of these towns are somewhat west of Innsmouth. In the view from his hotel room's west window, the narrator spies the distant Rowley road to his right and the Ipswich road to his left (*DH* 346–47). This implies that Rowley is somewhat northwest of Innsmouth, and that Ipswich is to the southwest—a compass relationship we find verified by the author's "sketch-map" of Innsmouth in *Something about Cats and Other Pieces* (Arkham House, 1949, p. 174) as also by other verso maps and plans found with the autograph manuscript and notes in the John Hay Library of Brown University.

Finally, in "The Dreams in the Witch House" we have added support for a north-south compass relationship of Arkham and Innsmouth as the protagonist Gilman, drawn to walk north from Arkham, finds himself (after an hour) upon a "narrow road" in salt-marsh country leading toward Innsmouth.

So here we just about have it. The reader who refers to my modified "map" of Lovecraft's Essex County will find "Kingsport" at the "corner" of that coastline which runs southeast from Newburyport and "veers" seaward "toward Cape Ann." The Miskatonic's entrance to the sea is just above the great headland north of Kingsport's center, as in the "The Strange High House" tale. The river has to approach this point from the southwest, because Arkham, which fronts upon the river, is described as "leagues" westward of the dizzy headland, and because a western or northern approach would interfere with the course of neighboring rivers, all of which approach the sea from the southwest. Also, Arkham's urban center must be miles upstream, if the term "leagues" is not wholly poetic license.

Since the Innsmouth story has Innsmouth north of Arkham and northeast of Ipswich, and because Ipswich is less than three miles upriver from the coast, we can limit how far west of Kingsport we place Arkham's center. On my map, this works out to putting Innsmouth's center on the coast, northeast of Ipswich and just south of Plum Island. Arkham I then place dead south of Innsmouth and straight west of Kingsport. Rowley, in accordance with the story, is northwest of Innsmouth. Looking again at Arkham one sees the township extending somewhat west of the urban center—to accommodate the "blasted heath" country—and also somewhat north to allow for some hills "beyond" (or above) Arkham, as described in "The Silver Key" and other Randolph Carter tales. The northerly direction is assumed because Lovecraft uses elsewhere the term "beyond" to mean "above," as when he places the high cliffs "beyond" Kingsport in the "The Strange High House" tale. Such positioning is also consistent with Randolph Carter's prospect in "The Silver Key," where, from "Elm Mountain," he looks seaward to view the spires of Kingsport with no mention of the spires of Arkham in between; he is north of Arkham.

My modified map of Essex County also shows the coastline from Cape Ann upward to be longer than the actual coastline. Innsmouth, Bolton, Arkham and Kingsport have been added to the county, so, unless we plan to somehow shrink or smallify the other towns, we must stretch the coast to make room for the additions. This, I believe, points up an important distinction we can make between "Lovecraft's New England" and the "Wessex Country" of Thomas Hardy, with which it is sometimes compared.

In the "Wessex" region, towns are disguised: when Hardy alludes to "Wintonchester," for instance, it is plain enough that Winchester is meant. His "Emminster" must surely be Beaminster in the light masquarade of an altered name. So too, Shaftsbury, Blandford, and Winebome are recognizable beneath the assumed names of "Shaston," "Shallsford," and "Warbome." Hardy's towns are *real places*—"only the names have been changed," in order to make them more acceptable settings for imaginary incidents.

There is no "map-stretching" in Wessex, because nothing is added; what is already "there" suffices under assumed names.

How very different with Lovecraft! His Innsmouth is supposed to be south of Rowley and north of Ipswich—but conventional maps show these to be adjacent towns. We can see where Innsmouth is on the real map—it occupies that infinitely narrow border line that separates the two real towns. Impossible? Why, as a matter of fact it *is* impossible, and there's the point. Lovecraft said his towns "are typical but imaginary places" and that "it would be impossible to make any real place the scene of such bizarre happenings" as he proposed for his "hypothetical towns." So his towns are *not* real, though he takes "pains to make [them] characteristic of genuine New England seaports" (*SL* 3.432–33).

So real towns have *modeled* for Miskatonic Valley towns, but unlike Hardy's Wessex, the models are not to be confused with the fictions.

We cannot be far wrong, I venture, if we say that southern Essex County's Salem "sat" for Lovecraft's portrayal of northern Essex County's "Arkham." Also, we shouldn't be much amiss in suggesting that as Lovecraft prepares to paint in "Kingsport" or "Innsmouth," he is loading his palette with the appropriate tints and shades he has acquired in Marblehead or Newburyport. We needn't confuse the source of the artist's colors with the completed canvas.

A happier comparison might be made with the "Barsetshire" region of Anthony Trollope's novels. "Barchester" is vaguely understood to be somewhere west of London and east of the Salisbury that Trollope identified as the seat of his inspiration. Now "Barchester" is *not* Salisbury in disguise, nor does it *displace* Salisbury on the map. It is much *like* Salisbury, and it seems we must imagine actual towns along the west road (perhaps Basingstoke and Whitechurch) forcibly parted to allow a "wedging in" of "Barchester."

I think we're safe in assuming that Aylesbury is west of Dunwich, since Dunwich lies off the "Aylesbury Pike," and turnpikes, then as now, were named for their destination towns. The story's traveler in north central Massachusetts "rejoins the Aylesbury Pike" after a detour through Dunwich. Lovecraft's map of Arkham shows an "Aylesbury Street" leading westward, which we can assume is the beginning of the "Pike." A parallel to this would be Route 9, connecting Boston (on the coast) with Worcester in the south-central part of the state. In Boston, route 9 is called the "Worcester Pike"; in Worcester, it's the "Boston Pike." So if you detour prior to reaching Worcester, then the place you detour into is somewhat east of Worcester. So too, I reason, with Aylesbury and Dunwich.

The deduction that Dunwich is fairly close to the New Hampshire border depends upon Lovecraft's letter of August 4, 1928, to August Derleth, in which he said his Dunwich is "far northwest of Arkham" (*ES* 1.151). If we run a rule straight west from our Arkham location (west end of Cape Ann), we discover that there are precious few miles separating the ruler from the New Hampshire line. So, if Dunwich is to be in Massachusetts and northwest of Arkham, it must press within a few miles of that border.

The Town Names Considered

Of Kingsport

In December 1922, Lovecraft made the first of many visits to the adjoining towns of Salem and Marblehead. He was deeply impressed by the antiquities of these towns, and his enthusiastic descriptions of them in subsequent letters show unmistakably in their color and style that Salem and Marblehead, respectively, shaped "Arkham" and "Kingsport" from this date forward. However, the use of the fictitious towns, and the names given them, actually predate this initial visit.

In "the beginning," with the writing of "The Terrible Old Man" in January of 1920, Kingsport is given as a coastal village located in some New England state unspecified. I know of nothing to suggest Lovecraft intended further use of this setting until after his first visit to Marblehead. It is not until he writes "The Festival" that we are able to say that Kingsport has any specific location or well-defined character. It would be incorrect, therefore, to assume that the name of that earliest Kingsport in "The Terrible Old Man" was intended to represent a Massachusetts seaport, to the exclusion of Rhode Island, Connecticut, New Hampshire, or Maine.

As discussed previously, *-port* is a common enough suffix along the Atlantic coast, and the prefix *Kings-* is by no means uncommon. Maine has a Kingsbury, New Hampshire a Kingston, and Massachusetts has a Kingston on its south shore; but closer to Lovecraft's home—within an hour's "cycling" southwest of Providence—is the coastal county of Kingstown with the village of Kingston within it. The town is often mentioned in Lovecraft's letters. Also, we must recall his fondness for the New York Kingston's Dutch antiquities—and it is not improbable that the state of Tennessee's substantial town of Kingsport was known to the author. At any rate, we have little need to suppose that Lovecraft pored over the old charts when he set about naming his little fishing village; the components of *Kings-* and *-port* were long familiar and "close at hand" in his experience.

Of Innsmouth

"Innsmouth," I would think, is a more creative choice of name, English coastal towns often have the name of a river in their prefix: thus old world Plymouth on the south coast is found near the "mouth" of the river Plym, and Cornwall's Exmouth is by the opening of the Ux. Lovecraft's invented coastal English town for his early tale "Celephaïs" may have been what he termed a "whimsical reversal" of Exmouth—his "Innsmouth" being posited near the estuary of a supposed river "Inns"—or perhaps "Innis."

We may be on firmer ground when we guess what factors might have converged to recall the name of "Innsmouth" to mind when the author set about inventing a town patterned on Newburyport. "The Shadow over Innsmouth," of course, has a pivotal scene in which the narrator is entrapped in the Gilman House, which he fears is "one of those inns where travelers are slain for their money" (*DH* 344).

Also, there can be little doubt that this story was Lovecraft's "answer" to Algernon Blackwood's John Silence story "Ancient Sorceries," which contains numerous similarities in plot, setting, and mood to the later tale. In both, we see a man prisoned in the heart of an ancient, odd, and remote village whose semi-human habitants share secret hellish rites. In both cases the prisoner's upstairs hotel room window gives upon a courtyard near a "cobbled marketplace," and likewise, both narrowly escape by moonlight only to learn, subsequently, of an ancestral connection with the strange townspeople. The word "shadow" appears fourteen times in Blackwood's text; even three times in one paragraph. There are fifteen allusions to the "courtyard," and fourteen mentions of the "inn," as well. We also note the "ancient inn yard" alluded to in the initial entry for the year 1928 in Lovecraft's *Commonplace Book*—an entry obviously inspired by Blackwood's tale. Then too, in Sonnet IX from *Fungi from Yuggoth*—where the setting appears to be Innsmouth—the stage is a "dark courtyard."

Finally, we may consider one of that converging network of streets which spill into the aforementioned Market Square of Newburyport. The street I am thinking of takes its name from the nearby presence of a hotel which served the travelers of Essex County's coaching days. The street is famous for its continuation of antiquities: here shops of ancient brick (with black and gold signs) crowd a narrow passage quite as they did in early Federalist times. And where but Newburyport could this uniquely quaint and colorful street be found? I speak, of course, of venerable *Inn Street!* God save the King!

Of Arkham

"Arkham" first appears briefly in "The Picture in the House" (December 1920), where it received a single mention as the destination of a traveler in the "Miskatonic Valley" region of Massachusetts. Other than this vague reference to a location in an equally fictitious valley, we are told nothing of the town; and I find nothing to suggest that the author at this date envisioned a series (or "Arkham Cycle") of stories staged within or near this or other fictitious towns. However, we again hear of Arkham as the seat of the imaginary "Miskatonic University Medical School" in "Herbert West—Reanimator," completed in the summer of 1922. Little more specific is added to our knowledge of the town: a street name here, a cemetery there, a pond, a farmhouse, and a hill. Had Lovecraft any actual Massachusetts town in mind here, he left precious few clues to identify it. It is not improbable that he was reminded of Rehoboth's Great Meadow Hill—often visited in his teens—when he placed a "Meadow Hill" in his "Arkham." I find indications, also, in the popular history, color, and folklore of Rehoboth of influences upon the plot and atmosphere of the "Picture" tale, and make a case for this elsewhere.

Still, I do not see nearly enough evidence to suggest that Rehoboth was "Arkham's" *original* model; in fact, I don't see that Arkham in the stories of the early '20s requires a precise model. Later stories would demand a more thoroughly informed setting, and Lovecraft would come to travel more extensively in Massachusetts in order to gather and absorb impressions to fill his descriptive needs. But for now, he was content to draw from his cursory acquaintance with the Bay State, acquired during his early visits to nearby towns like Rehoboth—and would draw also, I suppose, upon features of his native Rhode Island, such as might serve as descriptive counterparts of Massachusetts features he wished to portray.

Few, for instance, doubt that Lovecraft's familiarity with the great quadrangle of Providence's Brown University informed his creation of "Miskatonic University," which—no surprise here—is also set in a quadrangle in the author's map of Arkham. And the name "Arkham" itself, I believe, may have its basis in Lovecraft's Rhode Island experience.

Among the landmark events of Rhode Island history—right up there with Roger Williams crossing the Seekonk or the burning of the *Gaspée*—is the building of Slater's Mill on the Pawtucket River in 1790. Schoolboys of Lovecraft's day knew the story of the Lancashire inventor who combined the cotton-spinning jenny with a series of contoured rollers to afford better control of the carding process. The manufacture of cotton, linen, and woolen fibers was revolutionized by this gentleman's new "spinning frame," for which he was knighted. In the 1780s, a millworker named Samuel Slater brought the coveted secrets of this machine to New England; and with the support of investor Moses Brown, he made Pawtucket, Rhode Island, the site of this country's first successful textile industry.

Slater is credited with starting a factory movement that spread to every New England state—and beyond. But the names which attached to the cotton and woolen worsted works and mill towns harken back to that Lancashire inventor and the English riverside town where he developed the new frame. Of course, this was Sir Richard Arkwright—and "Arkwright Machine" is the name of his famous invention. "Arkwright factories" designates the mills operating in a multitude of "Arkwright towns," which enlarged or sprang up with the advent of the new process. Even the names of some of these towns honor the man—or the town where the process was born, Bolton, in Lancashire. "Bolton" will be found throughout this country: New England has "Boltons" in four of its six states. Rhode Island, additionally, has (or had) a town on the Pawtuxet River named for the inventor himself. Since it has been assimilated by the town of Fiskville, the much-diminished village of Arkwright seldom appears on current maps of the state, though it persists under this name as a district of the greater town. Today it is virtually unnoticed outside its neighborhood, but antiquaries and students of regional architecture have long esteemed Arkwright for its remaining examples of the early millworker's cottage.

I think it no stretch to suppose that when Lovecraft first contemplated town names for his "Miskatonic Valley" settings, typical names or name-elements associated with this once-thriving industry of the several New England states would cross his mind. Ark- may be a somewhat uncommon prefix: an Arkwright and an Arkport are in western New York, while in England and Ireland we find Arkley and Arklow. Nonetheless, Lovecraft had Arkwright, Rhode Island, within an hour's bicycle journey from his home. Need we look further?

Two additional considerations persuade me that this was his line of thinking: in the Herbert West tale he installs another town "near" Arkham, which he names "Bolton," telling us that it is a "factory town," and that the "Bolton Worsted Mills are the largest in the Miskatonic Valley" (D 144). Also, less than a year after completing the tale above, the author, "fired with the spirit of antient research," went to "gather impressions" in Salem. Subsequently, we know he broadened his focus to include Salem's orphan Danvers and officialized the witch-country as his model—but what drew him to explore Salem in the first place may well have been that the "witch-town" was renowned for its Naumkeag Steam Cotton Mills—one of the world's largest Arkwright plants. If he required a town "model" with a dark and colorful past (such as could not be found in Quaker-based Rhode Island) which would be large enough to embrace a undversity, and which would have a mill-centered economy of a sort faniihar to him, then Lovecraft couldn't do better than "sound out the possibilities" of using the city of Salem.

At any rate, we see that only subsequent to his initial visits to Salem does Arkham take shape as a "witch-haunted" city. In "The Unnamable," we find Salem's beloved "burying-point," with its "root-engulphed" slabs, flat-top sarcophagi, ancient willows, and abutting colonial houses accurately depicted as Arkham's "burying-ground." Later, in "The Dreams in the Witch House," we find Salem's famous "Witch House" restored to its original architectural form as Arkham's "Witch House." Comparing the topography of Salem with Lovecraft's map of "Arkham" reveals startling compass correspondences between Salem's Gallows Hill, North River, and Mack Park Hill and Arkham's "Hangman's Hill," "Miskatonic River," and "Meadow Hill."

Of Bolton and Foxfield

Will Murray tells us that Bolton is the name of a real town in Massachusetts; and so it is—in eastern Worcester County. He also tells us that this real Bolton is, like Lovecraft's Bolton in the stories, "a factory town"—which it certainly is not. Settled alongside the appropriately named Still River, this tiny rural hamlet numbered but a few hundred agriculturally bent souls in the 1920s. Its closest approach to manufacture might be the comb works, which employed as many as thirty people prior to its closing during the Civil War.

But Lovecraft's "Bolton" in the fiction is a major textile producer located near Arkham, and, therefore, in Essex County—not Worcester. Now if the real Bolton is none of these things, then we must ask how it could be so grossly misrepresented by a writer who normally takes pains to depict New England places accurately. Here is my view of it: I do not think Lovecraft would intentionally misrepresent outward aspects of a given town, nor do I think he would guess at these blindly. The actual Bolton is among the smallest and quietest of the state's many towns. It would surprise me not at all to learn that Lovecraft *never noticed* that Massachusetts already had a "Bolton" when he concocted his own. If he ever came to know there was an actual Bolton, I suspect he would feel obligated at least to modify the name of the invented town.

As I write this, the world learns of S. T. Joshi's discovery of still another fictitious town. "Foxfield" appears as a sketch-map among Lovecraft's papers in the John Hay Library: a description by Will Murray, accompanied by a graphic rationalization of the map, appears in *Lovecraft Studies* No. 33 (Fall 1995). Intended for an unwritten story, "Foxfield" appears to be somewhat northwest of Arkham, and generally eastward of the "Aylesbury-Dunwich" area.

A monograph on Foxfield must wait until I have seen the original document, though I feel safe for now with the following. The intended novel likely relates to a string of ideas found in Lovecraft's *Commonplace Book*, which in current editions are numbered 130, 131, and 134. The town's name ties partly to a passage in Holmes's *Guardian Angel*, describing a "Witch's Hollow," illuminated at night by the phosphorescence of "fox-fire." This, at any rate, I find more likely than Murray's suggestion that the actual town of Foxboro in distant Norfolk County is involved. Also, I believe that the adjacent towns of Boxford and Topsfield—which are just northwest of the place where I think Lovecraft put Arkham, and east of the "north-central" region—had some influence. Topsfield, in particular, is noted in period guidebooks for its triangular town green, which appears to be a feature of the sketch-map's "Foxfield."

Of Dunwich and Aylesbury

Upon the "channel coast" of Suffolk, in England, the better maps will show a rather small town labeled usually as Dunwich, though sometimes as Dunwick. Anciently, Dunwich was a great city-seaport, a shire-town and seat of a bishopric, which came to be substantially damaged by storms in the late thirteenth century. From then to the present, relentless ingressions of tide have rent and swallowed Dunwich bit by bit, without satiation.

August Derleth, in the early '70s, would seem the first to suggest the possibility of a connection between Suffolk's sunken seaport and Lovecraft's same-named fiction (*Arkham Collector*, Spring 1971). But it is Kenneth W. Faig, Jr., I believe, who first pinpointed historic and folkloric elements of the region which could have engaged Lovecraft's interest, as well as means by which this lore might have come to his notice. In a 1977 article Faig presented several verses from Algernon Charles Swinburne's "By the North Sea," which treat of tombs with "bare white . . . bones protruded, shroudless, down the loose collapsing banks crumble . . . that the sea devours and gives not thanks," and graves which "gape and slide and perish, rank on rank." Faig offered a reasoned scenario in which we may easily imagine Lovecraft finding in the "Dedicatory Epistle" of a widely read edition of Swinburne's poetry the passage in which battered Dunwich in Suffolk is identified as the poet's inspiration.

Faig acknowledges it may also be that the antiquarian inclinations of Lovecraft led him through volumes of English travel, regional history, and color (of which there are many) that weave together Dunwich's fact and folklore. As one who has interviewed a good many English travelers on the subject, I can attest to the widespread knowledge among these tourists of the lore and legendry of Dunwich. I well recall one garrulous Yorkshireman telling of "t' bells as many heard a'ter dark a-ringin' 'neath t' waves."

Mr. Faig has also speculated that Lovecraft's interest in Dunwich may have sprung from his fascination with the theme of a sunken city, as found in Edgar Allan Poe's poem "The City in the Sea." He cites Lovecraft's "The Temple," which has this theme, and also "The Nightmare Lake," a poem exploiting the fascination of sepulchral discovery.

I find further evidence of Lovecraft's bent in Sonnet VIII of *Fungi from Yuggoth*, "The Port." Also, we can't forget Lovecraft's manifest delight in the "Dell" cemetery in Wilbraham, where the dead are frequently discovered by a rushy sylph-haunted stream, as described in his essay "Mrs. Miniter— Estimates and Recollections."

We must also bear in mdnd that Suffolk's Dunwich is in the very heart of "M. R. James Country." Nearby is Aldeburgh, which informed James's "Seaburgh," where a buried crown "disappeared by the encroaching of the sea" and where also stood "a Saxon royal palace which is now under the sea" in "A Warning to the Curious." Just a few miles further south is Felixtowe, the original of invented "Burnstowe," where "the sea has encroached tremendously . . . all along that bit of coast" in "'Oh, Whistle, and I'll Come to You, My Lad.'" Need we mention that the Bunstowe setting is again used in "The Tractate Middoth"; or that "Rats" happens in coastal Suffolk's Thorpness; or that others of James's tales are recognizably East Anglian in their settings?

I would certainly be hard pressed to put a precise order to the steps by which a writer of Lovecraft's disposition might have come to know of ancient Dunwich. But the steps themselves are easy enough guessed out. Whether by way of Swinburne, Poe, James, or the travel guides, Lovecraft had ample means with which he could acquaint himself with legendary Dunwich and its association with the notion of submerged or decaying towns.

While I am fairly certain that Lovecraft knew of England's Dunwich before he set about preparing his rural Massachusetts tales, I strongly suspect that a few more elements entered in to reinforce the appropriateness of this name for his setting. We know he was fascinated by the concept of a modern survival of ancient witch-cults, as suggested in the horror fiction of Arthur Machen and others. Particularly engaging to Lovecraft were the images of occult societies persisting in hilly ruralities, present-day continuances of actual Graeco-Roman deities hidden in dark valleys and shunned uplands, where standing stones encircle hideous rites. He read E. F. Benson's "The Man Who Went Too Far," which has a dweller by the "River Fawn" among remote sylvan hills, striving to regain the lost communion 'twixt man and nature, who dies 'neath the cloven feet of Sylvanus Cocidius himself. He read in Algernon Blackwood's *Pan's Garden* and "The Regeneration of Lord Ernie" (in *Incredible Adventures*), where elemental spirit-worship remains active in wilderness High Places; ditto John Buchan's *Witch Wood* (1927), hinting revenants of diabolism centered on a black stone in a landscape of old woods, "bare hilltops, bleak at season" in the Highlands. Other recent books of interest were Leonard Cline's *The Dark Chamber,* telling of an attempt to retrogress to a pre-human state that is foiled when the celebrant is savaged by his own mastiff, and Herbert Gorman's *The Place Called Dagon,* which involves witchcraft, "Black Books," "Sacred Goats," and a monolithic "altar" in a hill-encircled cul de sac of "western New England."

Such as these, along with the (then-respected) fancies of Margaret Murray, would doubtless influence some of Lovecraft's tales to come—but no author more so that the Welsh mystic, Arthur Machen. We know this from Lovecraft's wholesale adoption of Machen's descriptive lexicon of outland features. Machen cannot be the first to write of "wild" hills or "domed" hills, but he used the terms far more than was common. Remote and uncultivated uplands and woods are "wild"; wrought limestone is vested with subterranean meaning; a river fed by hidden springs courses in hieroglyphic patterns upon the valley's floor—these are the common backgrounds in many of Machen's tales, harkening to his rural Welsh boyhood. And here he may play out the witch-sabbats, appearances of daemonic spawn-of-deities-coupled-with-the-daughters-of-man and "praeternatural transmutations," the recurring burden of Machen's horror fiction.

In "The Great God Pan" most of these Archadian-Panic elements are brought into play as we encounter the daemonic aftermath of the union of a scientist's daughter and the god Pan. Helen Vaughan (rhymes with "faun," y'know) is discovered responsible for several suicides and pressed to take her own life. As death comes on, the woman's anatomy undergoes a ghastly shape-shifting of retrograde transformation which reveals the archtypal form of horrid Pan—just prior to the body's total dissolution.

Here was a theme Lovecraft could build upon. His eventual answer, of course, would be "The Dunwich Horror," written in 1928. As we have long understood, the sylvan backdrop for Lovecraft's unique development of the "rural deities" theme is founded amid the spectral hills surrounding Wilbraham. Gneissic "domed hills," "Cyclopean" stoneworks, scoured slopes, "hidden" brooklets, "snaking" river, huddled houses—all the Machenesque props were present in Wilbraham, along with a genuine (even then rare) "covered bridge" spanning the Chicopee at the village's northern approach. Enter upon this stage the favorite son: "dark," "goatish," thick-lipped, pointy-eared Wilbur Whateley, with his "dark trunks" and "fringed belt," as the entity neither human, beast, nor daemon (though confounded in tradition with all of these), and this newer, more "rationalized" Arcadae Panic is under way. However, before Lovecraft even set foot in Wilbraham, he was writing of a Machen-like countryside.

There seems to me little doubt that Lovecraft deliberately sought out New England counterparts to the old-world settings Machen and other writers had so powerfully employed. There is nothing new here: Dickens vested London with a special glamour, making it a place where wonders occurred in curious byways; Stevenson followed Dickens in this with his *New Arabian Nights;* Machen followed Stevenson with *The Three Impostors,* and Lovecraft would come to follow Machen.

His friend of several years, Edith Miniter, was probably quite helpful in this regard. A native of west-central Massachusetts, Miniter wrote short stories that drew upon her considerable knowledge as a New England folklorist and antiquary. It sees likely that it was Miniter who led Lovecraft to explore Boston's North End where he would find the "grassless parks," enclosed "courts," dark cobbled alleyways and tottering, jettied houses, which were old Boston's answer to the quaint London features employed in Machen's fiction. Lovecraft would use these to advantage in "Pickman's Model," which, in fact, opens with a thoroughly Machenesque dialogue. At any rate, I cannot doubt that Miniter, who knew Lovecraft doted upon such things, told him of the mysterious "dark days" of Monson, which fell early in September of 1881. Guidebooks of the period tell of that sun which rose as

> a ball of fire and by 7:30 a.m. was entirely obscured. The sky had a ghastly appearance, vegetation [had] the appearance of a thick coat of green paint. Lights were needed by 10:30 a.m. . . . [the] flames of a kerosene lamp had a peculiar bluish brimstone look . . . red flowers took a salmon color.

The "peculiar light" caused headaches and faintness among many and "bells sounded unusually loud."

In Monson's "dark days," combined with the reports of the Amherst meteor fall of August 13, 1819, described in Charles Fort's *The Book of the Damned,* Lovecraft had a sufficiency of excellently dreadful local color to enhance the realism of a country tale in the mode of Arthur Machen. And he could have had this information before ever he saw Wilbraham. Another influence was, I believe, a stark, barren, windswept valley that seemed a wound in the heart of a wild, hilly woodland before a city reservoir covered much of it. It lies less than a two hours' walk from where Lovecraft placed "Arkham." In Lovecraft's day, this "devil's garden" or "goblin's hop yard" or "Satan's yarb yard," as such rocky sand-scoured lots are traditionally named, went by a number of less common descriptions, including "deserted village," "Scottish moor," "little Salisbury Plain," "barren waste," "Dogtown Common," and (rather unusual) "the blasted heath." The full story is interesting, but somewhat digressive; I shall tell it another time— but I mention it, because the name this place is best known by, "Dogtown Common," very likely reminded Lovecraft of an invention of Machen's called "Dunwich Common" in a very engaging novel called *The Terror*.

I suspect it no coincidence that when Lovecraft described his recently finished "The Colour out of Space" to a friend, he used the word "terror": "something falls from the sky and terror broods" (*SL* 2.120). And in the tale itself the word is often employed in describing the frightful element.

Though highly original in development and mood, "The Colour out of Space" borrows and reworks a number of images from *The Terror*. Machen's setting is a "wild and scattered region of outland hills," "secret and hidden valleys," and streams "from some hidden well." There are "deep shadowy woods" and fields "stretching up" toward "wild and desolate" hillsides that fall into "sudden dips and hollows." Ancient cottages are said to be "remote from all other habitations," some to be "pulled down or . . . allowed to slide into ruin."

The primary setting is a sixteenth-century farmhouse, framed with "Ilex" (or holm oak) trees, ash, and pine, and having a nearby well which is famous for the best water in the country. The unknown "terror" descending upon the farmers manifests itself in a number of seemingly unrelated forms and modes of attack. Certain trees appear to move, though the air is "very still . . . so still that not a leaf stirred." Another tree has "changed its shape . . . since the setting of the sun" and is later thought "no longer there." In darkness, some leafage is "starred" with "wonderful appearances of lights and colours." Some boughs are "starred with burning"; a "quivering movement" is seen within it "though the air [is] at a dead calm," and "little worms of fire" seem to shoot through it. A hedgerow of trees has "lighted up somehow." A bystander wonders "what is all this colour and burning?"

Sound familiar? Also in *The Terror* an uncanny light like "white fire" flashes forth from a coastal farmhouse. At evening "a sort of brightness on the ground" is noticed—"a dim sort of light like . . . glow worms." Dead bodies turn up with faces perhaps "eaten away" by "strong acids"; others are mangled as though trampled by a mad beast; and previously gentle horses and dogs go mad, turning upon their masters. Some bodies appear asphyxiated as if by drowning—yet far from water. An entire family, the Griffiths, has turned mad, dying from thirst, though but yards from the famous sweet well. A prominent professor from the "university town" is called in to gage the mystery: a "Z ray" is hypothesized as the cause; later a heretofore unknown gas is supposed. And the famous well is briefly suspect. Finally, the terror is abated, though Machen hints it "may rise again."

So we are left with a sizable heap of stepping-stones. Enough to ford the stream; need we know their original order? Let us imagine Lovecraft knows of Dunwich in Suffolk from English travel books. He knows also of "Dogtown Common" from various local guidebooks. His interest is intensified by Swinburne, Poe, and James. He is reminded of the region as he hears of the impending flooding of the valleys north of Wilbraham from Mrs. Miniter. And he is reminded again of the name when he reads Machen's *The Terror*, whose invented "Dunwich Common" recalls Dogtown Common and its "blasted heath." He begins to think of Dogtown Common as the local model for a story involving an Amherst-type meteor as the cause of unknown terror to a rural household. Perhaps Mrs. Miniter's "dark days" lore could be worked in. And a reservoir, modeled partly on the recent Scituate, Rhode Island, plan (1926), might be brought forward at the end to "clean up."

That is one scenario. But, in fact, we could rearrange the order of these stepping-stones a number of ways and still arrive safely (and plausibly) at "Dunwich" each time.

Of course, "The Colour out of Space" contains no "Dunwich." It is an Essex County story, and relies on the author's familiarity with that region of the state. Set in Arkham's countryside, it has no need of an additional invented town.

But a year later, Lovecraft had seen Wilbraham—and seen its potential as a setting for a rural-deities tale after the general manner of Arthur Machen. For this reason, he utilizes a Machen-like terminology in describing Wilbraham in letters to friends. He is seeking and finding ways to work up a word-portrait of an imaginary decadent farm village of Machenesque pattern, but with color and details of history and folklore modeled after Mrs. Miniter's home town.

Again, whatever the order, a weighty pattern of associations is established. And in such a context, "Dunwich" as the name for a New England town visited by the author's rationalized version of "Panic Horrors" seems all but inevitable. It is Old World. It is associated with physical and social decay. It has come to the notice of writers and poets Lovecraft admired. Its use would be an additional salute to Machen—an homage.

In light of these considerations, is there any reason for sunken Greenwich, Massachusetts, to be involved? My answer may surprise you: a tentative "yes." First off, Lovecraft is known to have passed through Greenwich as he rode the "rabbit run" train southward from Athol toward Wilbraham. Greenwich was one (actually two) of the stations in the doomed valley where the train is known to have stopped, however briefly. Second, though this is only speculation, Lovecraft may have mentioned Greenwich among the other doomed valley towns in a Machenesque language he often applies to the central Massachusetts and southern Vermont landscape. Unlike "Dunwich," however, Greenwich Center was not part of the north central region. It was not huddled against domed hills: it was spread upon a broad river plain, well east of the nearest hill. It was not a particularly old settlement. There is really little here to compare with Wilbraham: Greenwich quietly excuses itself from the running.

Nevertheless, I can at least imagine Lovecraft, who always took pains to name his fictional places "wholly and realistically characteristic" of real places (*SL* 3.433), noting the "tone" of town names in this general region, such as Greenwich, Dana (as perhaps also Winchendon and Dunstable), and thinking "Dunwich" would not sound out of place among these. Possibly he also noted the local (orthographic) pronunciation of "Greenwich" (as opposed to "Grennich" variants elsewhere) and allowed his "Dunwich" to be sounded as spelt on that basis. Since the 1930s, Lovecraftians have labored assiduously to find the link between lost Greenwich and brooding "Dunwich." In recent years Andrew E. Rothovius, Kenneth Faig, Jr., Donald R. Burleson, and lately Will Murray have discussed or remarked upon the enticing similarity of names. I am in agreement with Faig and Burleson that some such tie is likely. But I suspect it is a modest tie.

As "Dunwich," according to Lovecraft, is based roughly on the countryside east of Springfield, "say, Wilbraham, Hampden, and Monson," so "Dunwich" would appear to be a satellite of "Aylesbury." Springfield is a county seat—a "shiretown," where court matters and records concerning such county towns as Wilbraham are handled. When Wilbur Whateley dies, a report of death is filed at "the court-house in Aylesbury" (*DH* 176), from which we may reasonably infer that "Aylesbury" is the county seat of this north-central region. It is at least reasonable to suppose that "Aylesbury," if not actually modeled on Springfield, "at least stands in" for the functional aspects of Springfield. Also, it is difficult not to suppose Lovecraft had in mind the southerly loop through Wilbraham which forms a sightseeing detour for travelers on Route 20, the old "Springfield Pike." The winding of stone wall-bordered roads through rolling hills to the "plains beyond" closely parallels the description of the route of HPL's hypothetical traveler in the opening of "The Dunwich Horror."

A tale of standing stones ought to recall Avebury and also "Stonehenge" on the Salisbury Plain. Salisbury (see also Trollope and James), of course, is already a town name in Essex County. Possibly Lovecraft thought of Aylesbury (from the Buckinghamshire market town) as a good "tone" equivalent, since it ties the forms of "Avebury" and "Salisbury."

His Principal Hobby

For years now, Lovecraft has been hoarding precious coin in order to visit or revisit these towns, sometimes in the company of friends—and broadcasting far and wide, by letter and postcard, the news of these visits. To a friend he writes, "I hope you can see some of these old towns some time—they are my principal hobby." If this is some elaborate "ruse" to conceal the influence of places like Shutesbury or Grafton, then certainly, no man has walked so long a journey 'round the cowshed to reach so questionable a goal.

While I have a deal of faith in the alternative to Mr. Murray's reading that I have offered, it is by no means the final word on this subject. I can say little more than that I think this reading plausible and consistent with Lovecraft's text and the geographic realities of his day. Its usefulness either will or will not become apparent to future explorers. I shall only claim for it the essential virtue of any potentially useful reading: agreement with ascertainable fact. Some may be disappointed with a relatively open and candid Lovecraft. A well-mounted assault upon the institution of common sense has never lacked a following, as popular discussions in the realms of fringe science continually demonstrate. But, in the long run, I believe that scholars will abide by the interpretation that stands up to the light of scrutiny and reason. Again, we needn't rule out the likes of Oakham and Rockport; in the long run they rule themselves out. As one sometimes privileged to escort interested readers through these settings, I can testify that a good part of what Lovecraft described exists today in much the same form it had when he discovered it. Indeed, this is the good part.

Quaint archaic Kingsport, where "solemn buoys toll free in the white aether of faery," is here to be enjoyed in all its "antediluvian" splendor in the village of terraced Marblehead. And just west of this, crumbling witch-haunted Arkham, by the rushing Miskatonic, has survived that horror which seeped through centuries as witch-cursed Salem, where the credulous yet delight in soft-serve sorceries. We shouldn't neglect dying, rumour-shadowed Innsmouth, which persists undead today as blear-visioned, palingenic Newburyport. Far afield, beyond busy Bolton, dank-wooded, fungeous Foxfield, and sleepy Sefton, we wind among the huddled hills outskirting decadent Dunwich by following the old "Springfield Pike" (Route 20) to wayside Wilbraham, where rolling, briar-bordered farm lots brood out the centuries. Massachusetts offers so many treasures of Lovecraftian setting, I cannot think why an informed traveler would choose to spend even a moment of his precious time among the currently proffered alternatives to the writer's own professed itinerary.

Works Cited

Faig, Kenneth W., Jr. "Swinburniana Leads to Dunwichiana." *De Tenebris* No. 3 (March 1977): 2–3, 6–10, 18–21.

Lovecraft, H. P. *Essential Solitude: The Letters of H. P. Lovecraft and August Derleth.* Ed. David E. Schultz and S. T. Joshi. New York: Hippocampus Press, 2008. 2 vols.

———. *Letters to Alfred Galpin.* Ed. S. T. Joshi and David E. Schultz. New York: Hippocampus Press, 2005.

Murray, Will. "I Found Innsmouth!" *Crypt of Cthulhu* No. 57 (St. John's Eve 1988):10–14.

———. "In Search of Arkham Country." *Lovecraft Studies* No. 13 (Fall 1986): 54–67.

———. "In Search of Arkham Country Revisited." *Lovecraft Studies* Nos. 19/20 (Fall 1989): 65–69.

———. "Lovecraft's New England: Haunted Backwaters." In *H. P. Lovecraft Centennial Guidebook,* ed. Jon B. Cooke. Pawtucket, RI: Montilla Publications, 1990. 21–24.

———. "Lovecraft's Arkham Country." In *H. P. Lovecraft Centennial Conftrence Proceedings,* ed. S. T. Joshi. West Warwick, RI: Necronomicon Press, 1991. 15–17.

———. "Where Was Foxfield?" *Lovecraft Studies* No. 3 (Fall 1995): 18–25, 38.

[*Lovecraft Studies* No. 39 (Summer 1998): 1–20]

Where Was Foxfield?

By Will Murray

H. P. Lovecraft filled his brooding fictional version of central Massachusetts with many portentous places—Arkham, Dunwich, Kingsport, Innsmouth, and other, lesser, hamlets. Without question the most obscure of these otherwise nameless places was Foxfield, Massachusetts.

You won't find Foxfield on any map of Massachusetts in our reality or Lovecraft's. But it is as authentic as Arkham, as remote as Dunwich, and as elusive as Aylesbury—a town mentioned in passing in "The Dunwich Horror," the *Fungi from Yuggoth*, but nowhere else. Foxfield is not the setting of any extent story penned for *Weird Tales*, but H. P. Lovecraft created it as surely as he created any of his more famous backwoods conjurings.

We would never know about Foxfield were it not for S. T. Joshi, who in June of 1994 happened to be prowling the Arkham House transcripts of Lovecraft's letters at Brown University's John Hay Library and came across a photostatic copy of a map of Foxfield. Clearly drawn by Lovecraft in his own crabbed writing, it was labeled:

Plan of Foxfield—for possible fictional use

No story set in Foxfield ever emerged from Lovecraft's pen. If he attempted any such endeavor, he presumably destroyed the abortive start, as he sometimes claimed to have done with certain unnamed tales. But thankfully the map survives, and through it we can catch a tantalizing glimpse of a corner of Arkham Country that would otherwise have been irretrievably lost.

The Foxfield plan differs from the surviving maps of Arkham or Innsmouth in that it shows a decidedly more rustic and less developed town than the fictional analogues to Salem and Marblehead that Lovecraft envisioned. In fact, Foxfield consists largely of a tiny village at one end of what is labeled a "state road." The map is dominated by this unnamed road, which forks just before it crosses the "Gorge of Passiquamstook." The few named sites lie on or near this gorge.

Curiously enough, the plan is laid out on a tilted axis, with the eastern compass point at the top of plan and the north-south line running left to right. Evidently Lovecraft envisioned the story narrator (who can doubt one would be involved?) traveling down the unnamed road only to be confronted by the fork in the road and very likely an Ominous Choice.

The northeast fork is labeled "old road" and crosses the "upper falls" of the Passiquamstook via a "rickety wooden bridge" before the way rises steeply. Branching off the old road are a valley where lie "traces" of an "abandoned road" whose bridge is "gone." On the other side of this gap lies a "steep hill" overlooking the "ruins of Shubael Tyler's mill."[1] The mill is naturally built on the gorge. Lovecraft provides the greatest amount of detail on this locality. Built in 1736, it was abandoned before 1767. It sits at the foot of the steep hill on another "abandoned road" that runs parallel to the gorge along its east bank. Apparently perched low on the hill is something Lovecraft cryptically labeled "reputed site of house built 1693."

The other fork, labeled "new road," crosses the gorge via a "concrete bridge" leading to a "declivity & Gardner's Brook," which runs parallel to and east of the Passiquamstook. For some reason Lovecraft thought it necessary to record that this road runs downhill as it approaches the gorge while the other side is graded and hilly. Ultimately the road runs all the way to witch-haunted Arkham on the Massachusetts coast.

Between the fork sits John Sawyer's mill, dated 1751, on the "lower falls" of the Passiquamstook. Like Shubael Tyler's mill, it sits on the eastern bank. But this mill is not described as a ruin, which suggests it may still be intact or operational.

Fortunately for us, Lovecraft exactly places Foxfield in relation to the rest of Arkham Country. According to his scribbled directions, to the southeast lies Arkham, while the Miskatonic River is oddly enough due south. This is curious because it strongly suggests the Miskatonic River runs along an east-west course, contrary to the three great Massachusetts rivers most often suggested as its inspiration—the Swift, the Housatonic, and the Connecticut, all of which run north-south. While it is possible that the Miskatonic so winds and meanders that for a stretch its course deviates significantly from a southerly course, the river does run easterly to empty out into the Atlantic at Arkham according to Lovecraft's own map of Arkham as published in *Marginalia*. This is confirmed by a line in "The Strange High House in the Mist" that refers to a section of the Massachusetts coast "where the great Miskatonic pours out of the plains

---

[1] The name Shubael appears to be of Biblical coinage. It means "captive of God." A tyler is a stone mason.

past Arkham" (*D* 277).

"Aylesbury-Dunwich" are due west—the direction from which the narrator is most likely to enter Foxfield. Aylesbury could be Shutesbury, a town west of the Quabbin reservoir. More probably, it is derived from Shrewsbury, which, although east of the Quabbin area, was the terminus of an important main road connecting Boston with the middle part of the state. In any case, this forked road may be the Aylesbury pike whose junction is mentioned in "The Dunwich Horror." In fact, the Arkham map depicts an Aylesbury Street that runs westerly out of Arkham proper. One assumes it is a connector road to the Aylesbury pike.[2]

Due north lies a town called Belton. This is apparently not to be confused with Bolton, an actual Massachusetts town cited in "Herbert West—Reanimator" and "The Colour out of Space," and said by Lovecraft to exist in the Miskatonic Valley. Lovecraft clearly wrote Belton. The name perhaps derives from Belchertown, a town south of the Swift River area and the present-day Quabbin Reservoir.

The Gorge of Passiquamstook runs through eastern Foxfield on a straight north-south line, as does Gardner's Brook. Both appear to be tributaries of the Miskatonic River. South-pointing arrows labeled "to Miskatonic" adorn both waterways. Like the famous Miskatonic, the Passiquamstook is a coinage that combines authentic Algonquian Indian root words into an original but meaningful original.[3] The root *passi* equates to muddy or mirey. *Quam* equals "long." And *took* (sometimes spelled *tic* or *tuck*) is a very common root meaning "river." Thus, Passiquamstook translates as "long muddy river." This suggests that the Passiquamstook is a dying or dead river and that its decline led to the abandonment of both mills.

The village portion of the map is remarkably bare of detail. A short, wide, nameless street right-angles off the state road, leading to Belton. An-

---

[2] The main road running from Boston to New York State in the days before turnpikes passed through Shrewsbury to stop one town over in Worcester. In its earliest incarnation it was called the Bay Path. Originally an Indian trail, it was widened for ox carts circa 1670. It was also known as Old Bay Road and Stage Road. A later turnpike, the Sixth Massachusetts Turnpike, picked up in Shrewsbury and travels west to Amherst through the heart of what is now the Quabbin area, including Oakham, Greenwich, and Pelham. It is possible that in Lovecraft's Massachusetts this was one continuous road called the Aylesbury pike.

[3] In my article "Roots of the Miskatonic" (*Crypt of Cthulhu* No. 45 [Candlemas 1987]), I speculated as to what Lovecraft might have meant by "red" mountain. (Miskatonic means "Place of Red Mountains.") It seems the area surrounding Deerfield is noted for its conical red sandstone hills, the most famous of which, Sugar Loaf, lies southeast of present-day Deerfield. These may be the inspiration for Round Mountain and the other strangely rounded summits described in "The Dunwich Horror."

other narrower street connects the far end of this to the state road, so that a grassy wedge is formed between them. This is labeled "green"—obviously a rustic town green. Neither street is named, but the three-way intersection is lined with well-spaced squares suggesting houses, so there is no escaping that this constitutes a village. That nothing here is named suggests that Lovecraft foresaw the story action bypassing this inhabited stretch.

Any attempt to date the Foxfield map is strictly conjectural. It is probably no earlier than 1927 because the names Dunwich and Aylesbury are mentioned—almost inescapably suggesting that Lovecraft drew the plan after penning "The Dunwich Horror" in the summer of 1928. However, the forked road appears identical to the one mentioned early in "The Colour out of Space," written in March of 1927:

> There was once a road over the hills and through the valleys, that ran straight where the blasted heath is now; but people ceased to use it and a new road was laid curving far toward the south. Traces of the old one can still be found amidst the weeds of a returning wilderness, and some of them will doubtless linger even when half the hollows are flooded for the new reservoir. (*DH* 54)

This suggests that the locale of "Colour" is very near Foxfield, if not identical to it. Lovecraft never gave that particular setting a name, but the absence of any blasted heath on the Foxfield map indicates that the plan is either highly localized or at worst closely adjacent to the terrain described in "Colour."

Whatever the exact date, the map is a product of the late 1920s. But what about the inspiration for Foxfield? Like certain other Arkham Country place-names, Foxfield is a portmanteau word, a conflation of two existing place-names to create an authentic-sounding but non-existent original, much the way Kingsport for example seems to be a conflation of the Massachusetts coastal towns of Kingston and Rockport. (It should be mentioned, however, that Kingsport is also the name of a traditional New England design for a decorative stairway baluster.)

Foxfield clearly derives its name in part from the eastern Massachusetts town of Foxborough (sometimes spelled Foxboro). Incorporated in 1778, Foxborough was named after British Parliamentarian Charles James Fox. Inasmuch as Fox was a staunch defender of the American Colonies, Lovecraft is unlikely to have named his town after a Rebel sympathizer. Foxborough is also far from the Miskatonic Valley area and is otherwise not remarkable, having been cobbled together from land taken from various surrounding towns.

The derivation of "field" is more difficult to determine. There are as many fields in the Bay State as there are seaports like Plymouth and Yarmouth, which lent their final syllable to ramshackle Innsmouth. There is for example a Greenfield, an Enfield, and a Deerfield, among others, all in north-central Massachusetts.

Enfield is very suggestive because it is one of the four Swift River Valley towns that were "discontinued" by the Metropolitan District Commission in the 1930s to make way for the Quabbin Reservoir—the very reservoir whose coming is foreshadowed at the end of "The Colour out of Space." Originally known as Quabbin, Enfield was settled around 1730. In 1787, it became the South Parish of Greenwich (the likely doublet for Lovecraft's Dunwich, which was also swallowed by the Quabbin) and incorporated in 1816.

Enfield is a likely candidate because it grew up around a grist mill and boasted saw, box, and grain mills, the earliest of which date from 1770. The first saw mill was built by Ephraim Woodward. A cider mill, built by Abijah Crombie, sat at the foot of Great Quabbin hill and was situated near a "skeleton bridge," according to Francis H. Underwood's 1896 narrative of old Enfield, Quabbin. Either might have been the inspiration for Shubael Tyler's mill. On the other hand, I can't imagine too many vintage Massachusetts settlements not equipped with mills—or wooden bridges over inconvenient rivers.

The most populous of the four discontinued towns, Enfield was a farm town comprised of an upper and a lower village. It was named after a early settler, Robert Field. (The prefix "En" was added, evidently out of Puritan modesty.) The town was bulldozed into non-existence and declared officially defunct on April 28, 1938. All that remain are the tops of its picturesque hills, which break the Quabbin's surface in the form of lonely islands. Two state routes—21 and 109—passed through Enfield during its twilight years, either of which night have inspired the state road on Lovecraft's map. A triangular green such as Lovecraft drew did exist in Enfield, but it was exceedingly small and it is unlikely that it constituted a green in the traditional sense of a town common. And if one were looking for the equivalents to Lovecraft's Passiquamstook and Gardner's Brook, they would be the Swift River and Beaver Brook, both of which ran through Enfield.

But is Enfield Foxfield? My past explorations into Lovecraft Country have demonstrated beyond reasonable doubt that he typically combined two or more locales to create his mythical hamlets, as he did when he combined Newburyport and Gloucester to create Innsmouth, or the Wilbraham area and Greenwich in order to arrive at rustic Dunwich. So, if Foxfield follows the expected pattern, we should look for another locale. Foxborough seems unfruitful. It is too far from the Miskatonic Valley region and all that Lovecraft seems to have gotten from it was the prefix "Fox."

A very suggestive Foxfield analogue might be Deerfield—and not simply due to the apparent animal motif in the town name. It happened to be one of Lovecraft's favorite Massachusetts localities. Located in the Connecticut River Valley, just a few miles west of the Swift River-Quabbin area, Deerfield is a unique locality, even today. It is more properly called Old Deerfield or, as Lovecraft called it, "Archaick Deerfield." Even before he first laid eyes on Deerfield, Lovecraft's letters mentioned it often. Waxing poetic in a letter to Donald Wandrei on March 13, 1927, he spoke of "the region of the upper Connecticut Valley where ancient Deerfield & Hadley dream. This Connecticut-Valley region has an architectural school all its own—examples of which I have of course seen only in museums" (*Mysteries of Time and Spirit* 51).

Visiting W. Paul Cook in Athol in August of 1927, Lovecraft first entered Deerfield. "I'll bet I'm getting three times as big a kick out of the Swift & Deerfield valleys as you did!" he enthused in another letter to Wandrei (*Mysteries of Time and Spirit* 151). "Deerfield is the summit of my earthly ambition—I've just gone broke on postcards!" He was referring to what was then and is still today called simply "The Street"—an elm-shaded thoroughfare dotted with Colonial-era homes painted in the sober reds, blues, and grays of the eighteenth century. Once most rural Massachusetts towns boasted of elm tree arches running down their main streets. Today, Deerfield's 200-year-old natural arcade is the only survivor in the entire state.

Deerfield architecture is an admixture of Colonial and Federal-style homes featuring unique properties—double-leaf doors and decorative fanlights of bull's-eye glass—seen nowhere else outside the Connecticut Valley. These simple designs are framed by baroque carven doorways profuse with keystones, rosettes, and classical pilasters, surmounted by distinctive pediments of the triangular and broken-scroll styles.

On subsequent trips to Athol in 1928 and '29, Lovecraft revisited Deerfield, obviously charmed by its main street. Even today, one can walk its elm-vaulted mile hemmed in by wild hills and valleys, and be easily lulled into thinking one were walking through an eighteenth-century village. To Lovecraft, it must have been the closest thing to heaven on earth.

Deerfield's past is anything but celestial. The town's history is steeped in tragedy and a commonplace horror. Originally it was called Pocumtuck, after the Indian tribe who inhabited the region. (HPL mentioned the Pocumtucks in "The Dunwich Horror.") Settled in the 1660s, it was the westernmost colonial outpost in the whole of Massachusetts at that time. By 1674, it was known as Deerfield. It was a thriving village where tobacco and pumpkins were raised until the advent of the King Philip's War, followed by thirty years of French and Indian attacks. Raided many times, after the Bloody Brook Massacre of September 1675 Deerfield was completely abandoned for seven years. During the infamous massacre of 1704, a combined raiding party of 200 French soldiers and 142 Catholic Indians attacked Deerfield and burnt it down. Of its 291 residents, 48 were killed outright and 111 forcibly marched to Montreal in the dead of winter. Twenty more died on that hellish trek.

Deerfield never fully recovered from that catastrophe. Although re-claimed and rebuilt, it never again thrived and is today an historical town preserved in the manner of Colonial Williamsburg, to which Lovecraft once compared it favorably. The town did boast several mills in its later phase, including a grist mill built in 1709–10, a corn mill in 1714, and a saw mill in the same year. Older than Enfield, its chronology is compatible with the 1693 house site noted on the Foxfield plan.

The 1693 date may be significant. According to "The Dunwich Horror," Dunwich Village was settled in 1692 by expatriates from Salem. Might not Foxfield also have been spawned by unhanged witches? In the same story Lovecraft wrote:

> Dunwich is indeed ridiculously old—older by far than any of the communities within thirty miles of it. South of the village one may still spy the cellar walls and chimney of the ancient Bishop house, which was built before 1700; whilst the ruins of the mill at the falls, built in 1806, form the most modern piece of architecture to be seen. (*DH* 158)

These details suggest that Foxfield antedates Dunwich and lies more than thirty miles from it—unless of course one discounts Foxfield as a true community. It is interesting that here Lovecraft might be describing Foxfield, but for some of the dates and compass directions.[4] Although west of the Quabbin, Deerfield lies firmly in the general area that is generally called Lovecraft Country. The town of Whateley is immediately south of

---

[4] Along those lines, it is worth mentioning that near the Bear's Den, a hidden waterfall in North New Salem that HPL visited in the summer of 1928 and mentioned in "The Dunwich Horror," the ruins of a corn mill built by David Lawson in the mid- to late 1880s still stand. It is one of three mills which stood in that area overlooked by a house on a hill. (The author would like to acknowledge the kind assistance of S. T. Joshi, David Schultz, as well as Don and Mollie Burleson in the preparation of this article.)

present-day Deerfield. And below it, the Wilbraham-Hampden-Monson area, which inspired and gave color to Dunwich. These are all Connecticut Valley towns, which exerted a peculiar fascination on HPL, as was evidenced by his 1934 memoir, "Mrs. Miniter—Estimates and Recollections":

> . . . the Connecticut Valley's backwaters present typical and tenacious phases of life not to be found elsewhere; phases contrasting sharply with the brisk, well-ordered, seaward-gazing, and often adventurous life of coastal New England and its vivid old ports.
>
> In the first Puritan days this region was a trackless wilderness covered with black woods whose depths the settlers' fancy peopled with unknown horrors and evil shadows. Then the Bay Path was hewn through to the settlements on the Connecticut, and after King Philip's War thin streams of pioneers began to trickle along it and branch off from it; cutting faint roadways and clearing meagre farmsteads on the silent rocky hillsides. Grim, low-pitched, unpainted farmhouses sprang up in the lee of craggy slopes, their dim, small-paned windows looking secretively off across leagues of loneliness. Life was hard and practical, and contact with the world very slight. Old tales and thoughts and words and ways persisted, and people remembered odd fancies which others had forgotten. (*CE* 1.379)

Suggestively, Lovecraft discovered Deerfield between writing the key Miskatonic Valley stories, "The Colour out of Space" and "The Dunwich Horror." Even the scant names mentioned on the Foxfield map—Sawyer and Gardner—are reflected those same stories. (Gardner, by the way, is a familiar Enfield name. And John Sawyer may be a corruption of the name of one of Enfield's earliest settlers, John Sawin.) In fact, there is an unmistakable adumbration of the Gorge of Passiquamstook early in "The Dunwich Horror" where Lovecraft warns that "Gorges and ravines of problematical depth intersect the way, and the crude wooden bridges always seem of dubious safety" (*DH* 156).

Obviously Foxfield is very close to the heart of Lovecraft Country—if not geographically the heart itself. For it is surrounded by all the great evocative place-names that define Lovecraft's Miskatonic Valley—Arkham, Dunwich, Aylesbury, and the mighty Miskatonic itself.

We may never know for certain what H. P. Lovecraft had in mind when he laid out Foxfield. His commonplace book makes no mention of any story centering around old mills. Two 1925 entries (130 and 134) about a New England region called "Witches' Hollow" are too general to point to Foxfield, although one does talk of a teacher who takes the wrong road and ends up in a weird hollow. And the 1693 home site does make one wonder if fugitive Salem (or Arkham) witches might not have constructed it. Entry 131, "Phosphorescence of decaying wood—call'd in New England 'foxfire,'" is suggestive but inconclusive. The town of Foxborough is the most plausible and likely source for the place-name.

Still, in the absence of a plot to go with the Foxfield map or a locale to go with "Witches' Hollow" (which was planned as a novel, by the way) the two do converge more than they diverge. But that is not the only unwritten story that does. The brief undated premise called "The Round Tower" (incorporated by August Derleth into his novel *The Lurker at the Threshold*) is also of interest. It reads:

> S. of Arkham is a cylindrical tower of stone with conical roof—perhaps 12 feet across & 20 ft. high. There has been a great arched opening (quarter way up) but it is sealed with masonry. The thing rises from the bottom of a densely wooded ravine once the bed of an extinct tributary of the Miskatonic. Whole region feared & shunned by rustics. Tales of fate of persons climbing into tower before opening could be sealed. Indian legends speak of it as existing as long as they could remember—supposed to be older than mankind. Legend that it was built by Old Ones (shapeless & gigantic amphibia) & that it was once under water. Dressed stone masonry shews odd & unknown technique. Geometrical designs on large stone above sealed opening utterly baffling. Supposed to house a treasure or something which Old Ones value highly. Possibly nothing of interest to human beings. Rumours that it connects to hidden caverns where water still exists. Perhaps Old Ones still alive. Base seems to extend indefinitely downward—ground level having somewhat risen. Has not been seen for ages, since everyone shuns the ravine. (*CE* 5.253)

At first blush, there is not much to connect this idea to the Foxfield plan other than the mention of a ravine and the unnamed extinct tributary of the Miskatonic, both of which suggest the Gorge of Passiquamstook. However, it is generally accepted that the tower that inspired the above was the controversial Viking Tower of Newport, Rhode Island. Briefly, it is a curious round fieldstone tower, presently roofless with a solitary window set high up, just as described. Some think it of Viking origin, others a Colonial windmill built by Governor Benedict Arnold. The latter theory is the one with the most supporting evidence, and for this reason it is popularly known as the Old Stone Mill.

WHERE WAS FOXFIELD?

When you add all those elements together, they certainly fit Lovecraft's map. With one exception: The Foxfield mill is west—not south—of Arkham. Still, the other similarities cannot be ignored.

In the final analysis, Foxfield, like the other Miskatonic localities, is neither here nor there, not quite this nor exactly that, but a subtle amalgam of Deerfield and Enfield with a dash of Foxborough added. We may not have the story Lovecraft intended to weave around this place of mystery, but at least the Foxfield map survives to point our imaginations toward this long-hidden frontier of the unknown.

Works Cited

Lovecraft, H. P., and Donald Wandrei. *Mysteries of Time and Spirit: The Letters of H. P. Lovecraft and Donald Wandrei.* Ed. S. T. Joshi and David E. Schultz. San Francisco: Night Shade, 2002.

[*Lovecraft Studies* No. 33 (Fall 1995): 18–23]

Lovecraft's Two Views of Arkham

By Edward W O'Brien, Jr.

T he imaginary town of Arkham, Massachusetts, seems to be a symbol of all that is mysterious, arcane, and menacing in the writings of Howard Phillips Lovecraft. It appears to function as the ideal home-town for many of his characters and provides an appropriate ambience for his stories. We may ask, then, just how did Lovecraft view his legendary town?

Arkham is actually mentioned in only a few of his fifty-odd stories, and in some of these there is no more than a passing notice of the place. The earliest reference seems to be in "The Festival" (1923).[1] The town is often alluded to cryptically, e.g.,"crumbling, whisper-haunted Arkham." Lovecraft never made an attempt to present a complete picture of Arkham as he did, or very nearly so, for Innsmouth.

Usually Arkham forms a shadowy, indistinct setting, and rarely has much to do with the action itself, except for "The Dreams in the Witch House"—the best source for Arkham material—and "The Thing on the Doorstep," though even here the town is chiefly background, its connection to the tale but slight, its own reality vague and veiled.

Lovecraft sees Arkham from two distinct perspectives, and the two views do not blend together easily. The dominant view, that it is a weird place, is stressed again and again in recurrent imagery. The other view, that Arkham is surprisingly a quite normal town, must be inferred, and I believe logically so, from certain descriptions of the town and its people.

Lovecraft wrote to August Derleth on November 6, 1931: "Vaguely, Arkham corresponds to Salem" (*SL* 3.432). But though its principal evil is the witchcraft of past days, Arkham cannot be a fictional Salem, because Lovecraft named both places in the same sentence of one of his

---

[1] [Lovecraft first cited Arkham in "The Picture in the House" (1920).—Ed.]

stories, and clearly distinguished one from the other (see "Through the Gates of the Silver Key" [*MM* 427–28]). It has been suggested that the "real Arkham—which Lovecraft claimed was settled by witches fleeing the Salem witch trials—was the tiny hamlet of New Salem, settled by emigrés from the original Salem. The nearby town of Oakham appears to have inspired the actual name, Arkham" (Murray 21).

Lovecraft wants to see his town as weird and evil. In "The Dreams in the Witch House" he writes of "the changeless, legend-haunted city of Arkham, with its clustering gambrel roofs that sway and sag over attics where witches hid from the king's men in the dark, olden days of the Province" (*MM* 262). This poetic, mellifluous sentence seems marred by the word "sway." To speak of swaying roofs is a bit much, as if violent storms were constantly sweeping over the town. But the following quotation from this story is even more suggestive of a dark and terror-stricken place:

> Sometimes he would take walks through shadowy tangles of unpaved musty-smelling lanes where eldritch brown houses of unknown age leered mockingly through narrow, small-paned windows. Here he knew strange things had happened once, and there was a faint suggestion behind the surface that everything of that monstrous past might not—at least in the darkest, narrowest, and most intricately crooked alleys—have utterly perished. (*MM* 264–65)

Once again, the language is extravagant (the houses described as tottering and the windows as leering) and the picture we get of Arkham is of a town still trapped in its evil past, unchanged since the eighteenth century, a town that even in our present day is menacing to the unwary, a place of black magic and secret sorcery. Yet no actual evil action is described; it is more a place of baneful atmosphere and aura than a town where one might be seduced into witchcraft or set upon by muggers. The key to Arkham's uncanny, eerie quality is mostly a matter of elder lore and legend, of nostalgia for a past still kept alive by the ancient dwellings which survive. In "The Colour out of Space," Arkham is "a very old town full of witch legends" (*DH* 54).

Arkham is not only the residence of Walter Gilman in "The Dreams in the Witch House," but that of Albert Wilmarth in "The Whisperer in Darkness," as well as the home of Edward Pickman Derby, his wife Asenath, and Daniel Upton in "The Thing on the Doorstep." Professor Nathaniel Peaslee of "The Shadow out of Time" also lives in this hoary town, and three other professors from Miskatonic University investigate the deadly doings at Nahum Gardner's farm in "The Colour out of Space." Nevertheless, only "The Dreams in the Witch House" is centrally involved with Arkham. For example, Peaslee merely alludes in a general way to "the traditions of horror, madness, and witchcraft which lurk behind the ancient Massachusetts town" (*DH* 369).

This, then, is how Lovecraft wants his readers to view Arkham: as a place of brooding, haunting menace, whose past evil, stretching back to Salem witchcraft days when unspeakable abominations were perpetrated, still lingers into the twentieth century, a town whose eldritch houses and narrow lanes still intimidate the modern visitor. He wants them to see it as a place of dark, occult mystery, where practices forbidden by church and state may still occur in secret behind those small-paned windows, under those apparently never-repaired sagging roofs, and down those still unlit, unimproved lanes. Tourists, beware! Go back, please, to your dull burgs like Jersey City, Bronxville, Newark, Montclair, and Glenview!

Lovecraft wants his readers to empathize with Randolph Carter in "The Silver Key": "Then he went back to Arkham, the terrible witch-haunted town of his forefathers in New England, and had experiences in the dark, amidst the hoary willows and tottering gambrel roofs" (*MM* 413). As can be seen, Lovecraft gets a lot of mileage from repetition of images that picture Arkham as an eldritch community.

Nevertheless, the logical implications of his exposition present quite another Arkham, for the insistent hand of pedestrian reality imposes itself constantly on Lovecraft's uncanny pen. Consider these facts: Arkham has, as he informs the reader, a national bank, an Episcopal church, a train station, building inspectors (!), a sanitarium, an historical society, markets, and two newspapers—the *Advertiser* and the *Gazette*. Among all the hoary legends and whispers there is even St. Mary's Hospital, apparently a Catholic institution with nuns and nurses buzzing around. We hope the roof of St. Mary's neither sways nor sags, and that no tentacled monster interferes with its auxiliary power system, though we recall that the "broad-minded" doctors there improbably helped the narrator obtain the copy of the dreaded *Necronomicon* from Miskatonic University (*D* 216). This unlikely scenario symbolizes clearly the tension between the two Arkhams.

Apropos of Miskatonic University, much has been made by fans of its occult associations with the *Necronomicon*. I suppose many readers think of M.U. as a very quirky institution, fit only for people like Gilman, Wilbur Whateley, and Asenath Derby. But remember, Miskatonic is a university, with all that implies: a plethora of the same academic courses taught at, say, Ohio State, Brown, or Princeton. The idea of people there being simply huddled nervously around a few strange forbidden books—books forbidden to students and even most of the faculty—and furtively registering for courses in occult arts, is of course preposterous. No reputable university would pander to or could survive such provincialism. Nor could the buildings at M.U. be "crumbling," for heaven's sake; no one would go there if they were except Asenath (who is few people's ideal coed).

The Miskatonic University Expedition described in *At the Mountains of Madness* leaves no doubt as to the modern scientific achievements of Arkham's famed institution. Its departments of engineering, physics, and geology make the trip to Antarctica possible. This world of successful technology is a far *Tekeli-li* cry from "witch-haunted" Arkham. No broomstick would get one to McMurdo Sound! And can you imagine the effect on tuition income at M.U. if eldritch Arkham were real? Long distance call to Union City: "Gee, mom, this is a weird college, all right! There's this kinky girl who . . . And the town! Last week I got bitten by a furry little weasel-thing they said was a million years old, and I had to go to St. Mary's Hospital. One of the sisters there said I should transfer to Notre Dame." What are the people of Arkham really like, as described by the gentleman from Providence? We catch hints here and there, hints neither debatable nor disturbing. In "The Colour out of Space" the editor of the *Arkham Gazette,* who ridicules the superstitions of country people, is described as "a stolid city man" (*DH* 63). In the same story, we read: "No use, either, in telling the city people at Arkham who laughed at everything" (*DH* 68). The citizens here seem cynical and skeptical about the otherworldly and strange, and the editor is shown as dull and not easily excited. In "The Dreams in the Witch House" good Mrs. Wolejko will not tell the Arkham police of the danger to her baby on Walpurgis night because "they never believed such things" (*MM* 288).

Nor is the degenerate town of Innsmouth anything like Arkham. "Innsmouth—that ancient, half-deserted town which Arkham people were so curiously unwilling to visit" (*MM* 278). But ought they not be unwilling, if Arkhamites are as normal as Lovecraft implies in the same tale? He also speaks of the "fine folks up in Miskatonic Avenue and High and Saltonstall streets" (*MM* 271). This is Arkham's old Yankee community of people with names like Peaslee, Derby, Upton, Elwood. It is difficult to imagine many of them—cultured, reserved, conservative—slipping over to M.U. in order to dip into the *Necronomicon.*
Then there is the Polish Catholic community of Arkham, which

could have saved Gilman if he had heeded it. This ethnic enclave centers around St. Stanislaus' church and Father Iwanicki. It includes people like Mrs. Walejko, Dr. Malkowski, Mary Czanek, Joe Mazurewicz, Paul Choynski, and Dombrowski, Gilman's landlord. They are the salt of the earth, and one cannot imagine them dreaming fondly of the old days in whisper-haunted Arkham, or hankering for any starry wisdom stuff. No, no. Mass at St. Stanislaus at nine, thank you! The Old American Ascendency on Saltonstall Street and the Polish enclave may live on opposite sides of the tracks, but both have too much robust common sense to do anything but shun uncanny doings. Each in its own way would endorse this placid view of their hometown from "The Strange High House in the Mist": "a lovely vista of Georgian steeples across leagues of river and meadow" (*D* 280).

What Lovecraft is depicting here is an Arkham that is a normal New England town, full of ordinary human beings who live like people everywhere. And of course it has to be this way. To be successful, horror fiction must be set against a background of customary, prosaic, rational, center-of-the-road human life. For every Richard Upton Pickman there ought to be a sufficient number of bread-and-butter people who staff your horrific story. Where Lovecraft possibly oversteps this rule, as in "The Outsider" or "The Shadow over Innsmouth" (which Kenneth Faig considers the darkest of his tales), he risks slipping into almost unrelieved nightmare, which no sane reader really wants. We have to have a Joe Mazurewicz on hand, reminding a Gilman to get his life in order.

How can we reconcile the realistic, necessary Arkham of reassuringly good people who stand sturdily against all cosmic horror, with a passage like this from "The Thing on the Doorstep": ". . . the ancient, mouldering, and subtly fearsome town in which we lived—witch-cursed, legend-haunted Arkham, whose huddled, sagging gambrel roofs and crumbling Georgian balustrades brood out the centuries beside the muttering Miskatonic" (*DH* 277)? When Lovecraft chose to write in poetic purple, he wrote things that the rational mind dismisses as not corresponding to reality, depicting an unbelievable Arkham that would have been condemned and razed by the authorities over a century ago. When he wrote in a simpler, sinewy style, he created an Arkham we can believe in. Still, the poetic prose has its place and contributes to the haunting mood of his tales; there is more to Lovecraft than *At the Mountains of Madness*. Without the poetry, without the passages I have quoted here, many of his best tales would lose their effectiveness. After all, Lovecraft is renowned for his ability to create eldritch atmosphere and setting. But we must clearly distinguish the two towns. Seen through the vague hoary mist of repititive yet poetic prose, Arkham is sinister; seen up close in bustling everyday life, it is healthy, peaceful, moral, safe.

Works Cited

Murray, Will. "Lovecraft's New England: Haunted Backwaters." In H. P. Lovecraft Centennial Guidebook, ed. Jon B. Cooke. Pawtucket, RI: Montilla Publications, 1990. 21–24.

[*Fantasy Commentator* 7, No. 1 (Fall 1990): 31–34]

V. Influences

Hali

By Marco Frenschkowski

Hali certainly is one of the most curious names in Lovecraft's mythological universe. He—or it—is mentioned in his stories and poems—as far as I can see—only once: "The Whisperer in Darkness," in a long list of mythological allusions, has "the lake of Hali" (*DH* 223). A major mythological idea Hali never became, but a "lake of Hali" is frequently alluded to in the stories of August Derleth. Most readers will be aware that Lovecraft's fiction can only seriously be studied by taking into account the difficult text history. Alas, it's the same with Derleth. Here is one instance: In the story "The Lair of the Star-Spawn," co-authored with Mark Schorer in the summer of 1931, in the version printed in the volume *Colonel Markesan and Less Pleasant People* (1966), we have the following familiar-looking quote: "The Great Old Ones fought these evil beings. . . . Hastur was exiled to Hali in the Hyades, Cthulhu was banished to the lost sea kingdom of R'lyeh" (70). Familiar, because Derleth used almost the same words in describing his mythology in so many later tales. But in the original publication of that story (*Weird Tales,* August 1932) the relevant sentence reads: "The Ancient Ones fought these evil beings. . . . Hastur fled into outer space. . . ." Hali is not mentioned. So there is a text-critical problem for Derleth as well; he adjusted his earlier stories to his later views on "correct" mythology. Derleth denied that very obvious fact: "none of them [these tales] has undergone revision," he writes on the cover of *Colonel Morkesan.* Any serious research on Derleth's interpretation of Lovecraft will have to compare his manuscripts, early and later printings, and so on. As currently most Lovecraftians regard Derleth as an abysmally bad writer (an opinion that I do not happen to share), there is little hope for a corrected or critical edition of his stories. This kind of research can't be done in Germany (where I live): there is not even a complete set of *Weird Tales* in any German library, and we have to rely on scattered copies of this and other magazines in our private collections. And the manuscripts of course are not available to me (interlibrary loan with American universities has become increasingly difficult during the last few years).

HALI

Not only Derleth, but also other writers of the Lovecraft circle used Hali, e.g., Donald Wandrei in "Colossus" (*Astounding Stories,* January 1934) (". . . a universe more distant than Carcosa and Hali" [*Colossus* 151]) or in that enigmatic and fascinating cascade of horror, "The Lady in Gray" (*Weird Tales,* December 1933) (". . . the twenty-three sleepers where Hali raises its black spires in Carcosa" [*Eye and the Finger* 5]).[1] I do not intend to exhaust this topic, but some few clarifications on the matter of who or what Hali was might be welcome. Lovecraft regarded Bierce as the ultimate source relating to Hastur, Hali and Carcosa (see *SL* 2.148), an opinion in which I believe he was wrong.

Bierce mentions and even quotes Hali in "The Death of Halpin Frayser" and "An Inhabitant of Carcosa." In this last tale the narrator—the ghost of Hoseib Alar Robardin—ponders the words of Hali on a possible resurrection of the spirit in the place where the corpse is buried. Hoseib Alar Robardin (a name that is not correct Arabic, by the way) discovers his own grave. It seems to me probable (though I cannot strictly prove it) that with the city "Carcosa" Bierce had Carcassonne in mind, which in Roman times was called Carcaso[2] (he may have simply got that wrong, giving the name from memory and not looking it up, or he wanted the two names to sound similar but not identical). This city had been under Arab rule from 720 till 759 when it was captured by the Franks. The main reason for this identification is that in Carcosa Arabic is no longer spoken when Hoseib returns from the realm of the dead, but some "barbarous chant in an unknown tongue." That of course would not be possible in any city, say, in Arabia or North Africa. Carcassonne is famous as one of two cities in Europe (Rothenburg ob der Tauber is the other one) that still virtually looks like it did in mediaeval times. Bierce will have had only limited knowledge on that fabulous town, old Carcaso, now French but once Arabic.[3] But that's not my main point here. Hali is obviously to be regarded as some Arabic sage, who has substantial things to say also on occult matters.

These tales by Bierce are the immediate inspiration of Robert W. Cham-

---

[1] For a general overview of Wandrei's work see my article "Donald Wandrei," *Quarber Merkur* No. 77 (1992): 18–28 (in German).

[2] Mentioned in Pliny the Elder, *Natural History* 3.3.6 and Claudius Ptolemaeus, *Georg.* 2.10.9, also in several inscriptions (Carcaso or Carcasso). For details see Ihm, "Carcoso," in *Paulys Realencyclopädie der classischen Altertumswissenschaft* 3, 2, 1899 (rpt. Stuttgart 1970), 1575f. The Ravenna geographer has the name as Carcassona, the Tabula Peutingeriana as Carcassione. The name has no obvious Celtic affiliation and may be of Iberian or perhaps Punic origin.

[3] Cf. ". . . one with the marvels of Carcassonne and Samarcand and El Dorado and all glorious and half-fabulous cities." "He" (*D* 266). This is the only mention of Carcassonne by HPL.

bers's use of Carcosa, Hastur, and Hali in his 1895 volume *The King in Yellow*. In "The Repairer of Reputations," in "The Mask," and in "The Yellow Sign" a "lake of Hali" is mentioned and it seems not to be on this earth, but on some other planet. Chambers skillfully evokes a place "thin and blank, without a ripple or wind to stir it, and . . . the towers of Carcosa behind the moon" ("The Mask"). "We spoke of Hastur and Cassilda, while outside the fog rolled against the blank window-panes as the cloud waves roll and break on the shores of Hali" ("The Yellow Sign"). Why did Chambers make out of the sage Hali in Bierce, of all things, a lake? I have never been able to find an answer: does any reader of this article know?

So far we are on safe and well-trod ground. Where did Bierce get the name Hali? It has been suggested that his sources may have been some hints in the novels of Sir Walter Scott, e.g., *Kenilworth*, chapter 18, or *The Surgeon's Daughter*, chapter 13 (see Tierney). This cannot be proved. More important, it seems to me, is that *there is a well-known Arabic personality connected with the magical tradition quoted as "Hali" quite often in mediaeval and Renaissance sources,* and there are also one or two lesser personages known as "Hali." "Everything depends on a good encyclopaedia" ("Suggestions for a Reading Guide" [*CE* 2.202]). If Lovecraftians would more often take to heart that advice of their master, some of the guesswork connected with mythological and literary matters would cease. Richard L. Tierney has seen the correct identification, but he has not given (as far as I know) any details. It is quite correct that "Hali" most often simply means Khalid ibn Yazid ibn Mu'awiyah, heir to the caliphate and "deeply interested in medicine, astrology and alchemy" (Sarton 1.495). Our most important source on him—as on so many other Arabic authors—is the famous *Kitab al-Fihrist* of Abu al-Faraj Muhammad ibn Ishaq al-Warraq, usually known as Ibn Abi Ya'qub al-Nadim. This work—since 1970 also available in an excellent English translation by Bayard Dodge—has been rightly called a "survey of Muslim culture"; it is the most erudite bibliographic compilation produced in the golden age of Arabic literature, completed about the year 990. Al-Nadim (pronounced An-nadim) mentions Khalid ibn Yazid four times and attributes a few books to him, all of which are probably lost (226, 581 , 586, 850f.; but see below). Here are the most interesting passages.

"Khalid ibn Yazid ibn Mu'awiyah was called the 'Wise Man of the Family of Marwans'. He was inherently virtuous, with an interest in and fondness for the sciences. As the Art [alchemy] attracted his attention, he ordered a group of Greek philosophers who were living in a city of Egypt to come to him. Because he was concerned with literary Arabic, he commanded them to translate the books about the Art from the Greek and Coptic languages into Arabic. This was the first translation in Islam from one language into

another" (581). And some pages later al-Nadim writes: "He was an ora-
tor, poet and man of literary style, as well as a man with comprehensive
interests and vision. He was the first person for whom books on medicine
and the stars and also books on alchemy were translated" (850). Khalid
ibn Yazid had been heir to the caliphate when his brother Mu'awiya died
in 683, but he soon retired and lived his last years in Egypt, as a private
citizen. He died in 704 or perhaps 708. Other Arabic sources give more
details.4 Now this is so to say, the "historic Hali," with whom we are not
much concerned. Later this patron and friend of scholarship was himself
regarded as receiving secret alchemical knowledge, and many books have
been attributed to him. It has been a subject of some controversy whether
any of these alchemical treatises can be regarded as genuine.5 Be that
as it may, Khalid became a famous figure in the history of Alchemy and
was often mentioned in later alchemical literature, which loves to quote
auctores antiquissimi—but quite a lot of these quotes are spurious. Now
many Latin works on "the Art" are only translations from Arabic originals,
and here he is latinized sometimes as Calid (or more completely as Calid
filius Jazidi), but also and especially later as Hali. It is rather difficult to
decide what in those later alchemical compilations is genuine tradition,
and what is simply spurious lore attributed to the great wise man known
from classical Arabic literature.

To give only one well-known example in the famous *Rosarium Philosophorum* (rose-garden of philosophers), first printed in Frankfort in
1855[6] but also known from many manuscripts, Hali is one of the main
authorities. This was one of the major works on alchemy in the sixteenth
century; it was also an important inspiration of Carl Gustav Jung's fasci-

---

[4] Two examples: Ibn Khallikan's *Biographical Dictionary*, tr. de Slane, 4 vols. (London:
W. H. Allen, 1843–71), 1.481; Al-Mas'udi, *Les Prairies d'or*, 9 vols., tr. C Barbier de
Maynard and P. de Courteille (Paris: Société Asiatique, 1861–77), 8.176 and often.
See also Fuat Sezgin, *Geschichte des arabischen Schrifttums, IV. Alchimie—Chemie—
Botanik—Agrikultur bis ca. 430 d. H.* (Leiden: Brill, 1971), 120–26 (Sezgin's work is the
most complete monograph on Arabic literature in existence) and M. Ullmann, in *The
Encyclopedia of Islam*, 2nd ed. IV (Leiden: Brill: 1978), 929f.

[5] The classic monograph on this question is Julius Ruska, *Arabische Alchemisten 1.
Chalid ibn Jazid ibn Mu'awija* (Heidelberg: Carl Winter, 1924). See also Edmund O.
von Lippmann, *Entstehung und Ausbreitung der Alchemie 1* (Berlin: Springer, 1919; rpt.
Hildesheim/New York: Georg Olms, 1978), 357–61, 483 (still the best general history of
alchemy). For more recent literature see especially Sezgin, 1. c.

[6] Recently reprinted in facsimile with an important translation: *Rosarium Philosophorum:
Ein alchemisches Florilegium des Spätmittelalters*. Ed. and explained by Joachim Telle, tr.
L. Claren and J. Huber (Weinheim: VHC Verlagsgesellschaft, 1992; 2 vols.). For a more
extensive comment on that work see my review in *Blätter fur Pfälzische Kirchengeschichte
und Religiöse Vollkskunde* 61 (1994) (also in *Ebernburg-Hefte* 73 [1994]).

nating but deeply problematic psychological interpretation of alchemy.[7] Three dicta are quoted from Hali's *Liber secretorum* (book of secrets), a Latin alchemical tract derived from the Arabic. At least one of the treatises attributed to Hali is also available in English: Lee Stavenhagen, *A Testament of Alchemy, Being the Revelations of Morienus . . . to Khalid ibn Yazid . . . of the Divine Secrets of the Magisterium and Accomplishment of the Alchemical Art*, ed. and transl. from the oldest manuscripts (Hanover, NH, 1974). Morienus (also called Morienes and Marianos) in this tradition is the Greek teacher of Hali. The Arabs of course knew that their alchemical doctrines had almost completely been derived from Greek (that is, Byzantine) sources. Hali's name is sometimes also given as Calid: Latinizations were not very consistent, and it seems the identity of Calid and Hali was often known. But sometimes they are two different persons: in a fifteenth-century tract "Haly" is not pupil but teacher to Morienus: perhaps simply a misunderstanding (see Ruska 1.204). He is also mentioned in other Arabic and Latin works, which I do not want to discuss here at length.

As I said, there have also been a few lesser personalities sometimes known as "Hali." The classic work on these questions (knowledge of Arabic authors in Europe) is still Moritz Steinschneider, *Die europaischen Übersetzungen aus dem Arabischen bis Mitte des 17. Jahrhunderts,* which first appeared 1904/5 and has been reprinted in one volume by the Alkademische Druck- und Verlagsanstalt (Graz, 1956). Steinschneider was an erudite Jewish bibliographer on many topics, who had a marvelous knowledge on all aspects of Jewish, Christian, and Islamic literature, especially in the Middle Ages. His books deserve still to be read by all interested in the contact of cultures.[8] I'm mentioning this mainly to contradict the prevailing superstition that a new monograph on a historic topic is usually better than an old one: sometimes the great works of erudition of the nineteenth century are still more complete than anything our century has produced. But back to Hali. On pp. 3f he gives details on eight alchemical and astrological works attributed to one or several authors called Hali, Haly, or simply Ali (though that common name is not usually transliterated Hali), whose identity is doubtful, but whose writings have been translated into Latin, German or Italian.

Lovecraft, (who, all his erudition notwithstanding, had only a very limited knowledge of Arabic matters) probably did not know anything of all this. It seems to me most likely that Bierce from somewhere (from Scott?)

---

[7] Jung used the text as contained in the alchemical collection *Auriferae artis, quam chemiam vacant, volumen secundum* (Basel 1572, rpt. 1593 and 1610).

[8] See on Steinschneider the article by Menahem Schmelzer in the *Encyclopedia Judaica* (Jerusalem: Keter, 1972), 15.374–77.

snatched just the name Hali, Chambers got it all poetically wrong, and Lovecraft wanted to do homage to both.

Works Cited

Derleth, August, and Mark Schorer. *Colonel Markesan and Less Pleasant People.* Sauk City, WI: Arkham House, 1966.

al-Nadim, Ibn Ali Ya'qub. *The Fihrist of Al-Nadim.* Tr. B. Dodge. New York Columbia University Press, 1970. 2 vols. (continuous pagination).

Ruska, J. *Tabula smaragdina.* Heidelberg: Carl Winter, 1924.

Sarton, G. *Introduction to the History of Science.* 1927. Rpt. Malabar, FL: Krieger, 1975.

Tierney, Richard L. Letter. *Crypt of Cthuthu* No. 75 (Michaelmas 1990): 76f.

Wandrei, Donald. *Colossus: The Collected Science Fiction of Donald Wandrei.* Minneapolis, MN: Fedogan & Bremer, 1989.

Wilson, Alison Morley. *August Derleth: A Bibliography.* Metuchen, NJ: Scarecrow Press, 1983.

[*Crypt of Cthulhu* No. 92 (Eastertide 1996): 8–12]

Cthulhu's Scald: Lovecraft and the Nordic Tradition

By Jason C. Eckhardt

T here is little argument about the presence of Greek and Roman mythology in the writing of H. P. Lovecraft; one need only read the short story "The Tree," set in ancient Greece, to find this in its purest form, while references ranging from the mention of Attis and Cybele in "The Rats in the Walls" to the Latin epigraph for "The Festival" all belie the ancient cultures that Lovecraft loved so well. There remains, however, another mythology that Lovecraft admired whose influence may not be so readily observed: Norse mythology. While Lovecraft's love for the classical myths extended back to his early childhood, certain statements show that his love for the Norse myths was comparable. "I am naturally a Nordic— . . . a Viking . . . a drinker of foemen's blood from new-picked skulls" (*SL* 1.227), and again: "those yellow-bearded gods of war and dominion before whom my own soul bows as before no other—Woden, Thor, Freyr and the vast Alfadur—frosty blue-eyed giants worthy of the admiration of a conquering people!" (HPL to F. C. Clark, 12 September 1925; quoted in de Camp 236). Now, while it is a little difficult to picture the erudite author as an ax-wielding berserk, the sentiment is clear. His tastes were modeled after the Greeks and Romans, but he could not deny his Anglo-Saxon blood; and this writer will attempt to prove, through a series of comparisons, that this Teutonic background was a subtle but undeniable influence in Lovecraft's stories.

Starting at the very beginning, the Norse worlds were said to have been created from a chaos of mingled fire and ice. Where these two worlds, Muspelheim and Niflheim respectively, met, a huge giant named Ymir and his cow were created. The first gods were created by the heat of the cow's tongue as it licked at the rime on the edge of this chaos, and these gods went on to kill Ymir and, hurling his body into the pit of the chaos, created the world from his corpse. Lovecraft's pantheon is headed by two monstrous entities named Yog-Sothoth and Azathoth, and it is noteworthy that this latter is referred to as "the idiot Chaos" ("Nyarlathotep," sonnet XXI of *Fungi from Yuggoth*). There is certainly a very heavy Egyptian sound to these two names, but there remains a similarity between "Yog-Sothoth" and "Yg," one of the many names of the Norse god Odin. As "Yg" translates to mean "the Terrible One," a name appropriate for either Odin or Yog-Sothoth, this seems a good parallel; but it only extends so far. A far better parallel could be drawn between Yog-Sothoth and Ymir, also seeing Azathoth as the chaos out of which Ymir sprang. Lovecraft, quoting from his fictional *Necronomicon*, tells us this about Yog-Sothoth:

> Past, present, future, all are one in Yog-Sothoth. He knows where the old Ones broke through of old, and where they shall break through again. . . . The wind gibbers with Their voices, and the earth mutters with Their consciousness. They bend the forest and crush the city, yet may not the forest nor the city behold the hand that smites . . . . The ice-desert of the South and the sunken isles of ocean hold stones whereon Their seal is graven. (*DH* 170)

Here we see the comparison extend to the frost-giants, descendants of Ymir and embodiments of storms and other natural phenomena. Like the Old Ones, their presence was felt in wild places and in the unbridled fury of nature, when they "broke through" from their realm of Jotunheim to the lands of men.

The references to an ice-desert and sunken isles are also relevant, considering the icy lands of the frost-giants, and the home of Ægir, a giant who made his home in a hall of gold on the ocean floor. These giants were at constant war with the Æsir gods, who were led by Odin, and again a parallel exists in Lovecraft. In *At the Mountains of Madness* the narrator discovers the history of the star-headed Old Ones, including the account of a fabulous war that the Old Ones waged against the octopoid minions of Cthulhu. This war ends in a truce, with the land given over to the Cthulhuoids and the seas and older lands left to the Old Ones. Similarly, the Æsir gods fought a war with another group of gods, the Vanir, also ending in a truce and an exchange of hostages. The two wars in Norse mythology as opposed to the one in Lovecraft can be explained as follows: the Vanir and the giants are never seen at the same time, with the exception of Njord, Freyr, and Freya, the three hostages given to the Æsir (and even then, Njord and Freyr wed giants' daughters), and thus can collectively be associated with the Old Ones. This can be extended further by examining the realms of the giants and of the Old Ones, both of which are frozen mountainous lands. Further, the narrator in *At the Mountains of Madness* equates the Antarctic plateau of the Old Ones' city with another plateau mentioned in Lovecraft, the plateau of Leng. This bleak tableland appears alternately in a land of dreams (*The Dream-Quest of Unknown Kadath*) and in an unspecified locale in central Asia ("The Hound," etc.). As the plateau of Leng, it houses a race of squat, uncouth people; and bearing this in mind, we can go on to equate them with the loutish frost-giants and the old Ones with the Vanir gods. One final note on this aspect is the locations of Leng and Jotunheim, both given as far to the mysterious east of the protagonists or narrator in each literature.

Returning to separate deities, there arises the awesome form of Cthulhu in Lovecraft's work, a being that perhaps resembles most the Norse god Odin. Both are rulers of their respective races, both are powerful magicians, and both are (or will be) resurrected from the dead. In Odin's case, he hanged himself—Odin sacrificed to Odin—to obtain more knowledge and magical powers. Here Cthulhu differs, having been dragged to the ocean floor by a natural cataclysm, but is destined to rise again to reclaim dominion over the world, much as Odin walked forth from the tree to rule gods and men. In both these beings, thought is a powerful tool: Odin sends his two ravens, Huginn ("Thought") and Muninn ("Memory"), out over the world each morning to see everything that happens, return, and whisper to him all that they have found. Similarly, Cthulhu sends out his dreams to the sensitive to help in his release from his tomb. Finally, there is a similarity between Odin's throne, Hlidskjalf ("Rock-Opening"), and his hall, Valaskjalf ("Shelf of the Slain"), and Cthulhu's "stone house" in the "corpse-city of R'lyeh" (*DH* 150).

While there appears to be a large influence by Odin upon Lovecraft's work, there is little if any by that other well-known Norse god, Thor, god of thunder. This would at first appear surprising until one recalls the nature of Thor: loud, brawling, drinking, sometimes stupid but always the common man's best friend. There is no room in Lovecraft's universe for such a being; the indifference of the cosmos to the doings of Lovecraft's characters precludes any saving influence, beyond blind luck, and this applies to Freyr as well, who, despite Lovecraft's statement cited at the beginning of this article, was a god of fertility and not war. These two beings were undeniably forces of good, but while Odin was their ruler, the same could not be said of him. He often tricked giants and people, and Loki once let it slip that Odin had often gathered with witches to do black magic. As Kevin Crossley-Holland has said, "He [Odin] is a terrifying god; maybe a god to be respected, but not a god to be loved" (xxvi). The same could be applied to Lovecraft's gods.

Following Odin and Thor in importance in the Norse myths is the colourful figure of Loki, and it is with him that we find perhaps the strongest presence in Lovecraft. The devious, mysterious shape-shifter, who taunts the very gods who shelter him, can be none other than Nyarlathotep. Starting with physical resemblances, Nyarlathotep is described as "wrapped in fabrics red as sunset's flame" ("Nyarla-thotep," *Fungi from Yuggoth*), while Loki's very name means "flame." The practical-joker Loki is mirrored briefly in *The Dream-Quest of Unknown Kadath*, when one reads that "around [Nyarlathotep's] eyes there lurked the languid sparkle of capricious humour" (*MM* 398), and again when it becomes plain that he has played a huge trick on Randolph Carter. Loki becomes increasingly cruel as the myths progress, finally slandering and vilifying the gods to their faces in the myth "Loki's Flyting"; and, again in *Dream-Quest,* we find Nyarlathotep "taunting insolently the mild gods of earth" (*MM* 407). Perhaps the strongest tie one finds between the two is their common ability to change shape. Loki is found at various times in the guise of a fly, a mare, a seal, a falcon, and an old hag; Nyarlathotep appears at different times as a goat-hoofed black man, a "three-lobed burning eye" (*DH* 115), and the "Crawling Chaos"; and is further described as having "a thousand other forms" (*MM* 403). One final note on this character is its "otherness"; for while both Nyarlathotep and Loki are grouped with the gods, Loki is in fact a jotun, of the same blood as the frost-giants, adopted by Odin; and Nyarlathotep remains the only one of Lovecraft's gods who is capable of taking another form and mingling with humans.

On the subject of Nyarlathotep, there is also a similarity between him and the Norse figure of Surt, Lord of Muspelheim, land of fire. There is also a physical resemblance here, as Surt's name describes him as "Black," while Nyarlathotep appears as a tall, black man in "The Dreams in the Witch House." The two share the element of fire as well; Robert Blake, in "The Haunter of the Dark," writes of the thing inhabiting the Starry Wisdom Church steeple as being "an avatar of Nyarlathotep" (*DH* 114), and he feels a great heat upon approaching it, as well as finding evidence of fire in the steeple itself. Again, the mention of a "three-lobed burning eye" is redolent of Surt and his flaming sword. Like Surt, Nyarlathotep is hinted at having a large part in the final destruction of the world, and it is fair to assume that, like Surt, he will bring fire upon the land.

There remain a few lesser echoes of the Norse imagination in the work of Lovecraft which deserve mention. One of these is the role of the dog, primarily represented in Lovecraft in the short story "The Hound." While the creature in this tale turns out not to be a hound at all, there is a reference to an amulet depicting a hound, said to be the symbol of the "corpse-eating cult of inaccessible Leng" (D 174). Once again we see a bond between Leng and Jotunheim; for the dog or wolf in Norse mythology is invariably a jotun in disguise, a cunning and bloodthirsty beast that delights in maiming and killing. In particular, the beast in "The Hound" echoes the hound Garm, the beast that guards the entrance to the hall of the dead, chewing on corpses. There are exceptions to this rule in each case—the two faithful wolves Frekki and Gerri sitting at the feet of Odin, and the German shepherd that kills Wilbur Whateley in "The Dunwich Horror"—but even these are merely servants doing their jobs, as opposed to the overt malignancy of the greater number. This is a far cry from Lovecraft's beloved Romans, who claimed their descent from the foundlings of a she-wolf. Conversely, the Norse shared an affection for cats with Lovecraft, as shown by their depicting Freya, goddess of love, in a cart drawn by cats.

Another, more subtle influence from the Norse myths may be the very temperament of the narrator. Resigned to the titanic churnings of fate, he is the true descendant of Freyr's servant Skirnir, who, faced with death, resolutely says, "Fearlessness is better than faint heart for any man who puts his nose out of doors. The length of my life and the hour of my death were fated long ago" (Crossley-Holland 56). Likewise, the Lovecraftian progatonist presses on in the face of madness and oblivion, realizing the futility of his puny actions yet still bothering to write them down in the hope that it will do some good. As with Lovecraft himself, it is pointless to try to picture his bookish heroes as mad-eyed warriors; but the same determination that fuels the Professor Armitages and Randolph Carters and Robert Blakes to dig a little further, to keep looking for that right incantation, even as the clouds assemble in all quarters of the sky, is the same determination that would keep a beserker slashing away in the midst of overwhelming hordes.

CTHULHU'S SCALD: LOVECRAFT AND THE NORDIC TRADITION

There are many features, this writer is sure, of the Lovecraft Mythos that conform not only to Norse mythology but to general mythological patterns as well. But it is significant to note this particular resemblance because of its many features and because it was one to which Lovecraft himself hinted. There is no question but that Lovecraft's mythos is a unique, highly imaginative, and powerful invention; and this writer hopes that this paper has only shown an unconscious though pervading influence from the Norse. For, as in the Norse creation myth, what Lovecraft did was to take many different ideas, the Norse among them, a veritable chaos of inspirations, and forge them into his own shining, new vision.

Works Cited

Crossley-Holland, Kevin. *The Norse Myths.* New York: Random House, 1980.

de Camp, L. Sprague. *Lovecraft: A Biography.* Garden City, NY: Doubleday, 1975.

[*Lovecraft Studies* No. 8 (Spring 1984): 25–29]

The Origin of Lovecraft's "Black Magic" Quote

By David E. Schultz

Lovecraft's "Black Magic" quote has long been suspected of being spurious. William Fulwiler voiced concern in his article, "Three Quotations and a Fabrication." He concluded that August Derleth was the originator of the quote, and that a letter from Lovecraft to Harold Farnese somehow figured into its genesis. Fulwiler correctly identified the major players in what has turned out to be a comedy of errors, but he fell short of solving the puzzle. Therefore, I would like to present the results of my own research on the matter, published initially in *Lovecraft Studies* in my article, "Who Needs the 'Cthulhu Mythos'?," in which I showed that the originator of the "Black Magic" quote was probably Harold Farnese.

August Derleth had written to Farnese on 6 April 1937 requesting the loan of Lovecraft's letters to Farnese, and also asking for information regarding two stanzas from *Fungi from Yuggoth* that Farnese had set to music. Derleth and Donald Wandrei hoped to publish Lovecraft's letters and began to gather them from Lovecraft's correspondents. Farnese responded to Derleth in a letter dated 8 April, saying: "In my correspondence files I must have at least two or three of his personal letters. These were voluminous letters and highly instructive and interesting, for which reason I kept them. In one of them, if I am not mistaken, he discussed various technical points of the construction of mystery stories of the higher type." Farnese said that at the time he did not know the whereabouts of the letters but that he would look for them. The Lovecraft collection of Brown University's John Hay Library contains seven letters from Farnese to Lovecraft, from 11 July 1932 to 9 January 1933. Farnese told Derleth that his correspondence with Lovecraft was of short duration, so he may not have received many more letters than those he acknowledged to Derleth. (As Dirk Mosig observed, one letter from Farnese merely asked why Lovecraft had not replied to his previous letter.) In fact, Farnese's correspondence with Lovecraft ended before Lovecraft moved from 10 Barnes to 66 College.

In a letter to Derleth dated 11 April, Farnese wrote:

> Pursuant to my promise to you . . . I am sending you today whatever correspondence I have of *H. P. Lovecraft.* I need not stress the fact that these letters should be highly interesting to you, for you will reach this conclusion after having perused them. The correspondence I unearthed from my files consists of two long letters and one postal card. If there was another letter, it has been destroyed, for I recorded the salient points in my scrap-book. It had entirely to do with our plans on collaborating on an opera, entitled: *Yurregarth and Yannimaid* or *The Swamp City;* we were not sure which name to use.

In the course of this letter, Farnese continued:

> HPL had trouble with the *dialogue.* He wrote: "*Dialogue of any form seems to tear the veil that I like to throw over my stories. Somehow, it seems impossible to cling to my technique of the weird, when I must indulge exclusively in dialogue!*" He also added: "*I am fascinated by your project of creating an opera, and wish with all my heart that I could help you. For you, a musician, and I, a writer, seem to see things in the same light. The story and plot of 'The Swamp City' pleases me mightily. I wish with all my heart that I could breathe life into the forms of Yurregarth and Yannimaid. And as to the sinister figure of Nickelman, a modernized version of 'Undine' should be a novelty to American audiences.*"

It seems unlikely that Lovecraft twice used the phrase, "I wish with all my heart." This statement does not appear in either of the two edited letters from Lovecraft to Farnese that appear in *Selected Letters* 4 (566, 22 September 1932; 570, 12 October 1932). Nor does another statement Farnese attributed to Lovecraft: "I am no student of music, but *it warms my soul!*" However, we do find statements in Lovecraft's published letters that are suspiciously similar to Farnese's descriptions:

> Regarding your suggestion that I cooperate in a musical drama with the score by yourself—I really feel quite overwhelmed by the force of the compliment! If I were able to do justice to such an enterprise, there is certainly nothing I would rather

attempt—for despite a profound ignorance of music, I am acutely sensible of its ability to enhance the effect of allied forms of expression. But over against this looms the fact that I have *no experience whatever in dramatic composition*—& how is a frank novice to evolve anything capable of correlation with the score of an accomplished composer? I am only too well aware that the construction of an effective drama demands a vastly greater fund of technique than one can pick up haphazard from the plays & operas one has casually & uncritically read or witnessed. Despite my tremendous admiration for things like Dunsany's *Gods of the Mountain* or O'Neill's *Emperor Jones*, I have never as yet employed drama as a medium of expression. Probably the reason is that in the sort of work I am trying to do human characters matter very little. They are only incidental details, & can well be left in the puppet stage—since the real protagonists of my tales are not organic beings at all, but simply *phenomena*. I doubt if I have the ability to handle human characters in a lifelike way, for they impress my imagination so much less than do the more impersonal forces of nature. This being so, it is clear that dialogue has never been of much use to me. If I had characters talk, it would be merely to register through them the abnormal mutations of their environment. To create the living figures necessary to vitalise a music-drama of any ordinary sort, therefore, would seem to me a task definitely beyond me. (*SL* 4.72, 22 September 1932)

Did Lovecraft write what Farnese said he wrote, perhaps in letters that remain unpublished? The words Farnese quoted do not sound like Lovecraft's own, but why would Farnese not have consulted the very letters he planned to mail even as he was writing to Derleth? Without consulting Lovecraft's actual letters to Farnese, the question cannot be answered with certainty, but it would seem that Farnese may have been paraphrasing, despite the fact that he transcribed the statements as direct quotes.

Derleth used both dubious quotations found in Farnese's letter of 11 April in *H.P.L.: A Memoir* (see p. 40) when discussing the opera Farnese planned to write with Lovecraft, though Derleth referred to it as "The Swamp." It would seem that Derleth copied the statements directly from Farnese's letters to him, instead of from Lovecraft's own letters.

Farnese's letter of 11 April is also the source for the "Black Magic" quote. As Farnese wrote:

Upon congratulating HPL upon his work, he answered: "*You will, of course, realize that all my stories, unconnected as they may be, are based on one fundamental lore or legend: That this world was inhabited at one time by another race, who in practicing black magic, lost their foothold and were expelled, yet live on outside, ever ready to take possession of this earth again."* "The Elders," as he called them.

Again, it is difficult to imagine that Farnese would attribute a quotation to Lovecraft that he did not actually copy from letters that he owned, but instead wrote down from memory, perhaps hoping at least to capture the essence of Lovecraft's statements to him.

In a letter to Derleth dated 21 April, Farnese acknowledged the receipt of his Lovecraft letters back from Derleth. He again expressed regret at having lost one of Lovecraft's letters, but said: "Yet I am glad to have been able to have given you all the salient points which I noted down in my book of reference. So I am pretty certain that nothing of value has been lost." Regarding Lovecraft's writing, Farnese went on to say, "He always made it clear to me that his endeavors covered a very small area of literature, but as he said in one of his letters submitted to you: 'I insist that it be treated with the same respect as any other corner of writing.'" When Farnese wrote this, he had Lovecraft's letters in hand, yet we find that he has now misquoted Lovecraft. Compare Lovecraft's actual statement from his letter of 22 September 1932:

> . . . I have always realised that . . . my especial province is fundamentally a very minor one; & that even if I achieved the level of literature, it would be merely a trivial phase of the "literature of escape." What I do insist upon is that this field, however minor, is a genuine and serious one; & not a mere aspect of naive crudity to be brushed aside by an enlightened age. (*SL* 4.69)

Other statements Farnese made in his letters to both Lovecraft and Derleth suggest that it was he, not Lovecraft, who was the source of the "Black Magic" quote. For instance, Farnese himself seemed to have had a preoccupation with Black Magic. In his letter to Lovecraft of 7 December 1932 he wrote:

> Here is a bit of news which might be of interest to you. One of the local Book Stores (Dawson's) [in Los Angeles] which goes in for collection of rare and out-of-print works, has a book on sale, which I saw once before in my life, in the library of a wealthy collector, the author's name of which I had forgotten.

It is the *Book of Black Magic and Pacts* incl. Rites and Mysteries of Goetic Theurgy, Sorcery and Infernal Necromancy by *Arthur Edward Waite*. . . . As far as I can remember it contains many invocations, incantations, spells etc. of infernal spirits and how to protect one's self when calling upon such spirits etc. Rather interesting, and perhaps just the proper background for some of your stories.

The title in question is *The Book of Black Magic and of Pacts: Including the Rites and Mysteries of Goëtic Theury, Sorcery, and Infernal Necromancy* (London: G. Redway, 1898) by Arthur Edward Waite (1857–1942).

Farnese's explanation of what attracted him to Lovecraft's writing also sheds light on the statements he attributed to Lovecraft:

What heightened my interest in HPL's tales and poems was the background (the underlying idea) against which most of his work was painted. He would have called it: "My pantheon." This background is not executed with the bold sweep of a brush, but is of a rather iridescent [*sic*] hue, shimmering through the network of his stories ever so palely. His idea of other entities (may we call them a race?) having lived on this globe, but expelled in time through the practice of what we would call Black Magic today. Yet these entities, these Elders, as HPL expressed it, are still "hanging on" in an outer circle, ever ready to take possession of this planet again, whenever an "inroad" should present itself. As he said, he did not dare to be too pronounced about it. A glimmer here, the strand of a cobweb there, was all that he permitted himself. With the light ethereal touch of a Debussy or Griffes he assembled his mosaic stones to lay the tesselated [*sic*] floor of his stories. (Farnese to Derleth. 21 April 1937)

It is evident that Farnese, not Lovecraft, had interest in Black Magic. It is difficult to reconcile the "Black Magic" quote with known statements Lovecraft made to Farnese. For example, Farnese wrote to Lovecraft: "If I comprehend your work correctly, I take from it the suggestion of an outer sphere (may I call it) of Black Magic, at one time ruling this planet but now dispossessed, awaiting 'on the outside' a chance for possible return" (3 September 1932; Mosig 112). Lovecraft's letter of 22 September appears to be a direct response to Farnese's query. In it, Lovecraft describes the elements he regularly employed in his fiction:

In my own efforts to crystallise [a] spaceward outreaching, I try to utilise as many as possible of the elements which have, under earlier mental and emotional conditions, given man a symbolic feeling of the unreal, the ethereal, & the mystical—choosing those least attacked by the realistic mental and emotional conditions of the present. Darkness—sunset—dreams—mists—fever—madness—the tomb—the hills—the sea—the sky—the wind—all these, and many other things have seemed to me to retain a certain imaginative potency despite our actual scientific analyses of them. Accordingly I have tried to weave them into a kind of shadowy phantasmagoria which may have the same sort of vague coherence as a cycle of traditional myth or legend—with nebulous backgrounds of Elder Forces & transgalactic entities which lurk about this infinitesimal planet, (& of course about others as well), establishing outposts thereon, & occasionally brushing aside other accidental forces of life (like human beings) in order to take up full habitation. . . . Having formed a cosmic pantheon, it remains for the fantaisiste to link this "outside" element to the earth in a suitably dramatic & convincing fashion. This, I have thought, is best done through glancing allusions to immemorially ancient cults & idols & documents attesting the recognition of the "outside" forces by men—or by those terrestrial entities which preceded man. The actual climaxes of tales based on such elements naturally have to do with sudden latter-day intrusions of forgotten elder forces on the placid surface of the known—either active intrusions, or revelations caused by the feverish & presumptuous probing of men into the unknown. (*SL* 4.70–71)

This may well be Lovecraft's most thorough explanation of the motivation for his fiction.

It seems that Farnese either ignored or forgot what Lovecraft wrote or misinterpreted it in a way that seemed more comprehensible to him, so that when Lovecraft explained what he really meant, Farnese merely considered Lovecraft to be affirming what he already suspected. He may have felt perfectly confident to "quote" Lovecraft from memory, when he instead merely expounded his skewed interpretation of what Lovecraft said. Or perhaps Farnese's notebook, with its "salient points" from Lovecraft's first letter to him, written down before Lovecraft attempted to clarify his work to him, was the source for the "Black Magic" quote. It should be noted that, in his letters of 3 September 1932 to Lovecraft and of 11 April 1937 to Derleth, Farnese's use of the term "Black Magic" seems hesitant.

It must also be mentioned that Farnese's memory was not particularly acute. In a letter to Donald Wandrei dated 15 September 1937, Farnese stated that Lovecraft ranked first among the contributors to *Weird Tales*, and that a writer he called "Bellknap Jones" was second. No such author ever contributed material to *Weird Tales,* and surely Farnese meant Frank Belknap Long. This lapse, and many others in his letters to Derleth, make his paraphrases of Lovecraft's statements very suspect.

Unfortunately, Derleth immediately seized upon the "Black Magic" quote as a concise, single-sentence précis of Lovecraft's antimythology. He first used it in print (with minor changes) in an article written about the time he received Farnese's letter of 11 April 1937, entitled "H. P. Lovecraft, Outsider." In that article Derleth singlehandedly started at least four long-standing errors of fact about Lovecraft: (1) that Lovecraft was an "outsider" or recluse; (2) that Lovecraft created the "Cthulhu Mythos"; (3) that Lovecraft's pseudomythology was a clear parallel to the "Christian Mythos"; and (4) that Black Magic was the motivating factor of all Lovecraft's stories. Derleth tirelessly used the Black Magic quote side-by-side with his own description of the "Cthulhu Mythos." When Richard L. Tierney queried Derleth about the source of the "Black Magic" quote, feeling that the sentiment expressed in it did not seem to jive with Lovecraft's stories or with other statements by Lovecraft himself regarding his own work, Derleth reportedly became angry. This is understandable. After all, Derleth had been using the quote for more than thirty years, and as far as he knew, it was a statement Lovecraft had made. However, after so long a time, he no longer remembered his source of that statement.

Derleth is certainly to blame for circulating the spurious "Black Magic" quote. However, Harold Farnese must be identified as its originator. There remains a slim possibility that Lovecraft did make the statement, and unless we find Lovecraft's letters to Farnese we will never know with certainty. However, from the evidence at hand, it appears that Farnese unintentionally misquoted Lovecraft and that he is, in fact, the author of the "Black Magic" quote.

Works Cited

Derleth, August. "H. P. Lovecraft, Outsider." *River* 1 , no. 3 (June 1937): 88–89.

———. *H. P. L.: A Memoir.* New York: Ben Abramson, 1945.

Farnese, Harold. Letters to August Derleth. State Historical Society of Wisconsin.

———. Letters to H. P. Lovecraft. John Hay Library, Brown University, Providence, RI.

Fulwiler, William. "Three Quotations and a Fabrication." *Crypt of Cthulhu* No. 46 (Eastertide 1987): 13–14.

THE ORIGIN OF LOVECRAFT'S "BLACK MAGIC" QUOTE

Mosig, Dirk. "H. P. Lovecraft: Myth-Maker." In *H. P. Lovecraft: Four Decades of Criticism,* ed. S. T. Joshi. Athens: Ohio State University Press, 1980.

Schultz, David E. "Who Needs the 'Cthulhu Mythos'?" *Lovecraft Studies* No. 13 (Fall 1986): 43–53.

Wandrei, Donald. Letter to August Derleth, 20 September 1937. State Historical Society of Wisconsin.

[*Crypt of Cthulhu* No. 48 (St. John's Eve 1987): 9–13]

Robert E. Howard and the Cthulhu Mythos

By Robert M. Price

What Is the Lovecraft Mythos?

Besides his actual stories and the enjoyment and thought they provoke in new generations of readers, H. P. Lovecraft's second greatest legacy to the weird fiction tradition was no doubt the "Cthulhu Mythos," or Lovecraft Mythos. This set of grisly gods and blasphemous books has provided a framework for many horror writers to cut their teeth and work out their writing skills. To understand what the Mythos is, we have to start not with the names and origins of the various deities, but rather with the philosophy underlying it.

Lovecraft was basically a nihilist and a materialist. That is, he felt that there was no reality that natural law and matter could not account for. Everything worked like one big machine. There was no god, no soul, no meaning or purpose. Why, you might wonder, did Lovecraft not kill himself? He did contemplate it from time to time, but what always kept him from it was curiosity and beauty. He felt sure the universe was just a collection of "stuff," but he had to know more about it. He hung on the news of the latest discoveries of science. And he felt the world, including some of the creations of humanity, was so beautiful as to make us pause for a lifetime to savor it.

So Lovecraft saw an ultimate void of utter meaninglessness, but he also could not help but see a penultimate world of fascination and beauty. We must understand this in order to understand his major fiction. I think it is fair to say that his major works can be divided into two groups, each of which depicts, as it were, one-half of his worldview.

Robert E. Howard and the Cthulhu Mythos

First, there are the "Dunsanian" or "Dream World" fantasies. In these, the brighter side of Lovecraft's philosophy is uppermost. This is nowhere more clear than in *The Dream-Quest of Unknown Kadath,* where he "spills the beans" at the story's end. The vista of supreme beauty Randolph Carter has pursued is none other than the New England cities so loved by Lovecraft himself—Salem, Marblehead, Providence, Boston. Yet in this story we are not allowed to forget that the happy and sunny "reality" of the dream-gods is subordinate to "the Other Gods"—blind, mindless, tenebrous monsters, whose ultimate throne is chaos! Every silver cloud, for Lovecraft, has a black and stormy lining!

Second, there are the Mythos tales. Here Lovecraft has taken off the gloves. He means to confront his characters (and his readers) with the awful truth—that the Universe is indifferent to humanity and in its blind, mechanical way will finally crush us as we crush an ant without ever knowing, making us as extinct as the dinosaur. In the stories, these merciless, superhuman forces of nature are symbolized by the "Great Old Ones," Cthulhu, YogSothoth, Azathoth, Shub-Niggurath, Nyarlathotep. They are going to destroy us, not because they hate us, but because we are in their way.

Lovecraft's characters gradually come to discover their danger by piecing together isolated scraps of knowledge: Armitage decoding Wilbur Whateley's diary and collating it with the *Necronomicon* in "The Dunwich Horror"; Thurston puzzling over his uncle's files and connecting them with an ominous news clipping in "The Call of Cthulhu"; Ward discovering his ancestor Curwen's journal and comparing it with old newspapers and genealogies in *The Case of Charles Dexter Ward.* Sometimes it is actual scientific or archaeological research which opens the door to oblivion, as in "The Dreams in the Witch House" and *At the Mountains of Madness.* At any rate, the idea is summed up at the beginning of "The Call of Cthulhu":

> The most merciful thing in the world, I think, is the inability of the human mind to correlate all its contents. We live on a placid island of ignorance in the midst of black seas of infinity, and it was not meant that we should voyage far. The sciences, each straining in its own direction, have hitherto harmed us little; but some day the piecing together of dissociated knowledge will open up such terrifying vistas of reality, and of our frightful position therein, that we shall either go mad from the revelation or flee from the deadly light into the peace and safety of a new dark age. (*DH* 125)

What sort of "scientific revelations" is Lovecraft talking about? Weapons of destruction like the H-bomb? No, this is to miss his point. He means not the destruction of the world, but the destruction of our worldview. Science would reveal the utter insignificance of humanity's place in the scheme of things. In fact, Lovecraft believed that it already had! He wrote of the disorientation caused by Copernicus and Darwin. Copernicus told us that our home planet was not the center of things. We are out on the rim, stuck off on a speck of dust orbiting a middling star in a minor galaxy. Darwin discovered that we are not qualitatively removed from and superior to the animals, as we had always thought. *Homo sapiens,* then, is neither the center nor the ruler of creation, but only a comic biped lost in a cosmic whiff of flotsam and jetsam. This news can be just as shocking and disorienting as Lovecraft said it must be. Witness the struggles of the medieval church to silence Galileo and of today's fundamentalists to combat Darwinism. They are, as Lovecraft said, fleeing into a new dark age of superstition.

Sometimes Lovecraft symbolizes the blind impartiality of the universe as the Old Ones, especially Azathoth. Sometimes there is no threat of destruction by aliens; it is merely knowledge of their existence (as in *At the Mountains of Madness*) that dwarfs us. Sometimes it is knowledge of the frightful secrets of the past that destroys (as in *Charles Dexter Ward* or "The Rats in the Walls").

So, now, what about the Lovecraft mythos?

Lovecraft scholar Dirk W. Mosig has pointed out that the "Yog-Sothoth Cycle of Myth," as he prefers to call it, refers to a body of *lore,* not a set of *stories.* The various stories all *draw on* this lore (as well as other sources) but they do not *belong to* the Mythos. Many writers and fans have ignored this crucial distinction, and the result has been complete chaos.

Anyway, what elements belong to the Mythos, as Lovecraft knew it? First, there are the gods: Cthulhu, Yog-Sothoth, Azathoth, Shub-Niggurath, Nyarlathotep. These appear in Lovecraft's own stories. A "second tier" of the pantheon includes Ghatanothoa, Rhan-Tegoth, Yig, Nug and Yeb, Gnoph-Keh, Kthun, and Noth-Yidik. These were specially created by Lovecraft for use in his "revision tales," ghost-written for various clients. Then there are the fabled grimoires: the *Necronomicon,* the Pnakotic Manuscripts, and *The Seven Cryptical Books of Hsan.*

In his lifetime, Lovecraft witnessed the elaboration of the Mythos by his friends. These (Robert E. Howard, Clark Ashton Smith, Henry Kuttner, Robert Bloch, Frank Belknap Long) sometimes lacked the philosophic punch of Lovecraft, but did keep the basically pessimistic tone.

Robert E. Howard and the Cthulhu Mythos

Enter Robert E. Howard

Robert E. Howard fits into the picture right at this point. Howard's stories represent no slavish imitation of Lovecraft; Howard definitely struck out in his own direction. But where he touches on the Mythos, it rings true.

His overt references to Lovecraftian lore are surprisingly few. In "The Thing on the Roof," "The Fire of Asshurbanipal," and "The Children of the Night," he mentions the *Necronomicon* (it does not appear in the Howard fragment "The House" finished by Derleth as "The House in the Oaks"). In "The Children of the Night" he gives a list of the Old Ones: "Cthulhu, Yog-Sothoth, Tsathoggua, Gol-goroth" (this last being Howard's own addition to the pantheon, also mentioned in "The Gods of Bal-Sagoth," though not in the Howard portions of the completed fragments "Dagon Manor" or "Black Eons"). "The Fire of Asshurbanipal" lists "Cthulhu and Koth and Yog-Sothoth." Yog-Sothoth and the mysterious planet Yuggoth occur briefly in "Dig Me No Grave," and "the Old Ones," "great Cthulhu," and Yog-Sothoth are all glancingly alluded to in "The Black Bear Bites." Finally, in "Worms of the Earth," Bran Mak Morn swears by the "black gods of R'lyeh." (The references to the star-headed Old Ones and the shoggoths from Lovecraft's *At the Mountains of Madness* that appear in the Cormac Mac Art tale "The Temple of Abomination" formed no part of Howard's original fragment; they were added by Richard L. Tierney who completed the tale.)

But simple name-dropping does not a Lovecraftian story make! Something lacking in many contemporary Mythos tales comes through loud and clear in Howard's tales: that dreadful awareness of ultra-worldly Powers who render human existence both tenuous and trite. Even in tales which basically belong to other genres, e.g., heroic fantasy or lost-race stories, this disturbing note creeps in like the distant whispered notes of El-Lil. We keep hearing of "the terrible black gods of ages past . . . to whom mankind was but a plaything and a puppet," "beings outside the ken of common humanity, foul shapes of transcosmic evil." Two quotations in particular remind us of the anti-human polemic of Lovecraft's *Necronomicon*. "Man was not always master of the earth—*and is he now?*" ("The Black Stone"). "Before manne was, ye Elder ones were . . . Men see ye tracks of ye talones but not ye feete that make them" ("Dig Me No Grave"). Listen to the *Necronomicon:* "Nor is it to be thought that man is either the oldest or the last of earth's masters . . . The Old Ones were, the Old Ones are, and the Old Ones shall be. . . . Their hand is at your throats, yet ye see Them not" (*DH* 170).

Perhaps Howard "got it right" because he had independently come to the same philosophical conclusions as Lovecraft. Reading Howard's tales of

DISSECTING CTHULHU

Kirowan, Grimlan, and others who have spent years seeking *and finding* occult realities, it may come as a surprise to read what Howard really thought of such individuals. In a letter to Lovecraft, Howard bemoans the credulity of Lovecraft's revision client William Lumley, who Howard says has "taken refuge from reality in misty imaginings and occult dreams." "There is to me a terrible pathos in a man's vain wanderings on occult paths, and clutching at non-existent things, as a refuge from the soul-crushing realities of life." Stripped of all such comforting illusions, Howard felt, a human being is left "writhing feebly on the jagged rocks of materiality, dying as any other insect dies, and knowing that he is no divine spirit in tune with some mystic infinity, but only a faint spark of material light, to be extinguished forever in the blackness of the ultimate abyss" (May 24, 1932). That is pure "Lovecraftian orthodoxy."

And like Lovecraft, Howard knew how debilitating it would be to have one's carefully constructed and self-flattering worldview knocked flat like a house of cards by some jolting scientific discovery. "Conrad looked all at sea. He was of that class of scientists who have the universe classified and pigeonholed and everything in its proper little nook. By Jove! It knocks them in a heap to be confronted with the paradoxical-unexplainable-shouldn't-be" ("The Voice of El-Lil").

Not only did H. P. Lovecraft and Robert E. Howard share a philosophical outlook readily translatable into horror fiction, once one "mythologized" the forces of the cosmos into personal Powers of evil, but once they had done so, their horror stories could took remarkably alike. For instance, compare Lovecraft's "The Nameless City" and Howard's "The Black Stone." In both stories, the protagonists are traveling adventurers who seek out all sorts of curiosities. Lovecraft's quester is hot on the trail of an ancient Arabian city, whispered of in campfire legends. Howard's vagabond cannot rest until he has seen for himself a mysterious obelisk in Hungary, which he has read about in connection with both the demonologist Von Junzt (author of *Unaussprechlichen Kulten*) and the poet Justin Geoffrey. Arriving in the respective vicinity of each, the adventurers pay no heed to the warnings they receive. At the site itself, both find that the object of their quest is a specimen of time-worn masonry, so old as to predate not only any known culture, but the human race itself. And eventually it becomes clear that the stone ruins are merely the tip of the iceberg. They are but the exposed remains of huge subterranean fortresses. Finally, the protagonists of both tales have ghostly visions of the long-dead inhabitants of the caverns below. Lovecraft's visionary sees "a nightmare horde of rushing devils; hate-distorted, grotesquely panoplied, half-transparent devils of a race no man might mistake—the crawling reptiles of the nameless city" (*D*

110). Howard's dreamer sees a soundless holograph of a frenzied bloody ceremony presided over by "a huge monstrous toad-like *thing* [that] squatted on the top of the monolith!" Awakening, both thrill-seekers are suitably frightened out of their wits.

Not only are the plot outlines point-for-point the same, but the stories are even introduced with identical devices. In each case, the narrator knows of a previous dreamer at the same haunted site who preserved his nightmares in verse. Both are even called "the mad poet."

"It was of this place that Abdul Alhazred the mad poet dreamed on the night before he sang his unexplainable couplet:

> That is not dead which can eternal lie,
> And with strange aeons, even death may die."
> ("The Nameless City" [*D* 98–99])

"And I suddenly saw a connection between this Stone and a certain weird and fantastic poem written by the mad poet, Justin Geoffrey's *The People of the Monolith.* Inquiries led to the information that Geoffrey had indeed written that poem while travelling in Hungary, and I could not doubt that the Black Stone was the very monolith to which he referred in his strange verse.

> They say foul beings of Old Times still lurk
> In dark forgotten corners of the world,
> And Gates still gape to loose, on certain nights,
> Shapes pent in Hell. ("The Black Stone")

Even the word "pent" appears in "The Nameless City" in a parallel context. The lizards evidence "the pent-up viciousness of desolate eternities" (*D* 110).

With all these similarities, it is hard to resist the conclusion that Howard borrowed substantially from Lovecraft's earlier story to create "The Black Stone." Yet we know from the publication history of "The Nameless City" that Howard could not have seen Lovecraft's story before he wrote "The Black Stone." The remarkable parallel is all the more remarkable for being spontaneous.

Another startling instance of the two men's eldritch imaginations running along the same course is an unusual image found in both Howard's "Dig Me No Grave" and Lovecraft's *The Dream-Quest of Unknown Kadath.* Lovecraft's novella was written about a decade before Howard's story but was never seen by him. In Howard's tale, the sorcerer John Grimlan gloats over his host John Conrad, "Not even in your dreams have you glimpsed the black cyclopean walls of Koth." In Lovecraft's tale, Randolph Carter, on an adventure that takes place in his *dreams*, finds himself at "that hellish tower of Koth with its Cyclopean steps leading to the enchanted wood" (*MM* 375). Figure *that* one out.

Other coincidences between Howard and Lovecraft can be more easily explained. The reader may have noticed that in "Dig Me No Grave," Grimlan tauntingly asks Conrad what he knows "of Yog-Sothoth, of Kathulos and the sunken cities?" Who is this "Kathulos"? Is this supposed to be Lovecraft's Cthulhu, spelled in a more pronounceable fashion? Actually, Howard's Kathulos is the same as the title character of his famous novella "Skull-Face," a desiccated mummy resurrected ages after the sinking of his native Atlantis. Noting later the similarity in sound to Lovecraft's Cthulhu, Howard suggested that the two might be merged. Lovecraft wrote him back, "It would be amusing to identify your Kathulos with my Cthulhu— indeed, I may so adopt him in some future black allusion" (August 14, 1930). Lovecraft did drop the name in a list of occult gibberish in "The Whisperer in Darkness," right next to other Howardian names: "L'mur-Kathulos, Bran"; but it was Howard who finally identified his Atlantean magus with Lovecraft's monster from R'lyeh in "Dig Me No Grave."

Nameless Cults

The most important instance of playful borrowing between Lovecraft and Howard was the creation of the "Black Book," *Nameless Cults* by Friedrich Wilhelm von Junzt. (Lovecraft provided von Junzt's first and middle names, and August Derleth supplied the German "original" of the title, *Unaussprechlichen Kulten*.) This tome of soul-blasting blasphemy appears in "The Children of the Night," "The Black Stone," "The Thing on the Roof," and Howard's portion of "Black Eons" (though the von Junzt quote heading that story is not Howard's; also, the book appears only in Derleth's portion of "The House in the Oaks").

Nameless Cults is obviously Howard's analogue to Lovecraft's *Necronomicon*. This is not only true of the conception of the book as a whole, but even of all of the intriguing details. The plausible and detailed publishing history of *Nameless Cults* is probably derived straight from similar data in Lovecraft's mock essay "History of the *Necronomicon*," penned in 1927 and sent around to correspondents including Clark Ashton Smith, Willis Conover, and probably Howard. Howard even shows himself familiar with details of Lovecraft's essay when he twice refers to "the original Greek translation" of the *Necronomicon*.

The shocking and mysterious death of von Junzt, his throat torn by invisible talons in a locked and bolted room, recalls the similar death of *Necronomicon* scribe Abdul Alhazred, who was "seized by an invisible monster in broad daylight and devoured horribly before a large number of fright-f rozen witnesses" (*MW* 52), a grisly fate narrated only in "History of the *Necronomicon*."

"As regards the hellish Black Book, if I can find some well-educated maniac, who hasn't been crammed with conventional occult hokus-pokus, I may have him write it for publication. If not, I may shoot myself full of dope sometime, and write it myself" (Howard to Lovecraft, May 24, 1932). Howard never did either. But he did tell us a surprising amount of important information as contained in *Nameless Cults*. In fact, the volume serves to connect several major areas of Howard's fiction. Of course von Junzt mentions the Monolith of Stregoicavar in "The Black Stone" as well as the Temple of the Toad in "The Thing on the Roof," but in "The Children of the Night" we find two tossed-off references not followed up in that story but central to two others. First is the god Gol-goroth who appears in one of the Turlough O'Brian adventures, "The Gods of Bal-Sagoth"; second is the cult of Bran which worships the stone image of Bran Mak Morn, an artifact that forms the basis for another Turlough tale, "The Dark Man," as well as providing a solid link to the Bran Mak Morn stories themselves (connected, in turn, to the King Kull series in "Kings of the Night"!).

Perhaps most startling of all is that in the Howard portion of "Black Eons," the character Allison tells his companion Brill about *Nameless Cults* and discloses that von Junzt is the source of all our "information" about the Hyborian Age! Allison basically provides a kind of thumbnail sketch of the history outlined in Howard's mock essay "The Hyborian Age," which one must therefore suspect of being a verbatim extract from *Nameless Cults* (though of course we have no direct evidence that Howard so intended this). It is no less tempting to wonder if Kirowan got his information about the ring of Thoth-Ammon (in "The Haunter of the Ring") from von Junzt's Hyborian section, since we first see the ring in the Conan tale "The Phoenix on the Sword."

Did Lovecraft mind the blatant imitation of his *Necronomicon* by Howard's *Nameless Cults?* Not at all! In fact he enthusiastically welcomed the volume into the growing phantom library of Mythos lore. Lovecraft often referred to the book in his own stories, mentioning it in the same breath with its older cousin the *Necronomicon,* as in "The Haunter of the Dark," when snooping Robert Blake stumbles upon a shelf of crumbling tomes in the Starry Wisdom Church: "He had himself read many of them—a Latin version of the abhorred *Necronomicon,* the sinister *Liber Ivonis,* the famous

DISSECTING CTHULHU

Cultes des Goules of Comte d'Erlette, the *Unaussprechlichen Kulten* of von Junzt, and old Ludvig Prinn's hellish *De Vermis Mysteriis*" (*DH* 100). (By the way, the second title is Clark Ashton Smith's creation, while the third and fifth are Robert Bloch's—by now everybody was playing the game!) So highly did Lovecraft esteem Howard's creation that he used it as the basis of one of his revision tales, "Out of the Aeons," ghostwritten for Hazel Heald. Much of the story is a flashback to ancient Mu, and the whole sub-narrative is presented as a summary from von Junzt.

So we have come full circle. Robert E. Howard both borrowed from the Mythos of H. P. Lovecraft and contributed to it one of its most intriguing bits of lore. Howard's Mythos fiction echoes Lovecraft's own with remarkable authenticity, a fact that may surprise us since most of Howard's fiction, being of the action-adventure type, is so different from Lovecraft's Gothic horror.

[*Lovecraft Studies* No. 18 (Spring 1989): 10–13, 29]

Divers Hands

By Stefan Dziemianowicz

There's a paradigm that they teach in Anthropology 101 for distinguishing between complex and primitive societies that goes something like this: complex societies, which have mastered the means of food production and transport, give each of the many types of fish they eat its own specific name; primitive societies, which subsist primarily on one type of fish, have only two names for fish—one for the type of fish they eat, and another that designates all other types of fish. Application of this model to Lovecraft studies is not as farfetched as it might seem. For many years, the corpus of Lovecraftian fiction and criticism was viewed as fitting the pattern of the primitive society: Lovecraft was the big fish, and those who wrote under his influence the undifferentiated (and all too frequently undistinguished) little fish; thus writing (both fiction and nonfiction) inspired by Lovecraft was separated into two simple categories, that written by Lovecraft and that written by anyone who was not Lovecraft (the infamous "Divers Hands" immortalized in the credits of such Arkham House volumes as *The Shuttered Room and Other Pieces* [19591 and *The Dark Brotherhood and Other Pieces* [1966]).

Some fifty-five years after Lovecraft's death, though, we are clearly at a point where it is necessary to view Lovecraftian fiction and the critical writing it has stimulated as something more complex and specialized, and for a number of reasons. First, Lovecraftian fiction has become virtually synonymous with Cthulhu Mythos fiction, and the Mythos, it cannot be reiterated too often, was not an invention of Lovecraft's but of August Derleth, who codified patterns implicit in the backgrounds of Lovecraft's horror fiction and promoted them as the ground rules for all subsequent fiction set in Lovecraft's universe. So many Mythos stories being written today in the wake of Derleth's instruction differ so markedly in conceptualization from Lovecraft's originals that they often appear to be two entirely different species of critter when put side by side.

Second, Lovecraft has become, paradoxically, a minor figure in the area of Cthulhu Mythos fiction. Though his work remains the source, it has inspired a mountain of pastiches, homages, and critical works by both fans and professionals that dwarfs his own contribution, in bulk if not significance. With writers like Derleth and Brian Lumley having written more stories incorporating Lovecraftian elements than Lovecraft himself, and critics such as Dirk Mosig, S. T. Joshi, and Robert M. Price having written more extensively on the meaning of Lovecraft's fiction than Lovecraft ever did (and promulgating their own distinct viewpoints on how to interpret that fiction), we can safely say that Lovecraft's fiction now constitutes only a small sub-subgenre within the larger subgenre of the Cthulhu Mythos.

But the main reason why it has become necessary to consider post-Lovecraftian writing as something more than simply a body of work connecting Lovecraft to his successors is the controversy it has provoked. Because Lovecraft expressed his intentions for his fiction in only the vaguest possible terms, the post-Lovecraftian readership has divided into factions at war over what does or does not constitute a Mythos tale. Reduced to its essentials, the controversy comes down to this: Does the Cthulhu Mythos refer to stories that share Lovecraft's cosmic viewpoint and embody his nihilistic philosophies regarding man's place in the universe? Or is the Mythos a subgenre of stories linked by their common use of extradimensional entities, necromantic texts, and geographic locales? Thanks to the specialty press and British publishing, most of the principal texts with which the lines for this battle were drawn are once more available to readers who wish to decide where they stand on the matter. The following is intended as a historicalcritique of this post-Lovecraftian fiction and criticism, one admittedly colored by the bias of the reviewer. (But then, breathes there a Lovecraftian who does not have strong opinions about what constitutes the best and worst, the correct and the incorrect, of the Mythos mélange?)

All discussion of—and argument over—the Cthulhu Mythos begins with August Derleth, recognized at one and the same time as the archangel who salvaged Lovecraft's writing from the pulps, and (by those less generously inclined) the archfiend of latter-day Lovecraft studies who distorted the meaning of Lovecraft's fiction for several generations of readers. If Lovecraft never fully expressed the intent or meaning of his fiction, save in the celebrated letter to Farnsworth Wright on the resubmittal of "The Call of Cthulhu" (*SL* 2.150) and his theoretical essay "Notes on Writing Weird Fiction," Derleth surely did, in essay after essay that received broader dissemination and more frequent reprinting than any of Lovecraft's own reflections on his work.

Documentation of Derleth's supposed heresy can be found in "A Note on the Cthulhu Mythos," the afterword (written in 1962) to his Cthulhu Mythos "novel" *The Trail of Cthulhu*. This is essentially a restatement of the interpretation of Lovecraft's fiction he had been promulgating in print at least since August of 1937, only five months after Lovecraft's death. Though Derleth has been dismissed in many circles as a second-rate writer whose true calling was as an editor, one could not find a more expertly written piece of propaganda (not meant in a pejorative sense, but in reference to a piece of writing whose intent is to persuade) than the first paragraph of this essay. In three simple declarative sentences, orchestrated with Love-craftian skill, he produced a statement that has probably stimulated more post-Lovecraftian writing than Lovecraft's own work. They deserve to be considered individually, and in order.

"The Cthulhu Mythos is a myth-pattern developed gradually by the late H. P. Lovecraft in the final phase of his creative work in the genre of the ma-cabre." No term has more bedeviled post-Lovecraftians than "the Cthulhu Mythos." Though most would agree that some concepts in Lovecraft's later fiction are more coherently and consistently expressed than in his earlier tales, many are loathe to single these stories out from the body of his work as somehow fundamentally different from what precedes them and to categorize them under a distinct name (particularly one so fraught with ambiguity as "the Cthulhu Mythos"). Indeed, as Dirk Mosig showed repeatedly in essays and commentaries in his amateur press magazine *The Miskatonic* (all twenty-seven issues of which were recently collected in two thick volumes by Kenneth Faig's Moshassuck Press, and will be discussed throughout this review), once one has pierced the superficial trappings of works as different as Lovecraft's Dunsanian fiction and so-called Mythos fiction, one finds essentially the same intent on Lovecraft's part: to deflate human ideals. Any attempt to distinguish a portion of Lovecraft's stories from his entire ouevre must be recognized as a conceit of the critic, and not ascribed to Lovecraft.[1]

Yet Derleth's choice of words implies the opposite. "Developed gradu-ally by" H. P. Lovecraft means something different from "is apparent in the fiction of" or "emerges from the later stories of" H. P. Lovecraft. Though Derleth notes later in the afterword that "there is much to indicate that in its initial stages at least, Lovecraft had no intention or plan to bring the Cthulhu Mythos into being as it finally took shape," and seven years later acknowledges in his introduction to the *Tales of the Cthuthu Mythos* that the Mythos was named "by Lovecraft's correspondents and fellow-writers,

---

[1] This is nowhere more evident than in the differences of critical opinion as to how many of Lovecraft's stories, and which ones, constitute the Mythos: 13 according to Derleth, 12 according to Mosig, 12 according to Lin Carter (different from Mosig's), and 3 or 4 according to Will Murray.

though Lovecraft himself never so designated it,"[2] *here* he implies deliberate invention on Lovecraft's part. Those who ascribe to Ramsey Campbell's understanding of Lovecraft's Mythos tales as "a step in Lovecraft's search for the perfect form for the weird tale" (*New Tales of the Cthulhu Mythos*) may see a different meaning implicit in Derleth's subtle choice of words. Where they might view the Mythos as a sort of perfection of the voice with which Lovecraft had been speaking all along, Derleth appears to have seen the Mythos as Lovecraft's adoption of a more suitable tone and dialect than the one he had spoken in before. Derleth's later observation that "There is, in fact, no hard and fast line separating Lovecraft's Dunsanian tales from the stories which are *definitely* part of the Mythos" [emphasis added], is self-contradictory. Clearly, he thinks that the Mythos begins at a specific point. It is for these and Derleth's other liberal interpretations of Lovecraft's writing that critics are hesitant to use the term "Cthulhu Mythos" when singling out works of Lovecraft's with an apparent mythic backdrop; many feel that to adopt Derleth's term is to sanction his categorization of the stories.

"*Lovecraft saw it as 'based on the fundamental lore or legend that this world was inhabited at one time or another by another race who, in practising black magic, lost their foothold and were expelled, yet live on the outside ever ready to take possession of this earth again.'*" We need not recapitulate here the origins of the spurious "black magic" quote attributed to Lovecraft (readers are referred to David Schultz's "The Origins of Lovecraft's 'Black Magic' Quote" in *Crypt of Cthulhu* 48). Evidence appears to indicate that the quote is Derleth's paraphrase of a paraphrase by a Lovecraft correspondent of something that Lovecraft might never have said. Despite speculations to the contrary, Derleth likely published it in good faith of its veracity, since he did not try to suppress the quote in Lovecraft's *Selected Letters* which it seems to echo, and which clearly contradicts it:

> Now all my tales are based on the fundamental premise that common human laws and interests and emotions have no validity or significance in the vast cosmos-at-large . . . To achieve the essence of real externality, whether of time or space or dimension, one must forget that such things as organic life, *good and evil*, love and hate, and all such local attributes of a negligible and temporary race called mankind, have any existence at all. (*SL* 2.150) [emphasis added]

---

[2] Presumably this refers only to August Derleth. I am unaware of any documentation that the term "Cthulhu Mythos" was used seriously before Lovecraft's death, or by anyone prior to August Derleth's coinage of the term.

The difference between the quote used by Derleth and that from Lovecraft's letter is the difference between a reading that stops at the surface of a Lovecraft story, and one that grasps its deeper implications. In Lovecraft's stories, both trustworthy and untrustworthy characters typically describe Mythos entities in terms of "good" and "evil." Black magic would presumably be one of many tools in the evil entities' bags of tricks. However, as Lovecraft shows time and again, his human protagonists—even those lucky enough to survive their ordeals and share with the reader the wealth of knowledge their experience affords them—are pathetically ignorant, and thus woefully unreliable in the revelations they impart. Lacking a system of appropriate references with which to describe the indescribable things they have discovered, a vocabulary that expresses the Unknown, even the most educated will lapse into the jargon of orthodox belief systems with which they are most familiar. The best they can hope to convey to the reader is a half-truth. It is a supreme irony of Lovecraft's Mythos fiction—one that seems to have completely eluded Derleth—that the concepts being dealt with are so esoteric and so beyond the scope of human comprehension that our language can offer only a poor approximation of what they are all about.

"Its similarity to the Christian mythos—as well as to other myth patterns common to both history and fiction—will be immediately apparent to the literate reader." Here is the climax to which the half-truths in this paragraph have been building, the assertion that has had critics as different as Mosig, Joshi, and Richard Tierney frothing at the mouth. *In theory,* of course, Derleth's observation is not incorrect. Implicit in Lovecraft's Mythos fiction is the understanding that the articles of *all* religious faiths—whether the cultish practices of Cthulhu's adherents or the dogma of Judeo-Christian belief—describe a need on the part of mankind to apprehend the workings of the universe through a system in which Man is securely at the center. Lovecraft recognized that this was the only way Man knew to comfort himself against the sort of existential despair Lovecraftian protagonists know at the end of a story, by which time they have come to the realization that man is merely an insignificant atom in the infrastructure of the cosmos.

In practice, however, Derleth rendered a distorted application of this aspect of Lovecraft's fiction, one that is summed up perfectly in a passage from the last Mythos tale to bear his individual byline, "The Seal of R'lyeh" (*The Mask of Cthulhu*):

> After all, the pattern in itself was not new. All religious beliefs, all myth-patterns, in no matter what systems of culture, are

basically familiar—they are predicated upon a struggle between forces of good and forces of evil. This pattern was part, too, of my uncle's mythos—the Great Old Ones and the Elder Gods, who may, for all I could figure out, have been the same, represented primal good, the Ancient Ones primal evil. As in many cultures, the Elder Gods were not often named; the Ancient Ones were, and often, for they were still worshipped and served by followers throughout the Earth and among the planetary spaces; and they were aligned not only against the Elder Gods, but also against one another in a ceaseless struggle for ultimate dominion. They were, in brief, representations of elemental forces—Cthulhu of water, Cthuga of fire, Ithaqua of air, Hastur of interplanetary spaces; and others among them belonged to great primal forces—Shub Niggurath, the messenger of the gods, of fertility; Yog-Sothoth of the time-space continua, Azathoth—in a sense the fountainhead of evil.

Was this pattern after all not familiar? The Elder Gods could so easily have become the Christian Trinity; the Ancient Ones could for most believers have been altered into Sathanus and Beelzebub, Mephistopheles and Azrael. Except that they were co-existent, which disturbed me, though I knew that systems of belief constantly overlapped in the history of mankind.

Here, one sees the inherent fallacy in Derleth's interpretation of Lovecraft's Mythos. Having gone to great length to establish that human myth-patterns all flow from the same source, Derleth presupposes that because these myth-patterns all embody the struggle between good and evil, then so must the source. This constitutes an extrapolation backwards from the myth-patterns themselves to impose their characteristics on the source, a little like assuming that God is an old man with a flowing white beard because the idea of the Judeo-Christian God was conceived within a patriarchal culture.

Derleth, it seems, was incapable (where Lovecraft clearly was not) of conceiving of a universe that was fundamentally morally neutral. Thus it became necessary for him to interpret Lovecraft's universe as one where myth patterns were secondhand distortions of a fundamental struggle between powers of good and evil, instead of one where human concepts of good and evil are themselves only human distortions of blind, amoral cosmic forces. It was Derleth's inability to see beyond the limits of the anthropomorphized universe such thinking implies that led Lovecraft to brand his protégé a "self-blinded earth-gazer."

At this point, it would be fair to ask how terribly Derleth's misinterpretation of Lovecraft perverted the field of post-Lovecraftian fiction.

The answer is: probably not nearly as much as anti-Derlethians would like to think. In his essay "H. P. Lovecraft: Myth-Maker" (*Miskatonic* #13) Dirk Mosig wonders, "How many would-be Lovecraft pastichists inadvertently wound up pasticing Derleth's own inferior imitations?" implying that the once pure stream of Lovecraft imitators had been tainted by misunderstandings handed down by Derleth. The truth is, there were very few good Lovecraft pastiches to begin with. Going through the table of contents of the original version of *Tales of the Cthulhu Mythos,* assembled by Derleth in 1969 largely from stories by Lovecraft's colleagues in the pulps, one finds precious few stories written while Lovecraft was alive—and presumably able to cry foul (of course, because he was a gentleman, he never would have done so) had he felt his concepts were being abused—that approximate his own achievements.

Certainly these would include Robert Bloch's "The Shambler from the Stars," probably Frank Belknap Long's "The Hounds of Tindalos," Clark Ashton Smith's "Ubbo-Sathla," and on the fringe Robert E. Howard's "The Black Stone," a fine story whose Mythos elements are little more than a nod of respect to Lovecraft. These four stories represent the best of their kind, insofar as they evoke the sense of awe and dread we describe as "cosmic terror." But they are only the tip of the iceberg of pastiches produced by the first generation of Mythos writers, the bulk of which read like horror stories typical for the authors who wrote them except that they have been laminated with Mythos patina. Derleth may not have written a pastiche that captured the essence of Lovecraft's fiction, but he was by no means the first or last against whom that judgment could be levied.

One could argue that Derleth's pastiches injured Lovecraft's reputation by encouraging critics too lazy to go to the source to judge Lovecraft, and anyone who wrote in the Lovecraftian mode, by his pastiches' lack of merit (see, for example, Damon Knight's celebrated hatchet-job on Lovecraft in the chapter "B-R-R-R!" in *In Search of Wonder,* where he faults Lovecraft for the flaws in the pseudo-collaboration "The Shuttered Room"). But most such critics were intent on finding fault with Lovecraft anyway; Derleth merely gave them an easy means to do so. It's possible that an entire generation of readers were turned off to Lovecraft through Derleth's work in the postwar years, when it clogged the pages of *Weird Tales* and several other magazines; however, it's not highly probable. The truth is, Lovecraft and company were already somewhat on their way out by that time, thanks to the shifting interest of the reading public from fantasy and horror to science fiction, and horror readers from the fiction of the early pulp years to more modern fare by Ray

Bradbury and Richard Matheson.

The worst effect exerted by the Derleth Mythos appears to have been on fiction in the fan press, a market not particularly known for having a powerful effect on professional estimations of an author's work. Why this should be is not easy to explain, since Derleth didn't exactly hold seminars for would-be Mythos writers and his fiction never was all that popular (just contrast Derleth's track record in paperback reprints compared with Lovecraft's). Nevertheless, when one compares the differences between Lovecraft's fiction and the stories collected in *The Mask of Cthulhu* and *The Trail of Cthulhu,* one finds a virtual roadmap to the problems that make so much amateur Mythos fiction so dreadful.

The problem in Derleth's stories from which all others flow is (to paraphrase Mosig) his tendency to overexplain the Unknown. The paragraphs from "The Seal of R'lyeh" quoted above are a prime example. Here, Derleth locks the Mythos entities into two distinct systems: One based on the struggle between good and evil, and one predicated on the existence of elementals (how they can represent two mutually exclusive systems at the same time is never explained; it's a little like trying to comprehend a universe in which the God of the Old Testament and the Wendigo coexist). Such categorizations render these beings' motives and natures perfectly understandable within a human or earthly frame of reference, making them seem closer in conceptualization to the gods of ancient Greece than to Lovecraft's expressions of the incomprehensible void.

Derleth's obsessive need to codify the Mythos this way, assign everything in it its proper place, and then invent creatures to fill the gaps such ordering created (this is what he perceived Lovecraft himself to be doing, expanding the myth-pattern in his work through the incorporation of lore donated by colleagues) reduced Lovecraft's cosmic abstractions into an anal retentive's fantasy.

Although we cannot presume Lovecraft's intentions, one suspects the reason he never indulged in a Derlethian elucidation of the Mythos is that a linkage of the myths behind the individual stories into one unified supermyth ran contrary to what he was trying to achieve. In Lovecraft's fiction, Cthulhu, Yog-Sothoth, and company are sometimes physically realized, but even then they retain their metaphorical value: by their alienness, they symbolize the limits of human understanding of the cosmos. They are a means to an end, only clues to larger, more unfathomable mysteries of the universe. But Derleth meant for his representations of these same beings to be ends in themselves; his protagonists, by and large, do not grapple with unfathomable mysteries, but with Mythos monsters that can be summoned, and then either vanquished or eluded. If one looks upon the Mythos as a religious construct, it could be said that Lovecraft appreciated the conceptual foundations of the religion while Derleth preferred its dogma; that Lovecraft worshipped what the plaster statues stood for and Derleth the statues themselves.

Now, the perfectly legitimate question put to Lovecraft purists is why any of this should matter. In his critical study *Lin Carter: A Look Behind His Imaginary Worlds* (Starmont House), Robert M. Price takes issue with those who dismiss Lin Carter for his career as a pasticheur, one so completely analogous to Derleth's that one might think of them as the Whateley twins of fantasy publishing. "Should we browbeat a dead man for not being the kind of writer we feel it is best to be, or that he could have been?" wonders Price. "The fiction itself must, I think, be evaluated strictly on its own merits or demerits." In other words, might our perspective on Derleth's fiction be different if, rather than comparing it to Lovecraft's (and what writer would bear up well under such a comparison?) we simply evaluated it on its own terms as a story?

Assessed in this context, the stories in *The Mask of Cthulhu* and *The Trail of Cthulhu* are *perfect* Mythos stories, insofar as they elaborate the scheme Derleth had worked out for the Mythos (which, after all, was his creation). But as weird fiction, they leave much to be desired, and the reason for this can be traced directly to the differences between how Lovecraft and Derleth employed the Mythos in their writing. Because Lovecraft never quite spelled out what the Mythos meant, or whether it should even integrate coherently, he was put in the position of having to recreate anew, in each story, the sense of mystery he used his myth-patterns to express. In this way, he was able to use Mythos elements dynamically, shaping them to suit the needs of his plots. Though echoes reverberate from story to story, no two of Lovecraft's so-called Mythos tales are exactly alike, except insofar as each is a self-contained expression of a certain set of philosophic principles. Should the definitions of Mythos paraphernalia in one story contradict those in another, so much the better! Such confusion only helps to deepen the mystery and convey the impression that confused human knowledge gives rise to inferior understandings of that mystery.

By codifying the Mythos, Derleth not only limited its possibilities as a vehicle for expressing cosmic awe and terror, he severely constricted the type of story that could be written around it. Put simply, once the framework he devised for the Mythos was put in place, only a particular type of story could be constructed around it. Repitition is to be expected in the five stories that comprise *The Trail of Cthulhu,* for Derleth wrote them as chapters of a novel meant to reinforce by repetition. But the lack of imagination that his other Mythos stories reveal as a consequence of having to follow the rigid guidelines he set down—a sameness that might have eluded readers who caught them only sporadically in the magazines of the '40s and '50s—is glaringly evident when those stories are brought together between book covers.

The typical Derleth story begins with a man either inheriting a family home, being called to a relative's home, or taking a house for rent. There, he comes into knowledge of the Mythos incunabula, which he usually shares with the reader in page-long catalogs of entities, books, and lore, what Lovecraft might have described as "bald catalogues" that lose their import as esoteric or forgotten knowledge through the sheer volume of data they contain, not to mention its accessibility to a layman. If the character is not himself destroyed by this knowledge, he is witness to someone who is. This scenario describes the events chronicled in "Beyond the Threshold," "The Return of Hastur," "The Sandwin Compact," "The Whippoorwills in the Hills," "The House in the Valley," and "The Seal of R'lyeh"—six of his eight stories in *The Mask of Cthulhu* and *Tales of the Cthulhu Mythos*. It is the foundation of all but five of the sixteen stories to be found in the volumes *The Lurker at the Threshold* and *The Watchers out of Time.*

Derleth also had a weakness for certain clichés of the Mythos might not have been so evident had he learned to vary his storytelling pattern. His early work, in particular the stories "Ithaqua" and "The Thing That Walked on the Wind," is chock full of characters who disappear only to be rediscovered in areas remote from their homes, looking as though dropped from a great height. Slightly later, he shows a fondness for narrators of Innsmouth stock who clearly (except to the narrators themselves) are destined to revert to their true heritage before the story's end.

Most unforgivable in the eyes of Lovecraft purists, the few times Derleth departed from his usual scenarios he blatantly cannibalized Lovecraft's fiction. "The Dweller in Darkness" evokes "The Whisperer in Darkness," "The Whippoorwills in the Hills" recalls "The Rats in the Walls," "The Horror from the Middle Span" borrows from *The Case of Charles Dexter Ward*, "The Shadow out of Space" xeroxes "The Shadow out of Time," and so on. These condensations of Lovecraft's work into his own is Derleth's worst indiscretion, for it makes it nearly impossible to consider his stories on their own merits. In order to appreciate the significance of the Lovecraftian tropes and motifs jammed into Derleth's stories, one must be familiar with the Lovecraft stories in which they originate (and next to which Derleth's, like anyone else's, pale in significance).

Was Derleth an innately unimaginative writer, or did he simply become tangled accidentally in the web of his realization of the Mythos? One suspects a little of both, but inclines toward the latter judgment. On the whole, Derleth's Mythos stories are not badly written. They avoid the adjectivitis that mars so many Mythos pastiches, and in some passages they are extremely evocative and atmospheric. If, as Mosig contends, Derleth reduced the tale of Lovecraftian horror to the equivalent of a vampire story, and in his articulation of the supposed battle between the Elder Gods and the Great Old Ones gave us a tale of cowboys and injuns on a cosmic scale, then what of it? Space opera is to Golden Age Science Fiction what Derleth's pastiches are to Lovecraft's fiction, and space opera can be quite entertaining regardless of our knowledge that better fiction can be written from its primary elements. Derleth's sin was that in his use of Mythos elements he failed to produce remarkable fiction: not fiction as remarkable as Lovecraft's, but fiction that lived up to the great expectations its concepts created. But then, how could he? The machinery of the Mythos that he assembled was so immense, and the results it was capable of producing so predetermined, that its reconstruction in every Mythos story completely frustrated (some would say relieved him of the obligation of) inventiveness.

This is obvious from a comparison of his two Mythos novels, *The Lurker at the Threshold* and *The Trail of Cthulhu*. In *Lurker* one finds possibly Derleth's best approximation of Lovecraft. Though told in three parts, the novel is essentially the same story told from three different perspectives. At least initially, Derleth uses this approach intelligently. The first part tells of Ambrose Dewart's ill-fated journey to his ancestral home in Arkham and ends with his presumed possession by his ancestor, Alijah Billington. In the second part, we witness the transformation of Ambrose through the eyes of his cousin, Stephen Bates, who is ignorant of the portents in Ambrose's increasingly peculiar behavior. These two chapters work well together, the second amplifying to a position of significance several minor details in the first. But then, instead of using a third perspective to further amplify these details just enough for the horror to work, Derleth oversteps the threshold of subtlety. Not giving his readers enough credit to intuit what is happening, he brings on Dr. Seneca Lapham (a fictionalized version of himself, who knows all the answers) to explain everything. Never mind that the knowledge Lapham possesses has driven lesser men—i.e., all of Lovecraft's protagonists—to despair. The Mythos needs to be explained so that its horrors can be thwarted, and Lapham does this with lightning-fast speed.

A similar example of how Derleth's Mythos fiction is held hostage to the dictates of the myth-pattern it must reveal is evident in *The Trail of*

Cthulhu, the first part of which Derleth was writing at approximately the same time he must have been preparing to publish *Lurker*. Another multi-perspective narrative, it holds out hope that its five different viewpoints will add up to a whole greater than the sum of the parts. But each of its five stories settles quickly into the same pattern: Dr. Laban Shrewsbury visits a young disciple, educates him about the Mythos, shows him an example of the Mythos at work in daily life, recruits him to stamp it out, and then helps spirit him away to a safe refuge. Rather than reinforce each other through the sharing of details, these five interconnected stories generate only an oppressive tedium as the overfamiliarity of their common elements neutralizes what little horror they possess. It hardly comes as a surprise that the better-written stories in these three volumes of Derleth's work—"Wentworth's Day," "The Dark Brotherhood," "The Ancestor," "The Fisherman of Falcon Point"—are those in which the plots are completely liberated from the obligation to delineate the Mythos in its entirety.

This, then, was the true legacy of Derleth's Mythos fiction: its repetitiousness and obsessive concentration on the minutiae of the Mythos, rather than what the minutiae pointed to. For proof of where Derleth's concerns lay, one need only turn to his introduction to the 1969 *Tales of the Cthulhu Mythos*. The first two paragraphs attempt an explanation of the cosmic underpinnings of Lovecraft's fiction. The next five pages catalog the lists of deities, eldritch tomes, geographic locales, and story titles contributed by Lovecraft and everyone else. If the bulk of Mythos fiction written today is any indication, Derleth may have played no small role in convincing would-be writers that writing Mythos fiction depends less on expressing—in the words of James Turner, in his introduction to the revised *Tales of the Cthulhu Mythos* (Arkham House, 1990)—"a certain convincing cosmic attitude," than it does on larding the pages with unpronounceable proper names and plagiarizing Lovecraft's plots. Like Derleth's, such stories are less works of fiction than critiques of all similar tales that have preceded them into print.

If the genealogy of the Mythos begins with Lovecraft and extends to August Derleth, then from Derleth the line of descent passes on to Lin Carter and Brian Lumley. It's hard to say whether either of these writers was directly influenced by Derleth, but both seem to have been encouraged by Derleth's example, and each has propagated a controversial aspect of his legacy.

The longest chapter in Robert Price's *Lin Carter: A Look Behind His Imaginary Worlds* (an enjoyable discussion of Carter's vast output that is neither uncritical nor apologetic with regard to his penchant for mimicry) is "The Statement of Lin Carter," a perceptive overview of Carter's forays into the Cthulhu Mythos following his immersion in it during his editing days at Ballantine Books. "Though Carter of course enjoyed the stories of Lovecraft, Derleth, Howard, et al.," writes Price, "he was so fascinated with the concept and system of the Mythos itself that he tended to view the various tales primarily as sources for the data that made up the Cthulhu Mythos." So it follows that Carter, like Derleth, began to write stories about the Cthulhu Mythos, rather than using the Mythos as Lovecraft did as "a spooky fog" in the background. But then, Carter had no interest in pastiching Lovecraft, says Price. His forte was the sequel, which he used (in his own words) for "plugging up some of the holes left by early writers in the rather patchwork fabric of the Mythos." This penchant manifested itself in stories through which he sought to embellish Derleth's own elemental classifications for the Great Old Ones, or match up "inhuman races with nothing to do [with] Old Ones with no one to serve them, etc."

Naturally, the best that Carter could hope to do in such stories was maneuver familiar characters and creatures into the appropriate positions to facilitate plugging the gaps he perceived. The shortcomings of such ambitions are apparent in the stories they produced. "Their purpose to provide data gets in the way of their purpose to tell an entertaining tale. We start to get the feeling that the narrative is just a regrettable necessity to be endured in order to bring about the next chunk of Mythos exposition . . . Some of the stories seem to exist only because Mythos lore has to appear in a published story to become 'official.'" Though Carter shared the same zeal as Derleth to shore up the Mythos, we find a different sort of problem in his fiction: Derleth's tales, though static and lifeless, are at least self-contained works of fiction like Lovecraft's; Carter's, on the other hand, depend heavily on reference outside to other Mythos tales, and often read like fragments by themselves. Small wonder almost none of them ever saw print anywhere but in the small press: they were written almost exclusively for Lovecraft junkies, who already knew the primary texts by heart. The average reader—i.e., the reader at whom Lovecraft aimed his own stories—would have been totally baffled by all the fuss.

Price's conclusion that Carter and Brian Lumley both got the idea to write sequels from Lovecraft's collaboration with E. Hoffmann Price, "Through the Gates of the Silver Key," is highly debatable. In Carter's case, it is much more likely that he saw himself capable of doing for Lovecraft what he and L. Sprague de Camp had just done for Robert E. Howard's Conan saga, writing new stories that in effect bridged the gaps between Howard's to create a full chronological history. Nevertheless, Price is on target in his reading of both Carter's and Lumley's work in contrast to Lovecraft's: "Carter's (and Lumley's) stories are less effective than Lovecraft's, since the Old Ones' secret is out, has been since the conclusion of the 'The Dunwich Horror,' 'The Whisperer in Darkness,' 'The Shadow out of Time.' But what critics fail to grasp is that Carter and Lumley *seem* less effective only because they are not striving for the *same* effect Lovecraft sought."

Though Carter's and Lumley's Mythos stories spring from the same impulse, there is a significant difference between them. Carter's sequels labor to supply information that is already implicit in the stories they bridge. By contrast, Lumley's sequels attempt to bring the Mythos kicking and screaming into the late twentieth century through the incorporation of historical events and scientific discoveries that have transpired since Lovecraft's day.

The idea behind Lumley's updating of the Mythos can be traced back to Derleth's *The Trail of Cthulhu*, in particular the final chapter, "The Black Island," which ends with the ludicrous spectacle of the U.S. Navy nuking R'lyeh in the hope of disposing of Cthulhu. Published in 1952 (and thus some time after Robert Bloch's "The Shadow from the Steeple," which ironically presented nuclear energy as an idea passed on to human beings by the Old Ones to hasten human self-destruction), "The Black Island" was written for a much different world than existed when the novel's first chapter, "The Trail of Cthulhu," was published in 1944.

Although Derleth's rendering of Lovecraft's timeless themes was not the most adept, he at least realized the importance of adapting those themes to a world that reflected the reality of postwar America. (It's not overreaching to assume that Lovecraft would have done the same, or to speculate what impact the dawn of the nuclear age would have had on the world view expressed in his stories.) In fact, Derleth appears to have encouraged writers to move the Mythos out of Lovecraft's Arkham country (where, naturally, it is always circa 1930) and into some more contemporary milieu in the hope of giving the Mythos a more modern appeal. Thus, the stories he chose from the newer Mythos writers for *Tales of the Cthulhu Mythos:* James Wade's "The Deep Ones" combined scientific study of dolphins with the fad mysticism of the 1960s youth culture; Ramsey Campbell's "Cold Print" portrayed the urban blight of contemporary Liverpool; and Colin Wilson's "Return of the Lloigor" (and later novel *The Mind Parasites*) captured the despair of a world coping with the harsh realities of modern war and crime.

But Lumley's radical reinterpretation of the Mythos, which can be found on full display in his 1974 novel *The Burrowers Beneath* and its 1976 sequel *The Transition of Titus Crow*, goes beyond mere updating of time and place. It entails a complete demystifying of the Mythos through contemporary scientific understanding. According to Lumley's Mythos, "the combined forces of evil, the Great Old Ones, are nothing more than alien beings or forces against which it will be necessary to employ alien weapons." In Lumley's Mythos, as in Derleth's, the Old Ones are not symbols for the suspension of natural law as Lovecraft saw them, but physically tangible beings with a stake in reclaiming the earth for their own purposes (a little like the space aliens of 1950s space opera and B-movies who came to Earth to steal the women). Nyarlathotep is the embodiment of the powers of telepathy (did you know his name was something of an anagram for it?), Shub-Niggurath the manifestation of miscegenation, and Azathoth, "the bubbler at the hub," simply another name for the nuclear blast. Their imprisonment by the Elder Gods (we are told) was achieved through the implantation of "mental and genetic blocks into the psyches and beings of the forces of evil and all their minions, that at the sight of—or upon sensing the presence of—certain symbols, or upon hearing those symbols reproduced as sound, those forces of evil are held back, impotent!" In other words, the Old Ones have been biologically programmed to run like superstitious natives when confronted by a starstone or appropriate chant.

In effect, Lumley's banalization of the Mythos anthropomorphizes Lovecraft's extradimensional beings more blatantly than Derleth ever did. They are depicted as having thoroughly human motives and desires, and thus seem no more threatening than slightly enlarged versions of the telepathically-endowed or starstone-encumbered men who chase them underground and across the ocean the way cops chase criminals over rooftops. Indeed, though characters in Lumley's novels constantly remind us of the need to think of the Mythos in a whole new light, the Mythos entities and their pursuers become little more than opponents in a ridiculous espionage scenario: the bad CCD (Cthulhu Cycle Deities) versus the good, scientifically enlightened Wilmarth Foundation (for Chthonic Surveillance).

Somewhere, in all of Lumley's renaming and reimagining of the Mythos, Lovecraft's sense of cosmic wonder gets lost. This is a shame, since there is merit in the idea behind Lumley's Mythos fiction—that all supposedly supernatural events can be understood in scientifically rational terms—that even Lovecraft might have appreciated (although in Lovecraft's universe, scientific understanding wouldn't have helped the human race one bit). As it is, the Lumley Mythos, with recurring characters Titus Crow and Henri Laurent de Marigny perpetually riding to the rescue against the Old Ones, is closer in spirit to heroic fantasy than to Lovecraft's cosmic horror fiction. Indeed, one sees the same spirit at work behind the stories that make up *Iced on Aran* and *The House of Cthulhu: Tales of the Primal Land, Volume 1.*

In the former (which evokes the proper names from Lovecraft's "Dream-land" fantasies but is clearly modeled on the work of Robert E. Howard and Edgar Rice Burroughs and consistent with three preceding volumes, *Hero of Dreams, Ship of Dreams,* and *Mad Moon of Dreams*) two roustabouts in Randolph Carter-land battle Mythos monsters with the same tactics Howard's Conan employs against slightly more mortal adversaries. In the latter, the first of three volumes of Lumley's sword and sorcery "Tales of the Primal Land" (followed by *Tarra Khash: Hrossak!* and *Sorcery in Shad*), the Mythos is subsumed as just one tiny element into the larger framework of myth that enshrouds the primal continent of Theem'hdra. The latter seems to present a very cosmic idea—an even larger Mythos into which the Cthulhu Mythos is incorporated—but as executed in the human-oriented tales of Theem'hdra, it is just one more way of reestablishing Man's place at the center of the universe.

August Derleth never had to face the type of informed criticism that greeted the publication of Lumley's Lovecraftian stories, but not because Derleth was a better writer. In fact, Lumley's work, along with the Lovecraftian fiction of Ramsey Campbell, Lin Carter, James Wade, Colin Wilson, Gary Myers, and Fred Chappell, was some of the first to appear in print outside the fan press following Arkham House's publication of Lovecraft's *Selected Letters* starting in 1965. The importance of this event cannot be overestimated, for it marks the beginning of modern Lovecraft studies. Prior to the appearance of the five volumes of *Selected Letters,* readers could only infer Lovecraft the thinker from the output of Lovecraft the writer. But with documentation of Lovecraft's thoughts over the course of much of his adult life, estimations of Lovecraft's writing—and what other writers could learn from it—changed radically.

Today most readers and critics of Lovecraft see his fiction and letters as extensions of one another. We have Dirk Mosig's example to thank in large part for this perception that Lovecraft's horror fiction is an expression of the same materialist philosophical principles expounded in his volumi-nous correspondence. Writing in his Esoteric Order of Dagon journal *The Miskatonic,* Mosig built on the foundations established by Richard Tierney to fearlessly challenge August Derleth's interpretation of Lovecraft and the Mythos. His "H. P. Lovecraft: Myth-Maker" in issue 13 is a seminal piece of Lovecraft scholarship, one that cites chapter and verse from Lovecraft's stories and letters to rebut the point of view on Lovecraft that Derleth had been promulgating in print for more than thirty-five years. In his zeal to defend Lovecraft's work against trivialization, however, Mosig failed to point out its inconsistencies: the confusion caused by Lovecraft's changing use of certain ideas and tropes over time is indeed the source of many different critical conclusions regarding his "intentions" or the "meaning" of his work. Thus, one suspects that the "correct" point of view lies somewhere between (at the two extremes) Mosig's and Derleth's—although undoubtedly much closer to Mosig's. As Mosig was wont to remind after most of his displays of erudition, "the reader must judge for himself." But having read Mosig's criticism, no one could any longer accept the party line on Lovecraft at face value.

The conclusion of Mosig's essay deserves to be quoted at length:

> Once all the distortions and misconceptions superimposed by Derleth on Lovecraft's work (and perpetuated by uncritical "fans" and disciples) are removed, what remains is a work of genius, a cosmic-minded ouevre embodying a mechanist materialist's brilliant conceptions of the imaginary realms and frightful reality "beyond the fields we know," a literary rhapsody of the cosmos and man's laughable position therein, which is likely to appeal to new generations of readers all over the world, for many years to come. The Lovecraft ouevre can be regarded as a significant contribution to world literature—may it be remembered without the "adornments," "embellishments," and "improvements" contributed by his "self-blinded, earth-gazing" imitators.

Beneath the obvious baiting of unnamed but recognizable perpetrators is the spirit that informs all of Mosig's criticism: belief in the seriousness of Lovecraft's writing, not horror fiction but as *literature*. What makes *The Miskatonic* indispensable reading for anyone interested in Lovecraft is the consideration with which Mosig treats Lovecraft as something more than the prized possession of a subculture of discerning fans. His sincerity is evident in "Toward a Greater Appreciation of Lovecraft: An Analytical Approach" (a Jungian analysis of Lovecraft's work) and "The Four Faces of 'The Outsider'" (which demonstrates how Lovecraft's work can be analyzed from Jungian, autobiographical, philosophical, anti-metaphysical, and other perspectives, each yielding up a lode of rich meaning that does not contradict any of the others), essays that opened many eyes to the depth of Lovecraft's work; in his inclusion of essays by Donald Burleson, J. Vernon Shea, James Wade and S. T. Joshi (including "Lovecraft Criticism: A Study" and "The Political and Economic Thought of H. P. Lovecraft," which anticipate, respectively, Joshi's landmark books *H. P. Lovecraft: Four Decades of Criticism* and *H. P. Lovecraft: The Decline of the West*); even in his highly opinionated reviews of L. Sprague de Camp's *Lovecraft: A Biography* and the Lovecraft poetry collection *A Winter Wish*. Reading Mosig's writing almost twenty years after it first appeared, one senses how exciting it was to be involved in Lovecraft studies at that time.

One also appreciates how Mosig's example helped to change the role of the amateur press in Lovecraft studies from the fannish preservation of enthusiasm over Lovecraft's work to the maintenance of his critical heritage. A good example is Harry O. Morris's *Nyctalops*, which, though started three years before *The Miskatonic*, demonstrates how the small press benefited from the labors of Mosig and other perceptive critics. Though *Nyctalops* was never exclusively a journal of Lovecraft studies—it published critical essays on the work of Clark Ashton Smith and Robert Aickman and an important essay on Ramsey Campbell by T. E. D. Klein that specifically praised Campbell for his growth from Lovecraft pasticheur to modern horror writer—Lovecraft's presence always loomed large in its pages. Once Mosig, Joshi, Price, Burleson and other critics began expanding the canon of Lovecraft criticism, *Nyctalops* and other small press magazines became the repositories for scholarly writing that academic and mainstream journals were too "sophisticated" to publish, as well as well-written fiction the modern horror field would just as soon have forgotten owing to its Lovecraft affiliation.

Issue 19, *Nyctolops*'s lamented last (scheduled for publication seven years ago but only just released at the end of 1991), shows how rewarding the pages of the small press had become by the mid-1980s. Five of eight articles are concerned with Lovecraft's fiction, and range in their treatment from Richard L. Huber's fannish "Lovecraft and Easter Island," to S. T. Joshi's "'The Tree' and Ancient History," a dissection of the historical background of a minor Lovecraft story, Jacqueline C. Shafer's philosophical study "H. P. Lovecraft: Aspiring Materialist," Joel Lane's intertextual analysis of the character of Nyarlathotep, "The Master of Masks," and "The Call of Khalk'ru and Other Speculations," Will Murray's comparative study of the work of Lovecraft and A. Merritt. Among the three fiction selections are two with Lovecraftian overtones: Robert M. Price's sequel to a Lovecraft revision, "The Strange Fate of Alonzo Typer," and Thomas Ligotti's "Flowers of the Abyss," which drops nary a Lovecraft reference yet perfectly embodies Lovecraft's aesthetic for the weird tale in that it creates "a vivid picture of a certain type of human mood." With its eclectic mix of the amateur and the professional, the serious and the humorous, *Nyctalops* published some of the best work of the post-Lovecraftian writers and became the standard by which other magazines, like *Crypt of Cthulhu*, are measured today.

Mention of Thomas Ligotti's name in conjunction with the area of Lovecraft studies calls to mind a comment made by Dirk Mosig in his

DIVERS HANDS

"Miskatonic Comments" column in issue eight of *The Miskatonic*: "A Lovecraftian tale by someone else does not have to belong to the Cthulhu Mythos, of course, although for some strange reason most of those bent upon pastiching HPL write Mythos pieces." It would be stretching a point to call Ligotti a Lovecraftian pasticheur, if only because his work is almost totally devoid of specific Lovecraftian references. Yet in his fiction we recognize the same effort to express the incomprehensible, the same gradual buildup from the "normal" to a vantage point from which the "normal" is revealed to be only seemingly so, the same image of a universe pockmarked with hidden traps and snares for the guiltless and gullible.

Ligotti is by no means the first writer to make us pause and ask what we mean by Lovecraftian fiction, if it is not synonymous with Mythos fiction. In his introduction to the 1980 anthology *New Tales of the Cthulhu Mythos*, Ramsey Campbell lamented the conventionalizing of the Mythos that had come with overuse of its set pieces and asked contributors "to return to the first principles of the Mythos—to give glimpses of something larger than they show, just as Lovecraft did." The result was a unique collection of stories that barely evoked the names we typically associate with the Mythos, yet still managed to communicate the sense of vast and powerful influences in the universe that dwarf all human endeavor. Memorable stories included T. E. D. Klein's "Black Man with a Horn," which simultaneously recalled the heyday of Lovecraft's pulp years and suggested horrifying possibilities encoded in the images of contemporary popular culture; David Drake's "Than Curse the Darkness" and A. A. Attanasio's "The Star Pools," in which the moral foundations of civilization are thrown into a quandary of relativism by large cosmic schemes; and Campbell's own "The Faces at Pine Dunes," which foregrounds a domestic situation against a horror so vast it can only be understood through the imagery of a bad drug trip.

Campbell's *Midnight Sun* can be seen not only as an extension of the themes addressed in "The Faces at Pine Dunes" and other of his Lovecraftian tales, but a convergence of the subtle Lovecraftian streak in his writing with the concerns of the contemporary horror novel. Though intimating forces of immeasurable age and proportion, *Midnight Sun* is the intimate story of Ben Sterling and his family. While a child, Ben hears stories of his great-grandfather's trip to the northwest in search of authentic folk legends, and his peculiar death shortly afterward. In the woods of the family estate, Ben encounters a presence that manifests itself as a series of shifting patterns in the snow. Though life events take him away from Sterling Forest as a boy, he is inevitably drawn back by a sense of familial duty as an adult. There, he is enraptured and becomes the earthly conduit for a force that could have crawled from between the covers of a Lovecraft volume:

> He was being watched by something capable of swallowing the stars. More than the glade was the focus it used to perceive, more than the forest which felt for an instant like a single organ, emotionally aware of him. The transformation spreading out into the world was itself a medium which the inhabitant of the dark beyond the stars was using to perceive the world. The world and the stars had been less than a dream, nothing more than a momentary lapse in its consciousness, and the metamorphosis which was reaching for the world was infinitesimal by its standards, simply a stirring in its sleep, a transient dream of the awful perfection which would overtake infinity when the presence beyond the darkness was fully awake.

Campbell's achievement in *Midnight Sun* is not only to give a clear idea of the horrible fate that awaits life as we know it, should this "something" realize its full potential in our dimension, but also to answer the question which numerous post-Lovecraftians have eluded or fudged over in their Mythos fiction: in the words of David Drake, "I wonder why those ones gave themselves so wholly to an evil that would have destroyed them first?" Of one mind with this elemental power at the same time that he is deeply devoted to his family, Ben reflexively perceives the "awful perfection" it intends as a gift to be bestowed upon his loved ones. The ominous sense of impending doom created by Ben's predicament is unprecedented in post-Lovecraftian fiction, and in nearly all of the contemporary horror novels whose conventions it employs. In contrast to Campbell, who has found a way to sublimate his youthful interests in Lovecraft so that they remain a part of the background of his writing yet never call attention to themselves, there is Thomas Ligotti, whose "The Last Feast of Harlequin," published as the lead story in *Grimscribe,* is his most Lovecraftian (and thus most uncharacteristic) story to date. The slowly building narrative and accumulation of realistic detail that characterize the story seem a reversal of the imaginative skills deployed in "The Flowers of the Abyss," "Nethescurial," "In the Shadow of Another World," "The Shadow at the Bottom of the World," and other of the thirteen stories in this volume, where one sees more a progressive chipping away at the foundations of the real by the apparently unreal, until distinctions between the two become meaningless. Yet in the funhouse mirror distortions of all of Ligotti's fiction we see reflected the same objective as in Lovecraft's painstaking use of the realistic to evoke a sense of cosmic outsideness: to destabilize our faith in the familiar through a glimpse from a strikingly unfamiliar perspective. As Dirk Mosig might have opined, the reader should judge for himself whether Ligotti's fiction is somehow more faithful to the principles of Lovecraft's work than are the writings of August Derleth, Brian Lumley, Lin Carter, and the host of Lovecraft pasticheurs who have added to the Mythos in the more than half-century since Lovecraft's death. But if the surest sign of an author's impact is when his aesthetics become a natural part of other writers' fiction, then perhaps the true carriers of the Lovecraftian tradition are those in whom its influence is the least recognizable.

[*Crypt of Cthulhu* No. 80 (Eastertide 1992): 38–52]

Suggestions for Further Reading

Berruti, Massimo. "H. P. Lovecraft and the Anatomy of Nothingness: The Cthulhu Mythos." *Semiotica* No. 150 (2004): 363–418.

Bouchard, Alexandre, and Louis-Pierre Smith Lacroix. "*Necronomicon:* A Note." *Lovecraft Studies* No. 44 (2004): 107–12.

Burleson, Donald R.; Joshi, S. T.; Murray, Will; Price, Robert M.; and Schultz, David E. "What Is the Cthulhu Mythos?" *Lovecraft Studies* No. 14 (Spring 1987): 3–30.

Carter, Lin. *Lovecraft: A Look Behind the "Cthulhu Mythos."* New York: Ballantine, 1972, 1976.St. Albans, UK: Panther, 1975. San Bernadino, CA: Borgo Press, 1993.

Carter, Lin. "H. P. Lovecraft: The Books." *Inside and Science Fiction Advertiser* No. 14 (March 1956): 11–16; Nos. 15/49 (May 1956): 13–23; Nos. 16/50 (September 1956): 24–31. In *The Shuttered Room and Other Pieces* by H. P. Lovecraft and Divers Hands. Sauk City, WI: Arkham House, 1959. In *Discovering H. P. Lovecraft,* ed. Darrell Schweitzer. Holicong, PA: Wildside Press, 2001 (rev. ed.; rev. by Robert M. Price and S. T. Joshi).

Carter, Lin. "H. P. Lovecraft: The Gods." *Inside Science Fiction* No. 52 (October 1957): 49–59. In *The Shuttered Room and Other Pieces* by H. P. Lovecraft and Divers Hands. Sauk City, WI: Arkham House, 1959.

Frayling, Christopher. "Dreams of Dead Names: The Scholarship of Dreams." In George Hay, ed. *The Necronomicon.* Jersey, UK: Neville Spearman, 1978; London: Corgi, 1980, pp. 149–70.

Frenschkowski, Marco. "Nodens—Metamorphosis of a Deity." *Crypt of Cthulhu* No. 87 (Lammas 1994): 3–8, 18.

Garofalo, Charles, and Robert M. Price. "Chariots of the Old Ones?" *Crypt of Cthulhu* No. 5 (Roodmas 1982): 21–24.

Hanegraaff, Wouter J. "Fiction in the Desert of the Real: Lovecraft's Cthulhu Mythos." *Aries* 7, No. 1 (2007): 85–109.

Jarocha-Ernst, Chris. *A Cthulhu Mythos Bibliography & Concordance.* Seattle: Armitage House, 1999.

Joshi, S. T. "The Cthulhu Mythos." In S. T. Joshi, ed. *Icons of Horror and the Supernatural.* Westport, CT: Greenwood Press, 2007, pp. 97–128 (Vol. 1.).

————. *The Rise and Fall of the Cthulhu Mythos*. Poplar Bluff, MO: Mythos Books, 2008.

Kingston-Brown, Nevil [*pseud.*]. "The Cosmology of Azathoth: Modern Physics and the Idiot Chaos." *Crypt of Cthulhu* No. 4 (Eastertide 1982): 15–22.

Laney, Francis T. "The Cthulhu Mythology: A Glossary." *Acolyte* 1, No. 2 (Winter 1942): 6–12. Rev. ed. in *Beyond the Wall of Sleep* by H. P. Lovecraft. Sauk City, WI: Arkham House, 1943. *Crypt of Cthulhu* No. 35 (Hallowmas 1985): 28–34.

Leiber, Fritz. "The Cthulhu Mythos: Wondrous and Terrible." *Fantastic* 24, No. 4 (June 1975): 118–21. In *Fritz Leiber and H. P. Lovecraft: Writers of the Dark,* ed. Ben J. S. Szumskyj and S. T. Joshi. Holicong, PA: Wildside Press, 2003.

Murray, Will. "The Dunwich Chimera and Others: Correlating the Cthulhu Mythos." *Lovecraft Studies* No. 8 (Spring 1984): 10–24.

Murray, Will. "An Uncompromising Look at the Cthulhu Mythos." *Lovecraft Studies* No. 12 (Spring 1986): 26–31.

Owings, Mark. *The Necronomicon: A Study.* Baltimore: Mirage, 1967.

Price, Robert M. "H. P. Lovecraft and the Cthulhu Mythos." *Crypt of Cthulhu* No. 35 (Hallowmas 1985): 3–11. In Price's *H. P. Lovecraft and the Cthulhu Mythos* (q.v.).

————. *H. P. Lovecraft and the Cthulhu Mythos.* Mercer Island, WA: Starmont House, 1990.

————. "The Lovecraft-Derleth Connection." *Crypt of Cthulhu* No. 6 (St. John's Eve 1982): 3–8. *Lovecraft Studies* No. 7 (Fall 1982): 18–23 (with editorial postscript by S. T. Joshi, pp. 23–24, 7). In Price's *H. P. Lovecraft and the Cthulhu Mythos* (q.v.).

————. "Lovecraft's 'Artificial Mythology.'" In *An Epicure in the Terrible: A Centennial Anthology of Essays in Honor of H. P. Lovecraft,* ed. David E. Schultz and S. T. Joshi. Rutherford, NJ: Fairleigh Dickinson University Press, 1991. New York: Hippocampus Press, 2011.

————. "The Mythology of the Old Ones." *Books at Brown* 28/29 (1991–92): 31–41.

————. "The Revision Mythos." *Crypt of Cthulhu* No. 11 (Candlemas 1983): 15–19. *Lovecraft Studies* No. 11 (Fall 1985): 43–50. In Price's *H. P. Lovecraft and the Cthulhu Mythos* (q.v.).

————. "Stephen King and the Lovecraft Mythos." In *Discovering Stephen King,* ed. Darrell Schweitzer. Mercer Island, WA: Starmont House, 1985. 109–22.

Quale, Thomas. "The Blind Idiot God: Miltonic Echoes in the Cthulhu Mythos." *Crypt of Cthulhu* No. 49 (Lammas 1987): 24–28.

Schultz, David E., ed. "Notes toward a History of the Cthulhu Mythos." *Crypt of Cthulhu* No. 92 (Eastertide 1996): 15–33.

Turner, James. "A Mythos in His Own Image." *Foundation* No. 33 (Spring 1985): 55–61. In *At the Mountains of Madness and Other Novels* by H. P. Lovecraft. Sauk City, WI: Arkham House, 1985.

Wetzel, George T. "The Cthulhu Mythos: A Study." In C.109, 110. Rev. ed. in *HPL,* ed. Meade and Penny Frierson. Birmingham, AL: The Editors, 1972. In *H. P. Lovecraft: Four Decades of Criticism,* ed. S. T. Joshi. Athens: Ohio University Press, 1980.

Zachrau, Thekla. "The 'Cthulhu Mythos': Between Horror and Science Fiction." Tr. L. G. Boba and S. T. Joshi. *Lovecraft Studies* Nos. 19/20 (Fall 1989): 56–62.

Index

INDEX

Horror for the Holidays

Edited by Scott David Aniolowski

"When the footpads quail at the night-bird's wail,
And black dogs bay at the moon,
Then is the specters' holiday – then is the ghosts' high noon!"

-- Sir William Schwenck Gilbert, *Raddigore*, Act 1

Holidays. Special days of commemoration and celebration. Feasts and festivities. Remembrance and revelry. But what dark things lurk just out of sight, in the shadows of those celebrated days? Forces beyond our comprehension, yearning to burst into our warm and comforting world and tear asunder those things we hold most dear. As the wheel of the year turns and we embrace our favorite occasions, let us not forget that beyond the light is a darkness, and in that darkness something stirs. Some nameless thing that brings us *Horror for the Holidays!*

Let dark fiction from Ramsey Campbell, Thomas Ligotti, Robert Price, Cody Goodfellow, and Lois Gresh adorn your holidays this season!

Coming Soon from

Miskatonic River Press

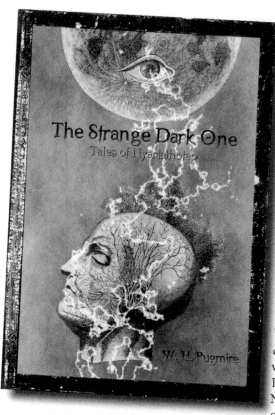

With

The Strange Dark One,

W. H. Pugmire collects all of his best weird fiction concerning H. P. Lovecraft's dark god, Nyarlathotep. This avatar of the Great Old Ones is Lovecraft's most enigmatic creation, a being of many masks and multitudinous personae. Often called The Crawling Chaos, Nyarlathotep heralds the end of mortal time, and serves as avatar of Azathoth, the Idiot Chaos who will blow earth's dust away. Many writers have been enchanted by this dark being, in particular Robert Bloch, the man who, through correspondence, inspired Wilum Pugmire to try his hand at Lovecraftian fiction. This new book is a testimonial of Nyarlathotep's hold on Pugmire's withered brain, and these tales serve as aspects of a haunted mind. Along with stories that have not been reprinted since their initial magazine appearances, The Strange Dark One includes "To See Beyond," a sequel-of-sorts to Robert Bloch's tale, "The Cheaters", and the book's title story is a 14,000 word novelette set in Pugmire's Sesqua Valley. Each tale if beautifully illustrated by the remarkable Jeffrey Thomas, who is himself one of today's finest horror authors.

Coming soon from

Miskatonic River Press

They Lie not Dead, but Dreaming...

Dead But Dreaming and *Dead But Dreaming 2*
are the new classics of modern Lovecraftian literature. Reviewed as
excellent tomes, they have been well received by fans of the genre for
years. The two books contain tales by Ramsey Campbell, Darrell
Schweiter, Donald R. Burleson, Joseph S. Pulver, Sr., and
W. H. Pugmire. Explore the darkness!

Dead But Dreaming and *Dead But Dreaming 2* are available direct
from the publisher at www.miskatonicriverpress.com, as well
from Amazon.com and other fine booksellers worldwide.

H.P. Lovecraft. Karl Edgar Wagner. Peter Straub. Those are a few of the names that stand tall in our genre and when it comes to Robert W. Chambers and his King in Yellow they agree, Chamber's beguiling tales of the King In Yellow and Carcosa are among the best in "Weird" fiction. Miskatonic River Press and Joseph S. Pulver, Sr. are proud and delighted to present an anthology of all new tales inspired by Chambers.

In haunted and splintered minds… Minds shackled to lonely places…
In the unbound shadows infesting hearts of beautiful woman with frantic sensations…
In an old house where biblical thrived…
In threadbare truths, disturbed by despair, cobwebbed with illusions…
In far cold Carcosa…

Lies madness.

In *A Season In Carcosa* readers will find the strange and mysterious places of heart and mind that spring from madness, and those minds and the places touched by it are the realms that are mined. Chambers' legacy of the worms and soft decay that spring from reading the King In Yellow play stir both new and established talents in the world of weird fiction and horror to contribute all new tales that pay homage to these eerie nightmares. In Carcosa twilight comes and minds lost in the mirrors of lust and fear, are awash in legacies of shadows not mercy. . .

Thomas Ligotti is beyond doubt one of the Grandmasters of Weird Fiction. In *The Grimiscribe's Puppets,* Joseph S. Pulver, Sr., has commissioned both new and established talents in the world of weird fiction and horror to contribute all new tales that pay homage to Ligotti and celebrate his eerie and essential nightmares. Poppy Z. Brite once asked, "Are you out there, Thomas Ligotti?" This anthology proves not only is he alive and well, but his extraordinary illuminations have proven to be a visionary and fertile source of inspiration for some of today's most accomplished authors.

Coming from

Miskatonic River Press

CPSIA information can be obtained
at www.ICGtesting.com
Printed in the USA
LVOW04s0246050117
519796LV00030B/559/P